65—

POLITICAL PHILOSOPHY FOR THE GLOBAL AGE

Mónica Judith Sánchez Flores

POLITICAL PHILOSOPHY FOR THE GLOBAL AGE
© Mónica Judith Sánchez Flores, 2005.

First published in 2005 by
PALGRAVE MACMILLAN™
175 Fifth Avenue, New York, N.Y. 10010 and
Houndmills, Basingstoke, Hampshire, England RG21 6XS
Companies and representatives throughout the world.

PALGRAVE MACMILLAN is the global academic imprint of the Palgrave Macmillan division of St. Martin's Press, LLC and of Palgrave Macmillan Ltd. Macmillan® is a registered trademark in the United States, United Kingdom and other countries. Palgrave is a registered trademark in the European Union and other countries.

ISBN 1–4039–6475–0

Library of Congress Cataloging-in-Publication Data

Sánchez Flores, Mónica Judith.
    Political philosophy for the global age / Mónica Judith Sánchez Flores.
        p. cm.
    Includes bibliographical references and index.
    ISBN 1–4039–6475–0
        1. Political science—Philosophy. 2. Political ethics. I. Title.

JA71.S2712 2005
320′.01—dc22   2004064918

A catalogue record for this book is available from the British Library.

Design by Newgen Imaging Systems (P) Ltd., Chennai, India.

First edition: July 2005

10 9 8 7 6 5 4 3 2 1

Printed in the United States of America.

CONTENTS

Acknowledgments

This book is the result of many years of reflection on the ethical basis of human interaction. During this time, I have been under the influence of various fortunate encounters as well as not very fortunate ones, which nonetheless have taught me important lessons on this subject. I could not possibly thank every single person who provided me with support and inspiration in this endeavor, and so I apologize in advance for failing to mention all the relevant influences. Explicit thanks are due to my professors at El Colegio de México: Francisco Gil Villegas, Mauricio Merino, Luis F. Aguilar Villanueva, Mª Carmen Pardo, Juan Molinar, Soledad Loaeza, and José María Pérez Gay, and at the University of Edinburgh: Emilios Christodoulidis, John Holmwood, Russel Keat, Kimberly Hutchings, and Zenon Bankowsky. I am grateful for the support that I have received from the *Centro de Investigación y Docencia Económicas* (CIDE), without which it would not have been possible to complete this book, especially from Carlos Bazdresch, Carlos Elizondo, Benito Nacif, and my colleagues and good friends Rafael Rojas and Covadonga Meseguer. Special thanks are due to my research assistants Francisco R. Pérez M., and Rodrigo Parral D., whose constant and unquestioning support was essential in getting the manuscript ready. I also want to thank Carmen Mata for always being there to solve all the mundane arrangements related to academic and administrative work. Additionally, I thank my family, especially mum and dad, and my friends whose love, support, and unconditional presence were essential for me to conclude this endeavor happily: Lorena Ruano, Juan Navarrete, Eric Magar, Eduardo López, Edgar Arredondo, Yasmeen Grant, and Elizabeth Jones. Finally, I want to thank Stuart Douglass, whom I have just recently found and whose presence in this world is for me a sign that love does make us whole.

1

LEGITIMATE REALITY AND
ETHICAL AUTHORITY

Modernity set itself in historical motion and progress after an emphatic rejection of religious dogma during the age of reason. The development of a Judeo-Christian *Western* type of sense of self produced the individualized habit of self-interpretation in a historical context, which eventually became a field of private subjectivity that in Modernity is ideally conceived of as autonomous. In this book, I argue that both history and autonomous individuality are essential principles of order and organization in the globalized world. Although history and individuality cannot be dispensed with in global interaction, they ought to be seen as *ideals* that emanate culturally from Europe, and not as essential aspects of universal humanity. This perspective on history and individuality will produce the basis to both phenomenologically *understand* the essence of history and modern individuality and *criticize* their ascendance. The critical stance is necessary toward history because it is imposed as the only *legitimate reality*, and toward autonomous individuality because it is imposed as the only universal principle for human morality. Nevertheless, the hermeneutic stance is necessary because these *ideals* have already become part of our experienced reality: We perceive ourselves as individuals and we perceive time as an indefinite sequence of events along which humanity strives for betterment and progress. But is this advancement *actually* happening or is it only a part of our imagined self-interpretation *qua* modern individuals? The answer to this question can only disclose a paradox: We are only ideally modern or Modernity is only a myth, yet already one that is relevant for modern global culture and disciplined interaction right now.

What could then be the basis to both *hermeneutically* understand and *critically* approach the legitimacy of the Western tradition of knowledge and interpretation of self, which has already been exported all over the world? I believe that both the hermeneutic and the critical attitudes are necessary in this endeavor. On the one hand, understanding is essential due to the fact that history and individuality are already part of the way in which many people beyond the West understand and interpret their reality—even if this self-interpretation is present simultaneously with nonliberal world cosmologies. And so, history and individuality are already part of individually imagined and emotionally cognized self-interpretations—but this is already part of their actuality: Modernity is real only ideally, but as such, it is the basis for the contemporary disciplined global interaction. On the other hand, critique is essential because Modernity's totalizing way of conceiving the self and its temporal structure of reality is based on universal metaphysics that leave any other conceptions at the margins of fiction and folklore. From this all-encompassing worldview, alternative views of reality are thrown into the same generic category of *otherness*—Modernity's alter ego—that obscures human diversity and various sources of order and creativity.

This book takes the above critical reflection as its starting point. I begin by discussing what I call the *postcolonial predicament*, defined, on the one hand, by the legitimacy of the accusation that postcolonial intellectuals make against the West and its totalizing pretensions, and, on the other hand, the failure of postcolonialism to articulate the voice of the other that was silenced by the violence of colonization. In this book, I propose that the failure of postcolonialism necessarily leads the debate toward posing the postcolonial legitimate accusation on a different theoretical basis. The alternative theoretical basis that I propose is constituted by the three ideal types of reality that I define conceptually in chapter 2, and develop theoretically in chapters 3–5. The types of reality that I propose constitute a sociology of religion that attempts an interpretation of the sacred sources of human ethos and morality—although I also consider their biological role. In these ideal types, I also engage in a discussion of contemporary positions about the sources of our morality—feminism, liberalism, and communitarianism—and how they relate to my ideal types. The exploration of our biological and sacred roots of ethical behavior and a critique of their contemporary theoretical discussion will be the basis to criticize the purely Western grounds on which the topic is discussed.

However, I believe that it is not enough to merely criticize the colonial West for canceling complete traditions and human worldviews: One ought to ask what may be the alternative legitimate basis for human order after having radically questioned the received modern substantive basis. This book is, thus, an attempt at providing an alternative substantive basis for human order that is appropriate for interaction under the present conditions of globalization. The Western worldview brought Modernity and modern institutions to fruition globally, and this is already an aspect of the world we live in. The autonomous and historical selves are already ways in which modern people interpret themselves all over the world. Nevertheless, to construct a common substantive basis for humanity, I argue that this modern conception of self ought to look beyond Modernity to find essential aspects of what it is to be human. I am speaking of human primitivity and spirituality that the secular modern substantive tradition does not contemplate as important, and even seeks to obliterate. And I argue that these aspects of being human are just as important for our integrity as embodied animals as well as for our integrity as ethical/moral selves—whatever our worldview. And so I propose to contemplate them as alternative views of reality that may be legitimized in world cosmologies other than the Western one, and that may offer useful sources of human creativity to complement it.

The theoretical construction that I propose in this book models the idea that the culture where we abide, our worldview, our cosmology is created by us and, at the same time, it is already creative of our conception of self. We can imagine this cultural creativity as a circle in which we contribute as much as the particular worldview that we are born into also contributes. The critical moment takes place in our human creative part of the circle and the hermeneutical moment, in the creative part that cultures or cosmologies may display: They shape human conceptions of self. We shape culture and we are shaped by culture, and this takes place at the same time, synchronically. What we perceive as reality is intimately entwined with what we believe to be reality, and so, it produces *us* (our sense of self) as we reproduce it in our daily practices. This means that while social reality is imaginatively constructed by social actors and interpreters, it also constructs emotionally the social actors' sense of self back: The moment that we perceive ourselves as "something," this imagined "something" becomes an intimate emotional experience of self that defines us. In society, we live *caught* within this activity that is partly intended and partly inherited by the business of living in society. We find ourselves already with it, and believing in it, to sustain our sense of self (and embodiment) by it; but the human creative moment entails that we are not necessarily trapped within our culture and we may be critical of it. If there were no ontological grounds for criticism, cultures would be static wholes that would not change. I will resort to the synchronous essence of cultural creativity throughout this book that will disclose the need to use both the critical and the hermeneutic attitudes toward what we believe to be real, our culture, our cosmology, our sense of self.

Following the Weberian methodology for a sociology of knowledge that engages in a constant self-interpretation, then, I relativize the notion of "reality" and consider it as an unfathomable and ongoing mystery, more readily ruled by paradox than coherence, which we must unavoidably deal with through our conscious experience and set of beliefs. But both paradox and coherence are ultimately mediated by conscious experience. As I have said, I assume that human consciousness is bootstrapped to its own created notion of reality in such an intimate manner that this notion of reality creates for human consciousness its notion of self back. This is illustrated by its *autopoietic* nature, as described by Humberto Maturana and Francisco Varela (1987) in their theory about life and cognition, which in this work is regarded as a useful metaphor for *consciousness*. And so, views of reality in this work are regarded as both humanly created and also simultaneously creative of the particular notion of human self. Legitimation in this work is therefore used to denote belief in a specific ideal type of reality. I argue that legitimate reality is genetically related to ethical authority, or to the principles of order that people follow in their daily interaction: These principles have sacred roots and this is the reason why the theoretical model of views of reality that I propose is essentially also a sociology of religion.

In the first section of this introductory chapter, I deal with how postcolonial intellectuals fail to give voice to the silenced other. Their politics of opposition and their use of the Western conceptual tools and methodologies are eventually self-defeating. This leads me to reject the dichotomy West/non-West and to diversify it into three types of views of reality as better analytical categories for an experience of self and for a common substantive basis for global interaction. In the second section of this chapter, I engage with the notion of reality: how it is that our modern understanding legitimizes it as objectivity, which, I will argue, is not without its sacred roots for claims of validity. These claims are rooted in an aprioristic connection of the human being with her transcendental identity and with the universal level of reality, as well as in belief on a godly made mechanistic cosmos of entities that lie outside of each other. This analytical critique is organized around Kantian metaphysics in his *Critique of Pure Reason* ([1781] 1929) and the interpretive methodology of Max Weber ([1904] 1949, [1905] 1958, [1922a] 1965, [1922b] 1987), and is based on theoretical developments in physics (Bohm 1980; Capra 1982, 1983; Prigogine 1984, 1997) that have transformed the Newtonian cosmos on which Kant based his reflections on science. This introductory chapter will illustrate how a legitimate view of reality also determines the legitimate cultural sources for ethical authority, which will then be diversified in the theoretical construct that will occupy the rest of the book.

THE POSTCOLONIAL PREDICAMENT IN MODERN POLITICAL PHILOSOPHY

What I call the *postcolonial predicament* is based on an accusation launched by a group of intellectuals against the way Modernity legitimizes itself by means of universally valid categories, such as *history* or *autonomous individuality*. It is contended that these categories emerge from a specific geographical center and cancel the legitimacy of diverse forms of knowledge and self-representation that lie outside what Europe or the West consider as legitimate reality. This epistemological accusation is framed within a history of violent colonization over most of the planet, traditionally interpreted by enlightened Europeans as a historical mission to civilize the world. The problem for a contemporary political philosophy that is informed by such history and experience is that, to this day, it supports this mission by means of substantive and universal claims about the self and her ethical life in society. This discloses the two-faced Janus nature of modern political philosophy: Paradoxically enough, on the one hand, the assumption of ontologically valid universal categories entails a cosmologically based negation of diversity or otherness and on the other, liberal politics seeks to organize heterogeneous and plural societies on the basis of a positive valuation of diversity and tolerance of otherness. I argue that postcolonial theory inherits the same paradoxical nature as Modernity: It refuses validity to monolithic individuality and yet cannot escape the modern trap of referring to, and thus defining, a monolithic other that was silenced by the violence of empire. I believe that one could apply to postcolonial theory the same criticism that Gadamer aims in his *Truth and Method* (1989) at Romantic philosophy: "Romanticism wages its war on a terrain defined by the adversary" (Ricoeur 1981, 67). The failure of postcolonial theory serves to clearly illustrate how any adversary to the modern *ethos* and view of reality is doomed to remain at the particularistic margins of political philosophy. This is the case of postcolonialism, feminism, and even communitarianism. However, the "post-" in postcolonial as well as postmodern representations of reality betrays their need to be bred from Modernity in a denied self-same image and likeness. In what follows, I will describe what I call the postcolonial predicament and this will be the basis to reconsider the analytical validity of the terms West and non-West to represent power struggles in the contemporary globalized world.

Modernity defines the terrain for postcolonial theory because postcolonial intellectuals find themselves in the predicament of needing to use Western tools for their own self-interpretation, at the same time as they aspire to speak for the unknowable other or the *subaltern* (Spivak 1988). Postcolonial theory needs the Western center in order to criticize and reject it at the same time, much in the same way as Marxism depends on an absolutist center, and post-structuralism and postmodernity on the absolutist negation of *any* center (Merquior 1986). But postcolonialism encompasses concepts and theoretical frameworks of both Marxist and postmodern analyses. It includes both the emancipating imperative of giving back the voice to the Gramscian subaltern *and* also the postmodern rejection of a universalizing meta-narrative. But, according to Leela Gandhi, these two perspectives are not compatible with each other:

> Postmodern/post-structuralist commentators argue that postcolonialism is in danger of becoming yet another totalizing method and theory. On the other side, Marxist and materialist critics have vociferously made the charge that postcolonial analysis lacks the methodological structure, and will to totalize, necessary for right thinking and left politics. (1998, 167)

Although Marxism provides postcolonialism with some key concepts, postmodern theory and post-structuralist methods are the main sources of such "critique," as they are congenial with the postcolonial agenda. As Gandhi suggests above and I discuss here, these post-critiques and their *nemesis* are in danger of reproducing the universalistic habits of Modernity. Postcolonialism mimics the postmodern rejection of totalizing meta-narratives as a methodology for a politics of opposition: the denunciation of terribly violent colonial imposition of narrative and identity. Such narrative, they contend, emerged from the particular Western world of white, male, and professional upper classes, and it was in their interest to make it universally valid. However, in its will to denounce the totalizing spirit of European Modernity, postmodernity defines reality as opposed to this spirit and inadvertently poses an alternative "universe." The postmodern kind of universality is disclosed as absolute uncertainty, diversity, and fragmentation—without even leaving us the consolation of nihility for consciousness to be existentially dissolved into. What is posed as "universal fragmentation" by postmodern critics and its accompanying methodology is *itself* the political agenda: to deconstruct the oppressive and imposed meta-narrative of Modernity.

This makes enough sense from a postcolonial position, yet as Arif Dirlik says, "the language of postcolonial discourse, . . . is the language of First World post-structuralism, as postcolonial critics readily concede, although they do not dwell too long on its implications" (Dirlik 1996, 303). The implications are related to the perspective where the postcolonial observers and rescuers of lost identities stand: precisely at the center of the Modernity that they want to reject. Bruno Latour's critique of postmodernity as a transformed version of modernism is very illustrative at this point. He contends that even though the modern drive to colonize the world was a ruthless, destructive, and arbitrary force whose consequences should not be trivialized, Modernity at least held dear the ideal mission of providing something new. Postmodernity in this sense holds only a teenager-like emancipating gesture:

> Modernization was ruthless towards the premoderns, but what can we say about postmodernization? Imperialist violence at least offered a future, but sudden weakness on the part of the conquerors is far worse for, always cut off from the past, it now also breaks with the future. Having been slapped in the face with modern reality, poor populations now have to submit to postmodern hyperreality. Nothing has value; everything is a reflection, a simulacrum, a floating sign; and that very weakness, they say, may save us from the invasion of technologies, science, reasons. Was it really worth destroying everything to end up adding this insult to that injury? (Latour 1993, 131)

In spite of this critique on postcolonial–postmodern methodologies, the postcolonial predicament that I have referred to is framed within the legitimacy of the postcolonial reasons for waging a battle against the worldview of totalizing Modernity *and* the impossibility for this battle to be fought with analytical weapons that have been forged precisely by the adversary's worldview. Therefore, I do not share the postcolonial theoretical perspective because the above type of analytical "battle" cannot be fought without once again refusing consciousness and ultimately insulting the ones this battle is supposedly fought for. However, I believe that there are legitimate reasons for fighting this battle, even if I refuse to conceptualize it as such when speaking from the perspective of globalization. I argue that if the postcolonial theoretical predicament illustrates anything at all, it is the need to drop the categories West and non-West to theoretically qualify power struggles. This is the reason why I propose alternative ideal–typical views of reality: To question the ascendance of one of them by putting these diversified human types of reality at the same level of importance for human life in the planet right now. I will do this in chapter 2, and it will set the theoretical basis for the development of the arguments in this book.

One of the main intuitions that has guided this work is a suspicion—analogous to Edward Said's own about *Orientalism* (1978)—that the West, as clearly situated in anything or anybody at all, contemporaneously, is an imaginary invention of many people's emotional involvement with both West and non-West all over the world. James Clifford (1988) has pointed out that Said himself is unable to evade embracing humanist and typically Western values in his will-to-oppose, and criticize European attitudes toward the conquered East. Further, to use such terms as Western and non-Western people within the intellectual circles of modern academia makes no sense. One must have already assimilated Western beliefs and categories of thought—must have conceived of oneself as a historical self—in order to participate in the debate at all. The factual emancipatory claims of the modern "rationalistic" discipline(s), even that of the postmodern and postcolonial intellectuals, produce the structural need for an ongoing "progress" of intellectual knowledge while it is created, revised, and reinterpreted as it is taught. And today, it is taught all over the world. The rationalist European tradition makes universalistic claims that have been used as legitimizing tools for colonial unifying of imperial violence. But imperial will-to-power *always* resorts to its "language of truth" in order to make legitimacy claims, be they cosmological–mythical, religious, universalistic, or scientific. This is a human constant, and not necessarily a specific bad habit of Modernity.

Further, what we conceive now as Modernity has already superseded the confines of the West. Even if it is originally tied to Europe, modern imagination organizes a global arena of interaction in which the whole world participates. While current global political power relations are necessarily tied to colonialism (past or present), it is already useless to lay the blame for this on a West that is no longer embodied in anything or anybody anymore. Its embodiment is really an enactment of Western values and categories of thought that go by the title of "reality." And so, I refrain from using categories such as the "West" or the "Western tradition of knowledge" as much as I can throughout this book, and in the rare occasion that I do, I mean to speak about a belief system that is already also an intimate aspect of many people living in the periphery right now (we find ourselves with it). Factual power relations among human beings, in particular (and living entities, in general), take place at all levels of interaction, and I believe that it is useful to attempt an understanding of one's own emotional, imaginary, and biological relationship with them. This is the subject of chapter 3, the primitive idea of reality that portrays people as animals of a certain species, embodied entities with biological needs who live in big groups. In chapter 3, I propose a model for human cognition that takes into account our vulnerability—especially as children growing up—and our conscious embodiment. I organize this model around what I call the *present moment of meaningful experience* that is always determined by a complex interplay between our imagination and our emotions, our past and our potentialities, and the systematic practice of human disciplines as well as the creative spontaneity of human life.

With the theoretical construct that I propose in this book, I want to portray at least a partial view of the complexities intertwined in human interaction, and especially *ethical* human interaction. In order to do this, it is important to realize that the West is not an analytical tool, but a traditional identity that defines itself with respect to an unknown (and unknowable) other. Currently, we can only blame for this estrangement our own beliefs of what we consider as *valid* knowledge, *valid* morality, *valid* humanity, and *valid* consciousness of self. *Validity* and validity claims are in the Weberian interpretive sociology intimately related to belief. And it is here that I find all pagan as well as monotheistic religions, intellectual philosophies, and mystic cosmologies to converge: Any type of symbolized knowledge must be accompanied by belief—even an intellectual–factual–historical–scientific one. In this book, in a phenomenological interpretation of self, this will be the basis to transform and diversify the categories West/non-West to produce a phenomenological basis for a *hybrid* experience and interpretation of self under the conditions of globalization. This type of hybridity is different from the postcolonial merely dichotomous one: I propose to re-examine the roots of the difference West/non-West toward a hermeneutical and tolerant interpretation of the modern self with respect to the excluded other. This phenomenological exercise will lead me both to critically question *and* to embrace the Western cultural inheritance in academic practice at the same time. In chapter 4, the historical ideal type of reality refers to this cultural inheritance and its achievements in the form of history and ideal individual autonomy.

What we call the West today has many faces and moving centers of power in the current global arena: It can be identified not only with advanced capitalism, the First World, consumerism, the arbitrariness of the powerful, and even with their painful arrogance, but also with liberal democracy, human rights, Modernity, academia, science, philosophy, *intelligentsia*, and humanist cosmopolitan ethics. While it is true that both the former and the latter groups of elements can today be observed and related to Western peoples, they can also be observed as common ideals and practices of peoples that we would consider today as peripheral. The failure of a postcolonial politics of opposition against the mythical West is that, currently, Modernity is embodied both nowhere in its purist and purifying aspirations (see Latour 1993) and everywhere in the world at the same time. What this means is that political opposition against the tyrant West becomes *ipso facto* an existential opposition against oneself. This inner opposition is the existential predicament in which hybrid identities find themselves. This is then a product, on the one hand, of an imaginary Modernity and our practical and emotional engagement with it at the same time, and on the other, of an imaginary past that is nonetheless very much practically and emotionally alive right here and now in us. The possibility, then, of a contemporary hybrid consciousness of self who lives within this existential predicament is the "object" of observation and analysis throughout this book. From this perspective, another (more general) instance of hybridity can then be observed in the human condition itself. In the embodied experience of being human, it is plain to see that we are all hybrids of nature and culture—animal and human—at the same time. The abased other in Western cosmology refers not only to the peoples who suffer the historical consequences of colonization, but also to women, children, and nature in general (the latter defined as *essentially* different from humanity). The unknowable other ought to be considered as infinite particularity and the legitimate source of various forms of knowledge and discipline that are relevant to human life (in particular) and to life in this planet (in general) right now.

The existential predicament referred to above, problematizes many of the instances in which the modern self perceives itself. A basic one in this book is the modern self's secular historical consciousness. If we look at this consciousness without questioning our imaginative and emotional participation in its reality at the same time, it becomes impossible to see the roots of its legitimacy *qua* reality. And so, a phenomenological reduction is necessary in order to contemplate the history within which we find ourselves as mere *appearance*. From the perspective of history as appearance, we can then discover that its production as legitimate reality is tied as much to imperial violence, as it is to the ongoing human production of sacred roots to reality.

As has been mentioned, one of the working hypotheses in this book is that the sacred roots to reality are never left behind by human beings, as one of the major myths of Modernity would have us believe. This will be discussed later at greater length with respect to specific traditions. Here, I want to advance that the phenomenological form of hybridity that I propose is not defined by a combination of opposites. Rather, it is phenomenological because being constituted of both nature and culture at the same time has an experiential essence, and its knowledge is regarded as a mixture of our primitive drives, our historical consciousness, and our spiritual aspirations.

From this standpoint of hybridity, I attempt a critique of the modern notion of objectivity as used to denote actual reality—or the only admitted type of legitimate reality. We can identify the source of the modern discipline of self-interpretation with the European Enlightenment as a mixture of (dis)continuities with the Christian order and dogma—with its own (dis)continuities with the Jewish cosmology—after rediscovering the Greek classics—with (dis)continuities of their own. The Western tradition, as we know it today, is created through disciplined observation of objective factuality or historical consciousness. This factuality is created by the constant discipline (ritual) of objective observation at the same time as objective observation is made possible by the disciplined experience of factuality itself. In this book, I argue that our modern objective view of reality—as well as any other type of view of reality—is tied to imaginary and emotionally cognized assumptions about reality. That is, here, human beings are regarded as a type of animal species that needs myth biologically to survive, to interact, and to sustain a meaningful sense of reality, and thus, of social order. I am aware that this assumption as a working hypothesis effectively means that *logos* and *mythos* overlap to become the same thing, but I hope that the reader will allow this extreme artifice initially in order to allow commensurability between the modern sense of self and its unknown other.

Objectivity, I believe, is the one notion through which the European tradition of knowledge can do violence to other views of reality in its universalistic and totalitarian assumptions. And yet, objectivity can also be a very useful tool in a specific type of appreciation of our immediate reality. And so, it cannot be wholly rejected or fought against through a politics of opposition, but I argue that it should be relativized and regarded as a useful myth. In order to criticize the conception of objectivity as the only source of legitimate reality, I engage with what it is that produces and legitimizes what we perceive as our immediate reality. Max Weber's interpretive sociology is very useful in this task as I argue that, in contemporary scientific knowledge (especially in physics), it has become possible to say that "subjectivity" is the basis for *any* kind of "objectivity" (see Delanty 1997). The traditional subject/object divide is radically questioned in this work as ontology; in epistemology though, the subjective and objective poles can be radicalized as ideal typical forms between which there lies a sea of complexity (which can also be seen as simplicity at the same time). The existential predicament of hybridity is situated amid complexity and uncertainty, and so, I believe that it is useful to resort to other (than European) traditions of knowledge in order to be able to live with this existential predicament, while refusing to resort solely to the usual totalitarian ontological assumptions of this tradition of knowledge. This is the reason why, in chapter 5, I propose the mystic ideal type of reality that organizes a universal center that is different from the one that contemporary Modernity stands on.

In the contemporary modern arena of global interaction, political legitimation is already tied to the particular shape and exercise of liberal democracies all over the world, but this legitimacy is sustained as a consequence of European colonization at the same time as contemporary political authority bases its legitimacy claims on belief in the "superior" modern notions of progress as wealth expansion and political freedom. In order to define his ideal types of domination, Max Weber relied more heavily in the latter legitimate belief than in awareness of the consequences of colonization. The European rational Enlightenment has traditionally based its claims of superiority on its cultural creation of a secular (civilized) path that unifies humanity around the ideal of a universally powerful moral individual. Although this could be regarded as a cultural achievement of the enlightened Europe, it was conceived within the Christian view of reality and in the spirit of rational theological speculation. When in rejection of dogma, the latter became secular, philosophers turned to their intellectual teachers (the Greek classics) within their European-Christian background. The Hellenic ideal of cosmopolitanism had inspired the Catholic drive to world conversion to achieve universal unification of humankind in Christianity. Humanist theology was the prelude to Reformation and to the achievement of secular universalist–humanist philosophy.[1] However, humanism keeps the inherently divided cosmos of Christianity, which also brings about the (always latent) possibility of a divided world and a divided human race:

> All humanisms, until now, have been imperial. They speak of the human in the accents and the interests of a class, a sex, a "race." Their

embrace suffocates those whom it does not ignore. The first humanists scripted the tyranny of Borgias, Medicis and Tudors. Later humanisms dreamed of freedom and celebrated Frederick II, Bonaparte, Bismarck, Stalin. The liberators of colonial America, like the Greek and Roman thinkers they emulated, owned slaves. At various times, not excluding the present, the circuit of the human has excluded women, those who do not speak Greek or Latin or English, those whose complexions are not pink, children, Jews. It is almost impossible to think of a crime that has not been committed in the name of humanity. (Davies 1997, 131)

Weber managed to translate the political arenas of the colonized world into theoretical evolutionary terms that, due to the imperial upper hand, evidently contemplated European countries as the most advanced stage. While Weber did not mean for this stage necessarily to be of a superior quality, he inadvertently organized a hierarchy with respect to which Modernity could identify itself as opposed to its own past *and* as opposed to the rest of the world (its own colonies) at the same time. There was only a small step—which in sociology Jürgen Habermas (1984, 1990a) explicitly took—to make the Weberian hierarchy into a structure that organizes the degrees of rational Enlightenment with respect to the proximity that interaction in any cultural situation has with respect to the modern style of order. In the current scenario of global interaction, this hierarchy is only acceptable in the rational–legal type of reality: In Modernity, it is valued for its ability to calculate outcomes and rationalize interaction. But Habermas's universalistic hierarchy becomes unacceptable very soon, when it takes a cosmic jump to assert that this value characterizes a superior form of human consciousness. While individually based rationality, impersonality, and even calculability might be essential to rule both civilized legal–rational interaction and mass production (and consumption), when it comes to organizations formed by human beings, the assumption of an enlightened rational and universalistic impersonality breaks down due to the particular animal and spiritual human elements involved in daily interaction—which are either systemically neglected by the modern lifestyle or insufficiently dealt with.

On the other hand, Weber's other ideal types of domination (traditional and charismatic) have come to be regarded as underdeveloped and unreflective domination structures of our days, which renders them primitive and undesirable per se. However, this produces a biased perception of institutions and organizations that relies too heavily in the absolutist assumptions of a universalistic type of objective rationalism. As Barbara Czarniawska has argued, organizations have been found to be preeminently cultural phenomena, intimately entwined with the consciousnesses that live in them (1992, 1997, 1998). Under the light of contemporary world globalization, the Weberian types of domination should be reconsidered in a phenomenological exercise of hybrid/modern self-interpretation that cannot regard itself at the apex of human consciousness anymore. This is the reason why I propose my three ideal types of reality in this book.

The Weberian ideal types of domination can be said to be theoretically mutually exclusive in terms of rationality, but empirically observed to be mixed with one another in actual social interaction— especially in these days of globalized interaction. Preeminently traditional and/or charismatic types of domination, according to Weber, still require an administrative structure, which he calls "organization" (Weber [1922b] 1987, 212). Legal–rational domination is based upon legitimate and systematic construction of such organization that will enable society to achieve specific ends pondered and pursued rationally. This formulation conveys the idea that due to the lack of stability in traditionally and charismatically dominated environments, it is possible (however deplorable or desirable) that they disappear through development or progress toward complex interaction, or that they become subordinated to the more stable rational structures that function on the basis of calculability and thus can be administrated. It takes this subordination for granted, making it into a theoretical assumption. Ironically, Weber considered impersonality and calculability as some kind of biblical monsters with apocalyptic superiority to anything else that would unavoidably bring about an administrative "iron cage."

However, it has become apparent in organizational studies and theory that a legal–rational structure on its own will not suffice for sustaining interaction among people, who *always* tend to develop some form of "collective action . . . based on interpersonal relationships, not a system of formal rules" (Czarniawska 1992, 18; see also March and Olsen 1989), which is generally identified with the traditional view of order. This amounts to an organizational prejudice against spontaneity and primitivity, a fear motivated by the belief in their potentially chaotic effects and an empirically groundless assumption that they will eventually be left behind in human existence. Ultimately, I will argue throughout this book that this prejudice emerges from a Christian cosmology that contemplates a divided universe of salvation (transcendence) and condemnation that relates the latter to sin and the inferior primitivity of embodiment. In Modernity, this division evolved into a social thrust to rationally dominate and control nature, contingency, and the primitive human aspect in civilized and disciplined interaction. Nevertheless, I argue that nonlegal–rational elements in organization can be said to come from spontaneous arrangements that can become very useful sources of order that should be considered as such theoretically.

The legal–rational type of legitimacy rests on the modern value of the individual self, while the other (traditional and charismatic) types rest on a higher estimation of the collectivity as a form of self. Weber defines legitimacy as based on belief and stresses that it should only be regarded as a probability, its presence or absence depending on individual prerogatives (Weber [1922b] 1987, 170–71). Nevertheless, the value of the individual is greater in the Western worldview than in the nonlegal–rational cosmologies because the interacting individual depends on her own personal awareness of rational interaction. Further, an ideal rational individual is ideally trained to recognize categories such as efficiency and cost reduction during interaction and the associated belief in the goodness of functionality, which should be possible to submit to rational scrutiny, while legitimacy in traditional or charismatic types of domination is based on much more communal values: belief in ancient tradition, strength in relation of kinship, the shared perception of the sanctity of the leader, mass ecstatic euphoria. Rationality and calculability in government ideally should produce public policy with material consequences that need to be justified rationally, while tradition and charisma are fulfilled in themselves, that is, ideally, they produce bonding and an immediate justification for order that is not rationalized because it is lived. The legitimacy of rationality and calculability is discovered in a historical time span: The process of legitimation is postponed to the analysis of the effects of the action, while the legitimacy of tradition and charisma is experienced in situ: Legitimation is the enactment of a perceived order. I propose to reformulate Weber's ideal types of domination toward an appreciation of tradition and charisma where they are not necessarily contemplated as inferior sources of unreflective "reality" and that can be useful and meaningful sources of order. The Weberian types of domination are built on the assumption of an individual basis for social order, and so, are displaced from conceptualizing a collective notion of self. This means that the phenomenon of authority in Weber considers its empirical manifestation as domination, but is displaced from considering willful subordination. Such willful subordination sustains disciplined practice and interaction as well as their creative spontaneous possibilities. We can consider the legitimacy of tradition and charisma—as Weber described them—as being different from that of the legal–rational type, by seeing that they are based on different conceptions of self and of time, and expressed in preeminently different verbal structures.

Nevertheless, as has been argued, in globalized current interaction, it is already a myth to consider that we can draw conceptual borders between cultures that coexist in the world today in different levels of syncretism. This is why the traditional modern self-interpretation as the highest manifestation of human consciousness is radically questioned in this work. Rather, I attempt a nonhierarchical theoretical construction in order to put forms of human knowledge at the same level of relevance to human life, which are nonetheless differentiated phenomenologically in three stages: primary, intellectual, and spiritual. Legitimate reality and its relationship with our experienced reality is equivalent to the relationship between the view of reality that is kept alive through disciplined practice and the view of reality that is experienced by virtue of our being alive and embodied in a humanly conscious manner. This involves our enactment of interaction through language and time, as our most immediate sources of a humanly experienced idea of reality. Language and time are immediate because they must be experienced and believed to convey reality at the same time as they sustain human interaction. I will expand on the constitutive roles of these two aspects of reality at length in chapter 2.

Globalization is generally related to economic interaction, but it would be a mistake to regard it as only this: globalization is the major producer of hybrid identities. Interaction is a creative source of social structures, and they reproduce themselves in institutions and organizations, which function in the background of interaction, laying common grounds for coordination of meaningful human activities. Weber's types of domination are useful tools for historical analysis, but they have an inbuilt bias toward the phenomenon of authority, which is too strongly seen as domination and not as willful subordination. I believe this to be related to a modern obsession with control and rational domination of experienced reality, but if we consider the aspect of willful subordination in legitimate authority, we are in a better position to explain how it is that belief systems produce human order through disciplined practices all over the world. This is congenial with a hermeneutical attitude toward human reality and is based in Gadamer's phenomenological rehabilitation of *prejudice, authority*, and *tradition* in his *Truth and Method* (1989). Nevertheless, I argue that the cultural achievements of the modern critical mind ought not to be abandoned. And so, in my conclusion to this book, I propose a *common human moral space* that encompasses both the critical and hermeneutic attitudes as well as the silent emotion of universal compassion, developed in chapter 5.

And so, in this work, human beings can be regarded as simultaneously equal but different to each other while being equal but different from animals, in particular, and nature, in general. This sounds like a riddle, but it illustrates the paradox of life, consciousness, and diversity, and the ethical difficulties involved in producing borders to differentiate peoples, cultures, phenomenal domains from one another, and this refers to the social sciences as well as the natural ones. I hope that the theoretical construct that I propose will also help to illustrate how the West and the non-West will not be seen at the same level of human consciousness unless our intellectual tradition of knowledge concedes to share phenomenologically its absolute inequality, its uniqueness—in which we are all very much delighted—with every other tradition of knowledge—however rudimentary in appearance. Our modern cultural inheritance helps us to produce relevant borders for a useful understanding of objective reality, but we would remain trapped by these borders if we did not have to engage in the business of constant interpretation and reinterpretation of their present relevance for all embodied humanity right now. In this sense, all human groups and their culture are regarded as engaged in this constant activity of interpretation in simultaneity with perception and disciplined practice. This discipline produces relevant and useful borders between ethical and phenomenal domains, but it is important to consider that symbols themselves may become rigid if seen as carriers of absolute aspects of reality. Imagined and enacted borders can be either useful or terrible, and the subtlety of this difference can only be grasped ethically in the awareness of our ongoing imaginative and emotional involvement with them. And so, this book is an attempt to look at human reality beyond the traditional confines of our Western tradition of knowledge. This tradition interprets itself as radically different from benighted spiritual and fantastic cosmologies, and yet, I argue that Modernity is not without its own sacred roots to reality.

"OBJECTIVE" KNOWLEDGE AND SACRED BELIEF

Kant's essay on Enlightenment ([1784] 1991) defined it as man's realization of the power of his rationality in order to leave his "self-caused immaturity." "*Sapere aude!*" was Kant's proposed slogan, which had already been adopted from Horace by Gassendi (Wade 1971, 20), and it involved courage. Such determination to leave the guidance of others in individual life specifically meant that people should stop the blind belief in religious dogma and use their reason and intelligence to lead a free life. The Enlightenment—or awakening to reason—implied a logical division of categories that, from then onward, would be developed to differentiate the enlightened understanding of the world from the traditional acceptance of religious dogma. The historical moment in which European philosophers had the realization of the power of their own individual rationality was charged with an epic sense of emotion in leading mankind to truth and freedom. I will argue that any search of this nature is based on faith and has an intrinsic spiritual stature. Science can be regarded as a discipline for contemplation of the self, a ritual or a tool to expand consciousness and create knowledge that can be intellectually shared and agreed upon. Although this search became secular in the enlightened worldview, it may work as an alternative *faith* that is capable of producing a belief system analogous to a religious one, which defines its own dogma—a veiled one under assumptions and aspirations of truth.

The history of Enlightenment is unavoidably linked with the history of Christianity; it represents a stage in the transformation of one of the most rationalized, organized, and expanded orthodox religions in the world (Harnack 1904, 1910; Tellenbach 1940; Baillie 1945; Green 1996; Davies 1997). Modernity emanated from the historical transformations that took place in preeminently Christian peoples, who remained mostly Christian and whose Christian conception of reality produced scientific thought. The European Enlightenment is the expression of the highest deification of reason in the known history of humankind, which currently shapes our perception of the world through political supremacy and the authority of science. Here, I attempt to unearth the values that create the current academic assumption that the Eurocentric scientific discipline for the creation of knowledge is superior to any other discipline with similar aims in the world. Although modern science is a major achievement of the human mind, I will regard it as a disciplinary achievement within an expanded spectrum of disciplined human creativity, which also includes our animal–primary link to embodiment and our spirituality.

This secular tradition of knowledge has an inbuilt mechanism of self-observation and interpretation that assumes progress as a principle of reality. But this is a specific type of progress, about which I will expand in chapter 4. I argue that the principle of progress, endemic in history and individuality, is lived as a disciplinary chore of secular purification. Ideal individuality is stripped of the human emotional aspect through the disciplined practice of leading her life according to universalizable principles. Objectivity in the scientific tradition of knowledge equally points at the universalistic pretensions of this tradition. In modern social life, progress is lived and experienced, on the one hand, as alienation from nature (urban life), and on the other, as the separation between the private and the public realms: My affections are lived and displayed only privately. In the public realm of interaction—where the scientific inquiry takes place—my emotional aspect remains hidden.

Nevertheless, this work is grounded in a hermeneutical reflexive spirit on the basis of which it regards itself as emerging from the scientific tradition of knowledge, or the modern world-*ethos*. What this means is that it is written within the scientific cultural inheritance of the author and her disciplined perception of reality. That is, I cannot imagine myself as being anything different to a Western individual: The colonial past of Latin America is so far behind that we have already embraced with hope and joy the quality of being Western, or the "other" West (see Merquior 1988; Carmagnani 2004). Nevertheless, from within the discipline of modern self-interpretation, I can only have the hermeneutical intuition that there may be other traditions of knowledge in the world that give no such symbolic importance to a notion of collective progress or of individual self. In them, this concern of what it is to be human might not be formulated in the same factual manner, but this is no reason to dismiss them as incommensurable with the modern perception of the predicament of what it is to be human, because they also come from human practice and experience. However, I use the intellectual descriptive symbols of our scientific tradition of knowledge and our type of "language of truth," while I simultaneously cancel the intellectual presupposition of a hierarchy of forms of human representations of reality that puts the modern one at the top. What we differentiate and compartmentalize as biological intellectual, imaginary, emotional, and spiritual qualities of being human are in this work considered as complementary characteristics that are present in us here and now as well as at all times. It is my basic assumption that, ultimately, the intellectual perspective can only be seen as a useful tool for concept formation, a disciplined means toward the knowledge of self, but the latter should dare to look beyond the limits of what we call objective reality, in order to reflect upon what it is to be human.

The main difference between science and any other form of ritualized religion is that science breaks down the traditional realm of the collective-sacred into the modern realm of the individual-sacred.

Hierophany or theophany—an experience of interaction with the divine or with God—produces the definition and clear conception of other-worldly reality as transcendence, beyond and above the world, which in turn opens the possibility of institutionalized disciplines and religions that strive for reaching transcendence (or salvation) and for living in the world according to the principles that emanate from the conception of the higher kind of reality. But after the age of reason in Europe, transcendence was equated to freedom and liberation from dogmatic bondage. Truth and knowledge were sought after as individual rational prerogatives, following reformed Christianity, which were eventually taken from the hands and texts of organized religion. Voltaire's famous promise to defend with his life somebody else's right to an opinion even if he himself did not share it, is an illustration of the enlightened ideal according to which universal individual human freedom transcends particular opinions. In the European enlightened social theodicy, tolerance would be "grounded on the brotherhood of man and the right to err" (Wade 1971, 27), for universal human consciousness—conceived as reason in Modernity—is believed and perceived to be based on the individual person. This European achievement created a systematized impersonal scientific discipline with no precedent in the known history of humankind.

According to Max Weber, science is "unique . . . in the provision of concepts and judgments which are neither empirical reality nor reproductions of it but which facilitate its analytical ordering in a valid manner" ([1904] 1949, 111). What Weber means by "valid" here explains his enlightened attempt at grounding modern social science on an objective basis. Following the neo-Kantian Heinrich Rickert, Weber developed his notion of objectivity for the social sciences at a moment when natural sciences appeared to be unquestionably, objectively grounded. However, in the light of relatively recent empirically based theories of physics—relativity and quantum theories—the Kantian conclusions must be revised, as they are based on the empirical observation of the classical mechanistic assumptions of Newtonian cosmology. Under the light of this discussion, I argue that the Weberian methodology for the social sciences becomes relevant to the methodology of science in general, that is, including the hard natural sciences.

I believe that the Weberian philosophy of science has such relevance today because Weber put into practice his scientific attempt at grounding knowledge both on empirical facts and objective judgment, but this objectivity is also based on personal awareness of one's own subjectivity, which only after having made it conscious, can be regarded as objective. Weber realized that there was no ontological divide between the subject and her object of cognition in the social sciences. His methodology in investigating social (cultural) phenomena turned him into one of the founding parents of sociology as a scientifically valid discipline. Although his methodological writings must be considered within the historical context in which they were produced, they convey a clear manifesto of the scientist as a philosopher.[2] Jaspers regards Weber as a philosopher because he embodied in his life and scientific practice a certain kind of philosophy. "All philosophers," says Jaspers, "have one thing in common: They are what they know; every philosopher is the lucidity of an unconditional being" (Jaspers 1964, 195). Weber's "being" goes beyond his work as a scientist, and if his controversial figure inspired the wealth of publications that it did, I believe that this is related to his uncompromising and honest search for truth that is reflected in his work. But this search is imbued in the Christian-enlightened attitude toward truth par excellence: It fetters its findings in imminence, and creates the charming figure of the solitary hero who is engaged in an eternal battle with the world. Weber refused to find refuge in abstraction and this turned him into one of the most charismatic scientists of our time.

In the contemporary times of postmodern assertion, beyond Weber's personal epic, and beyond the personal epic of the sacred individuality in modern theodicy, the current state of extremely differentiated and clashing conceptions of the social science leaves us perplexed with an equally extreme amount of loose ends. I believe that the present so-called postmodern condition and the atomization of identities and interests in contemporary Modernity are clear symptoms of what might come as a solution to the solitary, yet inwardly fragmented self: This work is an attempt to clarify why extreme subjectivity can only be solved in finding the universe within. But not in a relativist fashion, which can only create parallel, divided, fragmented, and clashing universes; this extreme subjectivity calls for the search of ultimate union, which can only be sought for if the immediate reality of what we regard as the world is bracketed and seen as mere appearance, following Husserl's phenomenological *epoché* (Ricoeur 1967b, 1981; Hammond et al. 1991). Weber did not do this, he was not a phenomenologist; he was a social scientist which made him demand experienced empirical evidence—the one that we can perceive and observe with disciplined objectivity. But he remained "between worlds," demanding conceptual clarity and never quite achieving it himself in his work, maybe realizing that the world's infinite diversity could only be partially captured by a margin of ambiguity, but always putting a conscious fight against this realization. His most lucid conclusions always ended up locating the reality of ethical–abstract conceptualizations (theoretical valuation) in the realm of the private individual consciousness. As Wilhelm Hennis has argued, Weber's basic concern was that of "the 'fate of humanity' under conditions of Modernity" (1988, 108), or the development of the characteristics that we conceive as what is great and noble in our human nature. But the universalistic assumptions made by Weber find themselves located in worldly existence "under conditions of Modernity" with its particular cultural inheritance and its view of reality. In this view of reality, human consciousness is based on the individual person and in the belief in a transcendental self that exists within every individual. Weber's neo-Kantian approach to sociological investigation embraces this belief (human consciousness based on the individual) in its conception of reality, and consequently, in its methodology to analyze cultural phenomena:

> The social-scientific interest has its point of departure, of course, in the *real*, i.e., concrete, individually structured configuration of our cultural life in its universal relationships which are themselves no less individually-structured, and in its development out of other social cultural conditions, which themselves are obviously likewise individually structured. (Weber [1904] 1949, 74)

Weber's methodology of concept formation is therefore situated in the modern consciousness of the thinking transcendental individual self whose existence amid an infinite diversity of phenomena gives meaning and relevance to the particular ones that the observer chooses to consider conceptually. The creation of such concepts in the social sciences, therefore, gives us knowledge about specific value relations in human beings, but tells us nothing objective (in the traditional natural science sense) about the preeminence of values related to the studied object. "If one," Weber says, "perceives the implications of the fundamental ideas of modern epistemology which ultimately derives from Kant; namely, that concepts are primarily analytical instruments for the intellectual mastery of empirical data and can be only that, the fact that precise genetic concepts are necessarily ideal types will not cause him to desist from constructing them" ([1904] 1949, 106). To Weber, concept formation would be useful only when it is backed by empirical investigation, but the knowledge created by the investigation as a whole would be grounded on knowledge of the self.

And here the relationship between theoretical values and practical valuation becomes clear: The transcendental subject must also be an embodied personality at the same time as she is transcendental. The practice of both science and universal morality depends on common belief in and contemplation of the transcendental subject that knows the universe, although this necessarily remains a spiritual experience and an intellectual ideal type. Kantian epistemology requires that the transcendental self be found by the scientist within herself in order to produce knowledge with universal validity. Kant said that it is impossible for us to accept the unity between the object of knowledge and the universe unless we also accept the unifying function of the knowing subject, the "I" and her a priori relationship to the universe. The object of knowledge must appear to us as a certain unity that might become problematic because it contains a multiplicity of elements and functions, but their unity is their origin: the awareness of the knowing subject. The thinking "I" or transcendental subject must *be* the universe through intuition in order to project it into an ordered unity of concepts. Nevertheless, Kant does not believe that these concepts can convey the transcendental meaning of the universe he sets limits to the human creation of knowledge. This stemmed out of his enquiries into the possibility of traditional metaphysics. The possibility of physical science and mathematics implies that understanding can only make an empirical use of its concepts and not a transcendental one. When the knowing subject conceives of the super-sensible as a given object, "he gets entangled in what Kant calls a transcendental illusion" (Luijpen 1964, 27). This is the kind of illusion that produces dogma in religious environments, which Kant encouraged men to escape from in order to lead their lives by the use of their own reason.

According to Kant, therefore, the scientific creation of knowledge could only refer to empirical appearances—to phenomenal occurrences—it cannot describe the "thing in itself" or the *noumenon*. Objects are given to concepts in intuition during the receptivity of impressions. Kant believed that the only kind of intuition available for the human mind was sense-intuition that allowed for the spontaneity of the production of concepts while receiving impressions through experience. According to Kant, intellectual-intuition is beyond humans, which would allow us to have access to the knowledge of the *noumenon*. For the subject to reach scientific knowledge about the world, it must assume the pure ideas of reason: "God," the "I," and the "world," a secular kind of Holy Trinity that involves the human self. These ideas are not really *known*, but in order to strive for the universality of science, we must, out of necessity, *think* them. They are the "pure concepts of reason" (Kant [1781] 1929, 316) and serve the function of directing understanding toward the universe.

However, the Kantian enthusiasm about achieving universal empirical knowledge through science and reason was tempered by the conclusions of the Scottish Enlightenment, which relied more heavily on the receptivity of impressions. Hume's most important point against the enlightened enthusiasm was that the concept of causality is only a subjective expectation aroused by the mechanism of association. This subjective expectation lies on beliefs, the ones that were given us while we were raised. If we attempt to harmonize in a hermeneutic fashion—if it is possible at all—the Kantian and Humean contributions to the philosophy of science, we could say that Kant contributed the imperative importance of contemplating the universe when doing science and Hume pointed at the—often ignored— principle of subjectivity involved in the confirmation of causality. On the one hand, contemplation of the universe is basic as an aspiration, even if it is impossible to translate the findings into words, for the latter are intrinsically finite, particular. On the other hand, confirmation of causality only means that there are bases for explanatory principles that can either help us agree about intellectual knowledge or be useful in our material everyday life. But our positivistic and scientific contemplation of the universe is based on the faith that we are mysteriously linked to it from within. This is the substantive basis for its claims of efficacy. The human inner link to universe is clearer among physicists who work with the biggest and smallest dimensions in sense experience. Our scientific explanations might prove to be useful in a practical sense only in the specific domain of experience where they are applied. This is the benefit of specialization. Technology and functionality derive from this and produce the expanded organizational capacity of the modern institutions, but they will never produce precise intellectual knowledge about the workings of the universe (in a sense that goes beyond sense experience). The Kantian impossibility to reach the "thing in itself" illustrates this point.

The model of knowledge developed by Kant can be rescued as a substantive aspiration of the hermeneutic tradition toward the ideal of universal integration of the knowing self. Nevertheless, there is always a margin of error as a scientific principle, or a distance between what I know based on theory and my empirical observation. This error points to an important warning needed for a "fundamentalist" belief in objectivity: Even if the error tends to be negligible with respect to the domain of experience in which we apply our theoretical abstraction, it can be mathematically shown that infinity still exists within that margin of error. Zeno's famous Achilles and the Tortoise *aporia* illustrates just this: There are infinite amounts of numbers between two points in any straight line and therefore we can break a line in two forever into infinity. But there are physical limits to perception of infinity in the world of sense-experience, so it is scientifically correct to reduce the error to the minimum possible range, and make it negligible in the domain of experience where it is applied. However, the scientist should not forget that to make it negligible in a specific domain of experience is no justification to ignore the infinity that it contains. Ever shrinking margins of error allow for further precision, but the significance of a decreasing margin of error also decreases marginally—the error cannot be canceled. Beyond the concept lies the diverse infinity of a universe that will not be apprehended by mere conceptual abstraction.

This might not have seemed relevant at the time when Kant wrote because, to him, the confirmation of the possibility of universal sciences lay on the then obvious universality of Newtonian physics, based on the precise functioning of a mechanical universe. Although Kant had been trained within the dogmatic rationalism of Wolff (Luijpen 1964, 9), he opposed the idea that pure conceptual operations of logic could describe universal reality (the "thing in itself"). But he also ended up rejecting the Humean idea that knowledge was based solely on changeable and concrete impressions, although this made him look into empiricism. Kant needed a source of necessary and universal judgments, and that was a priori knowledge, but the concrete experience that gave him an upper hand over the skeptics and impressionists was the apparent universal validity of the physics of Newton. Nevertheless, this appearance has been challenged in Einstein's relativity theory and in quantum physics, both of which have shown that Newton's physics apply only in a specific domain of experience: that of body-sized matter that moves slower than light (Bohm 1980; Capra 1982). Universal validity of intellectual knowledge can be regarded as a myth that carries fantastic imaginative assumptions in its very structure. However, these assumptions should not be seen as necessarily unreal because they point at what is important for the society that sustains the discipline, or the order-producing ritual.

One such useful but fantastic assumptions in the modern cosmos is the ontological assumption of a mechanical universe formed by discrete entities. Newton's physics is wholly based on what David Bohm calls the "mechanistic order" in his book *Wholeness and the Implicate Order* (1980). He contends that this kind of mechanistic view of the physical reality has been challenged by Einstein's relativity theory and also by quantum theory, but that it has remained at the center of the scientific cosmos and imagination:

> [T]he principal feature of this [mechanistic] order is that the world is regarded as constituted of entities which are *outside of each other*, in the sense that they exist independently in different regions of space (and time) and interact through forces that do not bring about any changes in their essential natures. The machine gives a typical illustration of such a system of order. (Bohm 1980, 173)

The entities are supposed to be formed of separately existent indivisible and unchangeable "elementary particles," atoms originally that later were divided into electrons, protons, and neutrons, and then into hundreds of different kinds of unstable particles, "and now even smaller ones" says Bohm "like 'quarks' and 'partons' have been postulated to explain these transformations. Though these have not yet been isolated there appears to be an unshakeable *faith* among physicists that either such particles, or some other kind yet to be discovered, will eventually make possible a complete and coherent explanation of everything" (1980, 173; emphasis added).

According to Bohm, the theory of relativity was the first indication toward the need to question the assumed mechanistic order of the universe. Einstein's relativity implied that the concept of independently existent particles was impossible, and he proposed to give a secondary importance to the idea of discrete particles. According to Einstein, reality should be regarded as constituted of *fields*, whose behavior is consistent with the requirements of the theory of relativity. "A key new idea," says Bohm, "of this 'unified field theory' of Einstein is that the field equations are *non-linear* [which] could have solutions in the form of localized pulses, consisting of a region of intense field that could move through space stably as a whole, and that could thus provide a model of the 'particle' " (1980, 174). But if any two of these pulses come close together, they alter each other so radically that the idea of independent and discrete particles is thus challenged as the essence of physical reality; a particle is thus seen as a useful abstraction furnishing valid approximations in a limited domain. However, Bohm says that Einstein's field concept still keeps the essential features of a mechanistic universe for being based on pulse-like entities that still reside outside each other, and for considering that only those separated by an infinitesimally small distance can affect each other. Einstein was never able to provide an ultimate mechanistic basis for physics in terms of a generally coherent and satisfactory formulation of his unified field theory, but Bohm says that it provided the basic intuition that the concept of particle is a useful abstraction from an unbroken and undivided universe (1980, 174).

According to Bohm, the more serious challenge to a mechanistic order came from quantum theory in the form of noncontinuity, non-causality, and nonlocality. The laws of quantum mechanics are not deterministic, they are statistical, and so, future individual events cannot be predicted uniquely and precisely. But according to Bohm, this feature does not essentially challenge the mechanistic order because independently existent elements are still seen as lying outside each other and connected by external relationships:

> The fact that (as in a pinball machine) such elements are related by the rule of chance (expressed mathematically in terms of the theory of probability) does not change the basic externality of the elements and so does not essentially affect the question of whether the fundamental order is mechanistic or not. (1980, 175)

Bohm isolates and refers to the three key features of quantum mechanics that do challenge the ontology of a classical mechanistic conception of cosmos and order on which the practice of science is based. *Noncontinuity* at a quantum level means that action is seen as an *indivisible quanta*, a whole that remains as such throughout changes of state; "it has no meaning to say that a system passes through a continuous series of intermediate states, similar to initial and final states" (Bohm 1980, 128); movement is discontinuous and the observed pulse-like entity can go from one state to another without passing through any states in between. *Noncausality* is based on the absence of determinism in quantum experiments and on the nature of experimental observation: "In the quantum context," says Bohm, "one can regard terms like 'observed object,' 'observing instrument,' 'link electron,' 'experimental results,' etc., as aspects of a single overall 'pattern' that are in effect abstracted or 'pointed out' by our mode of description. Thus to speak of interaction of 'observing instrument' and 'observed object' has no meaning" (1980, 134). Further, the observer is also part of the pattern of the experiment as pulse-like entities "can show different properties (e.g., particle-like, wave-like, or something in between), depending on the environmental context within which they exist and are subject to observation" (Bohm 1980, 175). *Nonlocality* is based on the peculiar nonlocal relationship between two entities that are far apart, such as electrons, which have separated after having initially combined into a molecule, that is, very small pulse-like entities affect one another at an indefinite distance after having interacted. What is remarkable about these discoveries is that they highlight the need to see physical reality as something that has no ontological division and that if there is any separation between the objects that we observe, it is mainly epistemological, based on our perspective and scientific style of observation.

Bohm problematizes this further and asks if instead of the typical attitude of looking at the mechanistic consistencies and applications of the relativity and quantum theories, their intuitions can be used to produce a qualitatively new perspective of observation of physical order, "from which both relativity and quantum theory are to be derived as abstractions, approximations and limiting cases" (Bohm 1980, 176). This new perspective would require a serious questioning of the Cartesian mechanistic cosmos and a different attitude toward our own thinking process, nature, and also the other in social science:

> Though physics has changed radically in many ways, the Cartesian grid (with minor modifications, such as the use of curvilinear coordinates) has remained the one key feature that has not changed. Evidently, it is not easy to change this, because our notions of order are pervasive, for not only do they involve our thinking but also our senses, our feelings, our intuitions, our physical movement, our relationships with other people and with society as a whole and, indeed, every phase of our lives. (Bohm 1980, 176)

Bohm suggests that we become aware of an unbroken continuum of reality, where distinctions should be seen as abstracted from that whole, in a similar way in which he highlights the oneness of the thinking process and its content. He believes that questions about the nature of consciousness cannot be properly expressed if we are caught up in the principle of a presumed essential separation of the elements of reality. He expresses this perspective in what he calls the "implicate order":

> We proposed that a new notion of order is involved here, which we called the *implicate order* (from a Latin root meaning "to enfold" or "to fold inward"). In terms of the implicate order one may say that everything is enfolded into everything. This contrasts with the *explicate order* now dominant in physics in which things are *unfolded* in the sense that each thing lies only in its own particular region of space (and time) and outside the regions belonging to other things. (Bohm 1980, 177)

Both implicate and explicate orders should be seen as perspectives on an intellectual contemplation of universal order that remains rooted in the belief on an essential human transcendental connection to that order. A scientist, such as Bohm, reflecting on this will not leave aside—as we are allowed to do in the social sciences—the basic assumption of investigating universally applicable principles of physics. Both the scientific contemplation of the universe and our imagined connection to that universe keep a transcendental *point d'appui* that the Kantian views on the philosophy of science explicate.

Science and philosophy differentiate or unify the universe artificially to indulge reason into observing a coherent kind of order in the world. Here, I want to emphasize that in spite of the postmodern views on the essential multiplicity of social reality (plurality turned infinite), whatever it is that we call universe remains a relevant category for intellectual contemplation of reality in the hard scientific way, the one that produces effective technology. Kant realized that physical sciences do not regard nature as a mere conglomeration of data, but as an interconnected whole that we can think of by means of concepts. Kant conceived intuitions and concepts as the elements of our intellectual knowledge, but he also thought that each intuition needed to be supported by a concept—and each concept by an intuition—to yield knowledge of the nature of the physical sciences (Kant [1781] 1929, 92). In order for this to be possible, the propositions that we formulate must *come* to us before sensible experience. In his "Transcendental Aesthetic," Kant accepts a priori forms of understanding that are impressed on the manifold data of intuition, which are reduced to a conceptual unity. For Kant, the possibility of the existence of physical sciences is only explained if we accept that this kind of knowledge about the world that obeys determinable physical laws cannot possibly come solely from experience. Nature, which is the sum of all appearances, is made an ordered whole through the intellectual discovery of a priori laws in the form of categories and concepts. Weber shares with the neo-Kantian school the idea that "it can be logically demonstrated that the reality confronting us in our daily lives is the structured version of something immediate and boundless" (Bruun 1972, 99). One can entertain the idea that explanations about our immediate reality, unavoidably yield models of that reality, which may be useful for understanding and functionality, but they remain imaginative models, ideal types, utopias.

As a consequence, the idea that we are intrinsically linked to the universe through Kantian aprioristic intuition is really only an act of faith: the certainty that humankind has an inner open window into the universe that can become conscious. And this faith may be regarded to be of identical nature to that of any other spiritual search. The difference of the Western enlightened discipline is that the scientist or philosopher can allow herself to *be* the wholeness of the universe through subjective intuition, but then she must translate the product of her contemplation into conceptual theory or explanatory systems that can be understood intellectually, and reproduced and verified empirically and publicly. This practice (or ritual), with demands of functionality (as a modern value), gives the scientist an environment of certainty within which an attitude of "rational domination of the world" thrives.[3] But the universal validity of intellectual knowledge is a myth that derives from the disciplinary belief in an individual human relationship with a universe that is originally spiritual as will be discussed below.

The essential Weberian scientific concern is to find out the subjective roots of practical valuation that gave rise to the development of the modern society in the direction of rational world domination. He found those roots in his sociology of religion, which he built in the shape of ideal typical formations. This brought him into sociology at a time when there was a need for a methodology of concept formation so that the discipline as a whole would gain the reputation of science (Hennis 1988). Thomas Burger argues that Weber was pushed into methodological argumentation "as a result of external circumstances" and "left off as soon as he could," and that his major methodological questions had been answered already by the neo-Kantian Heinrich Rickert (Burger 1976, 5).[4] However, it is possible to argue with Bruun that Weber went beyond Rickert's purely philosophical argumentation and logical categories by his use of his interpretive sociology and the close relationship between theoretical value relation and practical valuation: "Weber's attitude to the problem of value relation seems far more flexible [than Rickert's]. Of course scientific propositions and value judgments are two entirely different things; but in pointing to [practical] valuations as a frequent, and legitimate, condition of value relation, Weber hints at the possibility of a more extensive, if still controlled, interplay of practice and theory, interest and perception" (Bruun 1972, 106–07).

However, the Rickertian influence on Weber is clearly recognizable and Weber himself says that his incursions in methodology are bound up with Rickert's work (Weber [1904] 1949) and that of other neo-Kantians. According to Oakes, "in the philosophy of history developed by Windelband, Rickert, and Lask, Weber found an epistemology of the cultural sciences which, in his view, established the conditions under which knowledge of the historical individual is possible" (1987, 436). Rickert's logic created the possibility of contemplating history as a science with the objective stature of the natural sciences, but with a legitimacy of its own based on the individual uniqueness of the historically relevant events. What gives individual events their relevance is related to a valuation process:

> To attribute importance to the individuality of certain phenomena . . . means connecting them with some value in relation to which they acquire their importance . . . only this relation permits a selection from the infinite multiplicity of reality which respects the individual character of the phenomena selected, while being rooted in a firm criterion (viz., the value in question). (Bruun 1972, 88)

According to Rickert, the value in question would be relevant to everybody, meaning by this not just anybody, but everybody in a *Gemeinschaft*. This brings to mind the idea of intersubjectivity in a scientific community. However, without the scientific belief in the possibility of collectively invoking the transcendental subject in everyone in the community, the view of reality formed according to these principles is unable to overcome—at least in principle—its particularistic, locally structured nature.

Weber's ideas on value freedom in science accept that "a person may enter into two roles, being the source (or the recipient) of, alternately, scientific and valuational propositions, . . . the social scientist will often have to pass through a phase of practical valuation in order to be able to assume his theoretical role" (Bruun 1972, 106). The Rickertian "careful and deliberate" distinction between the object level and the research level is not found in Weber. He established a scientific practice according to which the scientist would look straight into her personal practical valuation. The scrupulous discipline of knowing and thus of contemplating oneself, would also make the scientist project her transcendental self-consciousness into the creation of proper theoretical value relations. According to Weber, only this scrupulous reflexive scrutiny of self will allow the scientist to create theoretical constructions that are useful to approach complex empirical reality. Yet these constructions must be systematically pondered against correct scientific proof, otherwise they are useless for the objectives of science.[5] In his essay on "objectivity," Weber considers concepts as correct if their empirical relation to the world could be recognized as such "even by a Chinese" (Weber [1904] 1949, 58). This refers to the ability of transcending particularistic cultural codes by means of scientific language.

Nevertheless—following the neo-Kantian school—theoretical value relations tell us nothing about individual perception of reality in itself, due to the established principle that immediate individual perception is a boundless infinite diversity of phenomena. Weberian methodology is rooted in a view of reality that divides the universe into real worldly phenomena and real transcendence, and whose only ground to make an objective claim is the conscious self-experience. To Weber, the relation between the concept and the object of study is always mediated by this conscious self-experience, through valuation. According to Oakes, Lask explored the relationship between the concept and its object and concluded that concrete reality cannot be derived from its conceptualization (as in what he called the emanationist Hegelian logic), but that it is lived in individual existence as the sole reality, and that its unique and unfathomable nature precludes the possibility of complete clear conceptualization. Therefore, the relationship between object and its concept is purely artificial as an "intellectual construct, reality [individual perception] is ontologically richer than the concept" (Oakes 1987, 439).

The relatively recent possibility of observation of physical phenomena at a quantum size has brought about similar conclusions: A different theoretical approach was needed at that level, because Newtonian all-encompassing theoretical physics described a more *local* kind of universe—one adapted to our body-dimensional experience of solid objects. Therefore, a broader theory was created that allowed for greater flexibility in measurement—through Heisenberg's uncertainty principle—instead of the discovery of numerical constants in the universe (or in the logic of the theory). According to Windelband, the natural sciences' *nomothetic* knowledge abstracts from the uniqueness of particular phenomena in order to concentrate on the patterns of behavior that govern the similarities of particular events, thus creating general laws, and canceling their uniqueness. In his view, historical science's kind of knowledge is *idiographic*, where "the purpose of knowledge is to comprehend the distinctive properties of the unique event itself" (Oakes 1987, 437). In history, those distinctive properties would be chosen according to general values that the scientist represents; in quantum physics, the phenomenon that the scientist decides to observe changes in (conceptual) nature according to the theoretical expectation that the scientist assumes in her experimental setting.

This allows for the possibility to say that both social and natural sciences have nomological characteristics, as well as idiographic ones. In order to produce useful concepts and theoretical constructs, they should encompass general observable phenomena (less so in history, but not in the rest of the social sciences). Idiographic uniqueness becomes important, in the hard natural sciences, by how much the experiment is influenced by the particular and individual person who is also a scientific observer, and in the social sciences, by the valuational closeness of the object of study: the conscious self. And so, what Weber pointed out to be the basis for objectivity in the social sciences applies to any kind of science, natural or social: What the current academia agrees to see as relevant and desirable for the expansion of intellectual knowledge, and what the initiated ones teach and accept as the leading paradigm has its basis in this intersubjective legitimacy. In this conception of reality, an intersubjective agreement—based on the strength of a rational abstract theory and evidence—is the basis for what we call objectivity.

Nevertheless, considering its basis on the individual conscious self, objectivity should always be regarded as an act of faith. This does not mean that objectivity is therefore faulty or impossible; it only means that the blind belief in absolute certainty through objective knowledge is a cultural scientific by-product of Modernity that, in practice, may acquire a dogmatic nature. In his defense of value freedom in the social sciences, Weber always opposed the formation of scientific dogma of this nature. To him, this was reflected in the confusion that science would be able to elucidate the actual validity of knowledge, which he strove to differentiate through keeping a clear distinction between empirical science and value judgments. "For even the knowledge of the most certain proposition of our theoretical sciences—e.g., the exact natural sciences or mathematics, is, like the cultivation and refinement of the conscience, a product of culture" (Weber [1904] 1949, 55).

On Weberian grounds, social science is such by virtue of the Kantian scientific unifying principle of contemplation of the universe—even if only as a transcendental belief, an aspiration, which realizes that any intellectual knowledge achieved in this manner remains a partial view of reality, with particular (local) significance. The social sciences should take seriously into account the possibility of everything being enfolded into everything else at the same time as we are able to distinguish discrete differences. This is the essence of synchronicity, and it can disclose the collective dimension of being human. Individual intention considered solely as the center of human action follows the principles of an atomistic Cartesian universe. And the ontology of this type of universe has already been empirically challenged by various modern philosophers and contemporary physics. The ideal modern self that we experience as an individual self can also be brought to conscious experience as a collective self imaginatively and emotionally. If we accept a hermeneutics of human consciousness that holds imaginative and emotional ways of experiencing itself as a united whole with other human beings, there is no reason why a collective self, beyond the modern individual self-conception, cannot be posed. This describes an ideal human self-experience that can be a legitimate source of knowledge.

It is in this spirit that I build three ideal typical views of reality as fictions or utopias that cannot be observed in their abstract purity, but that complement each other phenomenologically in human interaction. In a reflexive, hermeneutic spirit, the center for intellectual self-knowledge is individual consciousness, which is the perspective of the observer in the scientific tradition of knowledge. In this book, this perspective will be transformed into that of the *present moment of meaningful experience* in a phenomenological and hermeneutic theoretical position. I develop this perspective as a model for cognition in chapter 3 in order to be able to ground views of reality that are alternative to the modern one, in a consciousness of self that is not necessarily seen as essentially individual.

However, before building this perspective, I expand on the ideal types referred to above, and their relation to time and language in the next chapter. I then explain the theoretical justification for these ideal types in chapters 3–5 and I also concentrate on how reality is structured in the three types in order to organize different ways of approaching the ethical life of humans. I argue that this life is initially grounded on our biology and is eventually transformed by the symbological discovery (or invention) of transcendence. They also represent three different aspects of what it is to be human: our animality, our intellectual aspirations to truth, and our spiritual impulses beyond this concrete world. But it is important to say at this initial point that eventhough I use theoretical language to describe them, my ideal types are metaphors that I consider useful for heuristic purposes and—at best—they may be valid approximations in the observation of human interaction. Their validity is justified in terms of a point of intersection between practical valuation and theoretical valuation: the practice of science and its ideal aspirations to truth, but we should be aware that these aspirations are based on belief. This belief is of the sacred type, spelt out by Kantian philosophy of knowledge, which is not without its fantastic imaginative roots. These roots are nonetheless reproduced by human experience in social reality, sustained by the contemporary political world order and global interaction, and by the disciplined practice of scientific observation—which according to Weber, should be essentially practiced as self-observation.

2

ETHICAL AUTHORITY ACCORDING
TO THREE IDEAL TYPES
OF REALITY

In order to build the conceptual basis for a convergence of cosmologies, the basic premise of this work is that the ability to conceive and represent a "view of reality" makes *human interaction* different from any other phenomenon that an observer may call "interaction." The "substance" where a view of reality is formed is the experience of time and language in disciplined practice. Science and the modern worldview conceived as disciplined practice require human entities that regard themselves as either observers in science or as historical individuals in modern life. Nevertheless, in a disciplined search for knowledge—which can also be seen as a search for self-knowledge—an individual or an observer is already necessarily embodied and is herself already situated within a view of reality and cultural inheritance that she identifies with through her own particularly human interaction and experience of time and language. Currently, the modern view of legitimate knowledge construes reality as organized around the notions of a subject and an object that are separate from each other. "Objectivity" depends on the disciplined distance that a subject may take from her object of study. This analytical distance may be useful in the practice and understanding of science, but my contention is that, to take on board that the possibility of such separation is the only source of reality is analogous with assuming sacred or religious belief as absolute truth. Belief and legitimate reality are based on cosmological myths as well as on disciplined practice simultaneously.

In this work, religions and institutions are regarded as analogous to each other because they dictate the notion of legitimate reality, and this is reflected in the ideal principles expressed by prevalent discipline.

I argue that in contemporary modern interaction, the quality of order is different from that of the order of what is explicitly sacred by virtue of its relationship with time and language. In the "West," this difference is traditionally construed through a relationship to time that is progressive and that contemplates a movement from the reality of the sacred order at the center of human interaction to the reality of human rationality at the center of human interaction as a positive and desired transformation. But this modern self-interpretation, in its rejection of the sacred roots to reality, refuses to see that this progressive construal itself is sustained in human action (or nonaction), emotion, and imagination by those sacred (mythical) roots themselves. My argument is that the locus of legitimation is the relevant experience of time and language for either of the three ideally typical views of reality and their *institutionalization* as disciplines, even as the different types of time and language that are identified here are essential to the pragmatic *organization* of any culture that can be identified as such empirically. This is the reason why in this work legitimation is related to institutions and not to organization: Institutions, like religions, portray the ideal "form" of the discipline that human beings engage with in order to interact with experience, while organizations are a pragmatic mixture of that form with the unavoidable spontaneity of life. The ideal form of the discipline exists mainly in human emotion and imagination and this is related to the creation of belief in legitimate institutions and disciplined human interaction.

I suggest that what has been traditionally construed as difference between religion and rational institutions can also be construed as a continuum. This continuum has been identified by (new) forms of institutionalism as "path dependencies"; this is an image of social causation that "rejects the traditional postulate that the same operative forces will generate the same results everywhere in favor of the view that the effect of such forces will be mediated by the contextual features of a given situation often inherited from the past" (Hall and Taylor 1996, 941).[1] From this perspective, the sharp differences between tradition and Modernity become blurred, but can still be considered as differences of *degree*. This follows the experience that, while Modernity emanates from a specific geographical center in the world, the periphery is also already a part of it through currently sustained global interaction. At the same time, there is a popularly sustained myth—of the cosmological primary type—that Modernity progressively wipes out tradition; a suggestion that produces optimistic projections of a possibly *better* future as much as terrifying visions of administrated and utterly rationalized worlds. My own position here is to take fully on board Bruno Latour's claim that *We Have Never Been Modern* (1993). In this work, he contends that the project of Modernity is both suspended and sustained by its own inner paradoxes and contradictions. I would add that the modern methods to produce knowledge are at the same time traditional in their need for mythical assumptions of the cosmological type about reality. So nobody has ever been modern, yet Modernity is already the ideal basis of a global culture.

The difference in degree between modern and traditional interaction cannot be fully appreciated through a dichotomous relationship between the "West" and "non-West," or Modernity and tradition, where one of them is what the other is not. Tradition ought not to be assumed to precede Modernity in a sequential manner, mainly because it is part of the present social experience of both the center and the periphery in global world interaction simultaneously. This is the reason why this relationship should be brought to the contemporary world scenario in identifying various current cosmological beliefs, regardless of whether they seem to lack basis for reality in one's own tradition of knowledge and belief. In order to do this, I suggest a theoretical construction that contemplates three ideal types of reality; the structure of this ideal difference is essentially organized around the dialogical relationship between two concepts that constitute the conceptual axis of this work: "World" and "transcendence." Another important part of the conceptual framework of this book will be the notions of time and language that derive from each ideal type of reality, which determine the shape of the principles of ethical discipline—substantive institutions as defined in this work. However, I assume that all of the elements of the three ideal types of reality are complementary, that is, they depend conceptually on each other to be defined at all because the three of them constitute essential aspects of present human life. In the first section of this chapter, I justify theoretically and define conceptually the three ideal types of reality. In the second and third sections, I relate them to the notions of time and language that, I argue, are the materials in which views of reality are "carved."

THREE IDEAL–TYPICAL VIEWS OF REALITY

In his book *The Interpretation of Cultures* (1973), Clifford Geertz speaks about a pair of complementary concepts that he defines as *ethos* and worldview: "[T]he *ethos* is made intellectually reasonable by being shown to represent a way of life implied by the actual state of affairs which the worldview describes, and the worldview is made emotionally acceptable by being presented as an image of an actual state of affairs of which such a way of life is an authentic expression" (Geertz 1973, 127). What Geertz calls an "actual state of affairs" depends on whatever it is that a specific culture regards as real. "What all sacred symbols assert is that the good for man is to live realistically; where they differ is in the vision of reality they construct" (Geertz 1973, 130). He considers that, "for various individuals and in various cultures," religion fuses *ethos* and worldview and gives social values what he calls "an appearance of objectivity" (Geertz 1973, 131), which is what he thinks *ethos* and worldview most need to be successfully sustained.

Geertz's conclusions about social order help us clarify the organizational implications of a socially constructed view of reality, but he uses the symbol of objectivity (one that is regarded as legitimate reality in the West) in order to convey his link between reality and another worldview's experience of it. His general message is that another culture may hold an idea of reality that may not agree with ours, but that it is no less real to the bearers of the culture because of this. His is the relativistic Boasian standpoint in anthropology, where all cultures are seen as valuable in themselves (Bennet 1996). It is only from this standpoint that we can look at the modern tradition of analysis itself, and observe it as a culture, a worldview with a very particular type of *ethos*, which happens to be universalistic and factual. I will go back briefly to the discussion of the subject/object divide in order to illustrate the predicament of this Geertzian type of analysis, through which the anthropologist positions herself in the privileged perspective of observation to produce knowledge about a different culture, even while she does not claim superiority for her own cultural inheritance.

In order to carry out her analysis, the scientist must differentiate between subject and object as a methodological assumption. But, as has been discussed, this exercise of differentiation is itself based on a "myth" of separation at the very root of the modern tradition of knowledge. The methodological assumption of the clear divide between subject and object is an order-producing ritual in the worldview of science. Although recently, scholars are more willing to see ritual in scientific practice (Latour 1993), there is much resistance to identify ritual with the rationalized practices that produce secular knowledge and rational domination. Catherine Bell regards the generic concept of ritual as an analytical tool, based on the division between subject and object, that helps to give social shape to the dichotomy thought/action "that runs particularly deep in the intellectual traditions of Western Culture" (Bell 1992, 24):

> We do not see that we are wielding a particularly powerful analytical tool, nor do we see how our unconscious manipulation of it is driven not only by the need to resolve the dichotomy it establishes but also simultaneously to affirm *and* resolve the more fundamental opposition it poses—the opposition between the theoretician and the object of theoretical discourse. In other words, we do not see how such dichotomies contribute to the rational definition of a knower, a known, and a particular kind of knowledge. (Bell 1992, 25)

In Modernity, the kind of knowledge produced by scientific methods (or rituals) is the legitimate one. This knowledge is produced and coherently spelt out in the sequence of symbols that represent themselves and the world in the abstract possibilities of conceptual thought. But the critical discipline depends on the assumption of a vantage point (originally related to the Gaze of the Christian monotheistic God) that produces the rational ability to see the dichotomous relationships, which other cultures do not identify as the basis of reality. This vantage point belongs to the observer who is poised in a mimetic assimilation of the transcendental Gaze of God and who is able, from this vantage point of "pure" objectivity, to project universal knowledge into the abstract, sequential, scientific descriptions of "objective" reality. Even if this standpoint has been repeatedly questioned from within European philosophical enquiry—and this legitimizes the emergence of post-structuralist and postmodern theoretical constructs as well as various forms of existentialism and nihilism—in the realm of everyday life modern interaction, the privileged standpoint cannot be disposed of. In the collective practice of science, however, the absolute gaze of the scientist is transformed into a social consensus where the "objective" reality can be agreed upon:

> Hence the modern use of language has been driven increasingly to define the objective reality of the world, on the assumption that "objective" means real because it allows such consensus, and that "subjective" means unreal because it does not. The word "subject" in English means the observer of the objective, and it also has the political meaning of an individual subordinated to the authority of his society or its ruler, as in "British subject." It is not really possible, however, to separate the two meanings. The "subject" is subjected to the objective world, and not only subjected but almost crushed under it, like Atlas. (Frye 1982, 21)

The Geertzian relativistic interpretation of other cultures points at a metonymic correspondence in our use of the terms "objective" and "reality"; to us, it is not really possible to separate the meaning of these two concepts. However, a full exercise of relativism is impossible for an anthropologist who stands in the vantage point of an observer who is engaged in the activity of translation from the realm of the "other" to the realm of the modern objective tradition of knowledge as it is practiced today. This vantage point is sustained by contemporary cosmology, which implies a political order that is unavoidably entwined with the contemporary power structures of the world. A full exercise of relativism is needed that would imply a turn of one hundred and eighty degrees in order to analyze the "otherness" of European culture itself. The problem is that, in this attempt, our own universalistic grounds would be removed from under the feet of the privileged observer. The question that springs to mind is whether it is possible at all to realize this intellectual exercise, from the point of view of the observer, and regard the "Western" tradition as the "other" and as "oneself" at the same time. My own way of dealing with this predicament is to embrace the paradox and give intellectual knowledge only a metaphoric value, useful for understanding, yet mythical in its universalistic consequences.

According to Geertz, religion encompasses *ethos* and worldview in a given culture. In modern culture though, it is the institutions (legal–rational) that substitute for religion, and give the latter a marginal function in the private realm of human life. It is important to stress at this point that the current realm of global interaction is also situated in culture and belief, and therefore it is also based on an *ethos* and a worldview. Our modern institutions represent this *ethos* and worldview, but it is necessary to trace the ancestry of modern institutions all the way to the Christian religion, together with its own Judaic and Greek ancestries (Snell 1953; Jaeger 1962; Voegelin 1974; Nisbet 1994). It is this ancestry, I argue, that defines the present relevance of our contemporary use of the notions of a separate subject and object, the mechanistic cosmos that rules modern interaction, and our distinct sense for a factual type of history. The concept of *religion* is used in this work indistinctly from institution (legitimate belief), spiritual practice, or discipline, systematic form of worship, or social theodicy to describe the same phenomenon: the relationship between what Geertz describes as *ethos* and worldview of a culture, and their structural consequences in the cosmology that rules interaction. This relationship is necessarily ideal and, therefore, institutions here are regarded as possessing an aura of distance that is analogous to the charismatic aura of organized religion.[2]

An idea of reality, as portrayed in this work, may be couched in religions or (rational) institutions, cosmologies or the order of the world or the universe; it is rooted in what is really important for a given society, and in that sense, real. The concept of "religion" is linked to Christianity as a spiritual discipline and practice—and to the Judeo-Christian conception of God—and although it has been used to speak about other spiritual disciplines in the world, it was not created as an analytical tool but as a descriptive symbol of Christian "togetherness." Religion was something that the source of modern philosophy, the European Enlightenment, rejected in order to deify reason as a source of reality, which perpetuated a dichotomous opposition of the "real" and the "unreal." This is very relevant to this work because it attempts to show that Modernity has a mythological basis as much as any other known tradition of human knowledge. The modern view of reality is prevalent in global interaction, and therefore, we should be aware of its mythological basis. But this "mythology," as I have called it, cannot be disclosed unless—at least— the other two standpoints are conceptually constructed and identified with "other" world cultures. These standpoints must be built in the spirit of recognizing that they are also aspects of our own culture as they are aspects of every other culture—even if they are not culturally preeminent in ours. The problem is how to portray other generic views of reality that modern people can identify themselves with *qua* human beings. This would produce an empirically plausible counter-point to the modern worldview, formulated conceptually, which can at the same time be regarded as different but sharing its deepest existential concerns nonetheless.

I will construe three ideal–typical views of reality whose difference is essentially organized around an alternative dialogical relationship between "world" and "transcendence." The three ideal types are called the historical, mystic, and primitive types. Only the first one considers both world and transcendence as simultaneously real. The mystic type regards the "world" as illusory in nature and only transcendence as real. The primitive type regards reality as the "world." Thus, while the historical type is based on the dialectical tension of an "eternal" division, the mystic and the primitive types conceive of reality as essentially whole and couched in either of the two poles whose tension the historical view inhabits. I am aware that this alternative is also shaped by modern dialectics, but in a hermeneutic stance, I explicitly resort to my own cultural roots to reality. I do this in order to conceptually place the "other" within a perspective where she can also be "oneself" simultaneously.

In the historical view, reality is divided into an opposition—however ideal—between "world" and "transcendence." The other two typically ideal conceptions of reality that I propose are holistic in that reality is fettered either wholly in "world" or wholly in "transcendence," and the opposition between these two terms in those ideas of reality is either irrelevant or illusory. To an observer, the primitive conception regards reality as the "world" and the mystic conception regards reality as "transcendence." We are left with three typically ideal conceptions of reality whose empirical reference is linked with the prevailing spiritual practice in diverse cultural settings that, despite their diversity, can nonetheless be generally classified as primitive (reality as the "world" only), historical (reality as the "world" and "transcendence" at the same time), and mystic (reality as "transcendence" only). However, it is important to clarify that, although these views of reality are conceived in an idealized symbology and lead to an ideal classification of cultures from a specific perspective, they stress that they are empirically experienced in simultaneous and changing experiences of human consciousness in all kinds of cultures all over the world. The ideal types as such are analytical tools that help us identify which one of them is prevalent in any specific culture. And so, these three ideal types of reality are not mutually exclusive; they are complementary in human experience: All cultures have recognizable organizational features of the three types.

It is important to point out that the transcendentalist views (historical and mystic) legitimize the symmetrical opposite at the basis of their belief systems: In the historical view, the individual self achieved the status of a value in itself, while in mysticism, the collective mind is sacred (and it is not anthropomorphic). In the transcendentalist views, the idea of self that is idealized and given an institutional aura in the different types of views of reality tends either toward the transcendental individuality of human beings (the transcendental subject or the knowing Ego) or toward humanity unified in awareness of an immanent kind of collective entity that encompasses all, but that is not given a clear personality as in the God of the "religions of the Book." However, this "clean" symmetrical differentiation is mediated by the idea of transcendence, which is clearly articulated in the historical and in the mystic views of reality, but not in the primitive one. In the primitive view, oneness with the cosmos is a living experience of either collective or individual ritual, a sense of awe and veneration for the experienced mysterious characteristics of embodiment and the world, articulated in archaic symbols and myths, and induced by their cyclical mimetic enactment in synchronic experience. These practices bring about experienced awareness and renewal of the symbols of spiritual–organic union of life and death.

It is also important to mention at this point that the only conceptual tension with further dichotomous consequences in this tripartite differentiation exists between the two views of reality that contemplate "transcendence" as real. There is no conceptual tension between the transcendental views of reality and the primitive view of reality because the reality of the world is either controlled or engulfed by them—the more problematic tension is not conceptual but embodied in providing justification for violent colonialism. The conceptual tension between the transcendentalist views of reality is not experienced as such in global social interaction because, while the modern conception of reality, the historical type, produces the practice of what Weber called "rational domination" of *reality* (or experience), the mystic conception produces the practice of what I call "intuitive submission" to experience. Rational domination engages with the reality of the world and creates material organization that is most successful in coordinating world interaction; intuitive submission produces peacefulness as a substantive imperative and clear mindedness or awareness that is helpful in handling mundane experience, even as this idea of reality may consider the world as illusory. Both kinds of transcendental practice are aimed at colonizing the primitive idea of reality bringing it awareness of transcendence—without being able to abandon the grounds of embodiment and myth that wrap the mysteries of life and death. But transcendence lies beyond the concreteness of this world, as impersonated in the only God in Heaven, as infinity, as the eternal present mystic instant of Enlightenment, or as universal humanity.

The primitive type conceives reality as being only in the world, which due to diversity in nature, has created a huge range of stories (myths) where a mixture of human experience, emotional ties, and imagination speculate about the mysteries that keep the world alive and in constant renewal. But this is not an outward observation of phenomena, such as science; it is an inquiry toward the inner life of the human group that needs the group organically. Human beings need each other to survive as embodied animals. As we will see, this practical awareness may abandon human interaction only in extreme artificial circumstances (such as urban life). Nevertheless, the mythological realm of existence is a human characteristic of interaction and, even if it is left in the background of modern interaction as a source of the primeval root that links human to nature, it is still the foundation of social life:

> Mythology is not a *datum* but a *factum* of human existence: It belongs to the world of culture and civilization that man has made and still inhabits. As a god is a metaphor identifying a personality as an element of nature, solar myths or star myths or vegetation myths may suggest something of a primitive form of science. But the real interest of myth is to draw a circumference around a human community and look inward toward that community, not [essentially] to inquire into the operations of nature. Naturally it will draw on elements from nature, just as a creative design in painting or sculpture would do. But mythology is not a direct response to the natural environment; it is part of the imaginative insulation that separates us from that environment. (Frye 1982, 37)

It is pertinent to say with Frye that myth is never improved upon, nor is it abolished in any society (as in the assumption that progress in conceptual thought brought us away from myth). Its primitivity is linked to its organic present relevance to human and not to the "evolution of man" (where women and their domestic world are thought of as lagging behind—an appreciation that is linked to moral competence [see chapter 3]—together with children and "non-Western" peoples).

At the historical period of the European Enlightenment, what may be regarded as the historical origin of secular Modernity—or the age of reason—the historical conception of reality was redefined to reject the constraining dogma of the church. But the Christian dualistic and divided conception of reality in "world" and "transcendence" was kept in the rationally enlightened minds of the philosophers who could not have thought in the void and were thus subject to their cultural past "path dependencies." This differentiation of reality gives the modern conception an intellectual vantage point because it includes both world and transcendence as real; at the same time, it takes away the perspective of an experiential vantage point for other types of knowledge where these two categories lie undifferentiated. A disciplined rational domination of experience, along the Christian lines of time, eventually brought about science as a very powerful source of intellectual knowledge. However, there is a dogmatic trap here that every scientist should learn to avoid: One may believe that the discipline produced by this view of reality is the only source of valid knowledge.

The discipline of rational domination of experience constantly redefines itself to try to encompass intellectual knowledge of the infinite variation of phenomena that the world's constant change creates, while the discipline of intuitive submission to experience accepts the world as it is because its worldly nature as such is seen as illusion. These two attitudes characterize both "transcendentalist" views of reality and consider as important intellectual and spiritual knowledge, respectively. But a primitive type of (primary) knowledge rooted in the world and in myth is not only relevant to human, but it is also the basis of any other type of knowledge; as will be argued in the second section of chapter 3, it is the type of knowledge that human animals share with nonhuman animals. Knowledge in this work is not only conceptualized as intellectual knowledge, but there are also two other kinds of knowledge that should be taken into consideration when producing a substantive theory for human world order: Spiritual knowledge and the knowledge produced by a direct experience of the world—not mediated by any kind of explicit transcendentalism (primary knowledge).

Each of the three types of knowledge referred to correspond to each of the three types of views of reality and also have an ideal–typical nature in the sense that they are never pure, but manifest themselves as empirical mixtures in different symbolizations and degrees of relevance. Eventhough primary and spiritual knowledge lack precision in discursive expression, the realm of experience where they are expressed is real in its "actuality" for human interaction, in a way analogous to Mircea Eliade's idea that the sacred realm—where the imagined realms of magic, transcendence, and salvation lie—is also "objective reality" because it "manifests itself" (Bennet 1996, 118). Here, I would like to temper this position though, and accept the reality of primary and spiritual types of knowledge in as much as they organize experienced domains of present human interaction. Primary and spiritual knowledge are sources of organization that are barely noticed or recorded as they are expressed through practice that is embodied and enacted practically; their discursiveness is limited and ambiguous, but their presence is lived nonetheless.

Human consciousness is then ideally comprised of these three kinds of knowledge.[3] Intellectual knowledge is today represented through the scientific discipline of concept formation or factual knowledge, spiritual knowledge represents itself in universalistic revelation, the sacred "Word of God," Dharma, philosophical disquisition, or spiritual practice of various disciplines; and the primary experience of reality represents itself through compact symbols of local, particular, and embodied experience. In order to be able to contemplate a wider scope of human creativity, it is necessary to give these kinds of knowledge a conceptual existence within the framework of consciousness. It is necessary to represent them because, to the best of our knowledge, human experience creates and dwells in these representations of reality (which may also be said to create human experience back) and they persist in human life to this day through what is peculiar to our species: human language and a human type of embodied interaction. The three kinds of knowledge constantly interact with each other in human language and embodied interaction. Here, we are dealing with the complex process of consciousness that in this work is regarded as inseparable from embodiment. Language and embodied interaction undergo constant transformation through time but they can also be observed at the same time to keep a general form that we can identify. In order to concretize the difference between these kinds of knowledge and to define how they are relevant to human life, I must define types of time and types of language (verbal structures) and how these types relate to the ideal types of reality. One of the most important premises of this conceptual work is that the experiences of time and language, which are imaginatively and emotionally cognized, are used by human interaction in order to structure the immediate and boundless reality in front of us. This will be the object of enquiry in the following two sections of this chapter.

TIME: SYNCHRONY AND DIACHRONY

A "view of reality" emerges in embodied experience, emotion, and imagination, from the immediate need of our human consciousness to interact with each other and with the world. Through consciousness and embodiment, this interaction produces knowledge of various kinds that may be differentiated, on the one hand, according to each view of reality, and on the other, according to the legitimate experience of time within that view of reality. In the two holistic views of reality, the relevant experience of time for the purpose of legitimation lies on simultaneity (synchronicity): mimetic identification of ritual wholeness and the eternal present moment of mystic Enlightenment. In the divided view of reality of the historical type, the relevant experience of time that legitimizes expectation of eschatology or a constant "not yet"[4] of the project of Modernity is sequential and highlights past and future (diachrony): means-ends sequence, coherence of sequential, rational disquisition, and consciousness of history as a domain of reality that is relevant for a universal humanity. We owe the original distinction between synchrony and diachrony to the Saussurean structuralist analysis of language: synchrony is his axis of simultaneities and diachrony that of successions (Wilden 1972, 50; Merquior 1986). But here, I use the difference between synchrony and diachrony to be analogous with the difference between conscious and embodied awareness of simultaneity and the (human) experience of sequence either in natural events or in social ones. I argue that while Modernity has succeeded in showing the importance of the legitimate experience of time as progress and history, it should also look into the relevance of simultaneity within the organization of its own cultural tradition. I resort to Jaspers's (1953) construction of a historical *axial age* to illustrate this point.

Time may be experienced as a continuum of simultaneity that is comparable to space (but not identical with it) and which connects everything to everything else, but it may also be experienced as movement that is witnessed by the constant change and restlessness of everything that surrounds us.[5] To human consciousness, time is only identifiable through contrasts because otherwise its essence would be experienced as a mere flow of substances in nature: We need relevant marks that allow us to distinguish past from future in that endless flow. Human marks on time are produced in relevant experience of simultaneity that establishes meaningful points of reference in the flow of occurrences in the otherwise undifferentiated continuum. This makes us aware of two orders of events in time: synchrony and diachrony. The former denotes simultaneity and the latter, the movement from past to future. Synchrony is rooted in the present instant of human consciousness while diachrony is related to the relevant realms of past and future interaction with each other, with the world, with the sacred realm, or with eternity (transcendence).

This distinction is held by the three types of view of reality, in the sense that they are three types of human experience that we can distinguish conceptually. The historical view of legitimate knowledge is attached to a representation of time as (diachronic) progress and this displaces it from considering the synchronic realm of experience as a realm that can be legitimately considered as time-like.[6] Nevertheless, in order to clarify their realms of application to our concrete experience and perception, the opposition between synchrony and diachrony may be regarded as analogous to the opposition between being and becoming, but not as the Hegelian categories of Absolute reality, but as the position in which ordinary human self may find herself with respect to her experience. My contention is that, in the historical idea of reality, the realm of ordinary being is not relevant in its *suchness*[7] to our everyday living; we are mostly in chase of what it is that we are becoming (see Maturana and Verden-Zöler 1995).

In the previous section of this chapter, I spoke about the need to see the modern tradition in the position of the "other." I argue that the only temporal grounds from which this can be done is the synchronic realm of present experience. This is because an intellectual enquiry into the validity of other types of knowledge is couched on historical and evolutionary evidence that is itself already a structural feature of the modern tradition of legitimate knowledge. From a phenomenological perspective, we can see that progress, evolution, universal history, and any other kind of diachronic tale is constructed for the sake of the present moment of meaningful experience, for the possibility of present synchrony in functionality, in purpose, in understanding, in love. The only basis to launch a critique that unveils modern mythology is to regard diachronic human history, progress, and evolution as disciplined explanations—based on evidence—that we build in the present for the sake of present synchrony. This does not invalidate the diachronic tales themselves, but it allows us to contemplate their mythical aspects in their primary sense, which show what is really important for the culture under analysis, our modern liberal culture . . . which is already global.

And so, a synchronic perspective can help to create a space to point at the mythological assumptions entwined with the structure of a diachronic representation of time—such as the modern obsession with a constant kind of change that is supposed to wipe out the past progressively and unavoidably. In global interaction, universal history is relevant to every nation in the world and even if it was originally produced by Christian symbolism and empire, it is already part of the mythical conditioning of everyone who is in touch with the global realm of interaction. Historical relevance is organized and selected according to a specific set of values dictated by the prevalent conception of reality (see Weber [1904] 1949). Its source, the Christian view of reality, considers both world and transcendence real, but essentially separate, for the latter is fettered beyond the world. This is the root to a divided universe that would base interpretation of experience in a conceptual dichotomous relationship of opposite cosmological forces. This dual relationship in the modern tradition has been transformed into a methodological interplay of concepts that take place in an indefinite linear progression from the unknown to the unknowable;[8] but, it was originally based on belief in a circular cosmology that originated in Genesis and would end in Apocalypse.

The factual reality of the Bible myth here is irrelevant, because there remains a sense for a collective moral progress of humanity as a whole that, with all the potential beauty it holds, also makes cosmological assumptions that are relevant to the present idea of human consciousness, its *evolution* as a species and its *universal* history. In his monumental work *Order and History*, Eric Voegelin suggests that Modernity represents, as well as a break with its religious past, an unintended symbolic continuum with Christianity in its notion of the unfolding of time in universal human history. This religion sets the institutional present for itself in a "once and for all" event—the coming of the Messiah and the interaction with the divinity (hierophanic or theophanic events). "We have not moved so far away from Christianity as the conflict between the church and Modernity would suggest," says Voegelin (1974, 269). Modernity sets the absolute originality of its own present in symbols that Voegelin considers as deformed versions of the original Christian symbols produced by the hierophanic events. These "deformed" symbols were related originally to an aspiration toward transcendence, and became secular progress, evolution, and wealth expansion.

Theophanic events take place at the level of experiencing consciousness simultaneously with divine consciousness, which reveal the "dynamics of transfiguration" from darkness into light. This spiritual transformation was already embedded in the emotional and imaginative sources of the philosophers of the European Enlightenment, and was used as an important symbol for a rationalistic *transfiguration* in the same kind of synchronic "once and for all" event: the age of reason. According to Foucault, in his text *What is Enlightenment?*, Kant ([1784] 1991) regards the *Aufklärung* as an event where philosophy problematizes its own discursive contemporaneity in whose meaning, value, and philosophical particularity it finds "both its own raison d'être and the grounds for what it says" (Foucault 1988, 88). And yet, following Voegelin, I suggest that this construction of a contemporaneous (to Kant) rational self-awareness bases its "alternative" consciousness about historical reality and its progress on transformed symbols of the Christian reality, which it transforms and deforms in order to reject the religious undertones at same time. According to Voegelin, all the subsequent efforts to ground a philosophy of history beyond the Pauline tale only succeed in deforming the theophanic symbols of transfiguration into what he calls "egophanic" symbols where the thinker engages in a narcissistic contemplation of his own sphere of ownness:

> The variations on the theme of transfiguration still move in the differentiated form of the eschatological myth that Paul has created. This is an insight of considerable importance, because it permits one to

classify the ideological "philosophies of history" as variations of the Pauline myth in the mode of deformation. The symbols developed by the egophanic thinkers in the self-interpretation of their work, such as "*Wissenschaftslehre*," "system of science," "philosophy of history," "*philosophie positive*," or "*wissenschaftlicher Sozialismus*," cannot be taken at their face value; they are not engendered by bona fide analytical efforts in the noetic and pneumatic fields; they rather must be recognized as mythical symbols in a mode of degradation. The "history" of the egophanic thinkers does not unfold in the Metaxy, i.e., in the flux of divine presence, but in the Pauline Time of the Tale that has a beginning and an end. (Voegelin 1974, 269)

The efforts around the construction of a unified world church transformed the notion of transfiguration into collective expectation of an age of perfection, of the Spirit, one "beyond the establishment of church and empire" (Voegelin 1974, 268). But the original Tale was conceived in contemplation of divine presence, and even if we concede to regard it as myth, it gives sense to our present secular conception of progress, evolution, history, and moral conscience.

The notion of the contemplation of divine presence is important here in order to establish its link to the realms of synchrony and diachrony. I have mentioned that Voegelin regards the Christian symbol of spiritual transfiguration from darkness into light as the root to Western dichotomous relationships. However, this symbol of transfiguration is also present in the other transcendentalist type of idea of reality (mystic), and takes the shape of one or another symbol for spiritual Enlightenment, but it does not produce a philosophy of universal history in the Western sense. I will discuss some reasons for this in the second section of chapter 4. Nevertheless, the specifically Christian symbol of transfiguration serves as an axis that gives sense to diachrony in the Western worldview of a before and an after, but the transfiguration itself is a symbol that grounds its importance in synchronic experience and leaves a mark in time for centuries to come. The Christian tale of beginning and beyond describes a full cycle in the construction of spiritual consciousness that was contemplated as a historical cycle for all of humanity. But this Christian cycle rotates around the synchronic figure of the Son of God who is also the historical figure of Jesus of Nazareth.

In order to see how the above symbol organizes the whole conception of history and humanity throughout the ages, diachrony and synchrony must be placed in a relationship of direction with respect to each other. Synchrony is centripetal, establishing simultaneous relationships in human experience, whereas diachrony is centrifugal determining relevant difference (Frye 1982). The human experience of simultaneity contains the possibilities of symbolizing relatedness, and therefore, the ability to establish relevant marks in a continuum of flowing time that would otherwise remain undifferentiated. Synchrony and diachrony remain two ways of representing time as experienced by human beings. But eventhough these two orders of events in time depend on each other to be distinguished (experientially), they cannot be thought of at the same time (analytically). Going back to the typology of ideas of reality and types of knowledge outlined above, it is clear that the holistic views of reality (primitive and mystic) legitimize themselves in a continuous experience of the synchronic aspect of time, and the historical idea of reality legitimizes its divided view of cosmos in diachronic experience that unifies its divided idea of reality. "This is the basis," says Frye, "for the common place that Biblical religions have a distinctive sense of history" (1982, 83). Primary and spiritual knowledge are legitimized at the same time as they are experienced in synchrony; intellectual knowledge that depends on the sequence of the symbols that disclose it is legitimized in its effectiveness in diachrony. It could be said that the (primary) mythical tale has a sequence of its own, yet it is not engaged in faithfully describing objective and factual knowledge. Mythical primitive tales are engaged in directing substantive principles of human interaction and awareness. As Adorno and Horkheimer postulated it in their *Dialectics of Enlightenment*, they also lead to human consciousness.

Nevertheless, the basis for a symbol of transfiguration (Christian or otherwise) remains an idealized synchronic moment in time according to which the rest of the events—historical or irrelevant—may be organized in our factual idea of reality. It is an axis that the historical view of reality displays in religion, but that is necessarily hidden in the privacy of one's own mind in secular reality. The centripetal pull of the synchronic symbol defines sameness with transcendence, the divine example of the spiritual master, or sameness among human beings, and the centrifugal push defines difference and lays down a series of examples that spell out its doctrine and disciplinary precepts. Historically, this axis is the coming of the Messiah in Christian cosmology, and the age of reason in European Enlightenment in the cosmology of Modernity. But the need for a historical axis is also exemplified in useful constructions such as that of the axial age proposed by Karl Jaspers, who, in his *Origin and Goal of History*, transformed the particular Christian symbol of transfiguration into a historical age of spiritual Enlightenment and discovery of transcendence that unavoidably kept the Christian shape of the Pauline tale. In order for the historical time perspective to acquire dimensions of universal human history, an event or an age serves to organize its unfolding in a meaningful manner. This is where the axis of historical universality lies: It encompasses everyone on earth and gives each soul and nation a place in a cosmos that may be spiritual and eternal, or secular and constantly changing, supposedly subject to not only human agency but also human fallibility.

According to Jaspers, it was not until the axial age that diverse cultures in the world discovered the universe. What this means is that these cultures—or specific individuals scattered around these cultures—managed to conceive transcendence, not only as a symbol or an intellectual concept, but also as a certainty. Certainty is understanding as well as faith; this discovery, therefore, founded and laid the foundations for the great transcendentalist religions of the world whose practice survives to this day. After this age, various kinds of practices developed that strove for spiritual transcendence. The axial age contains the seeds of "humanity as we know it today" (Jaspers 1953, 2); when individual human beings developed the possibility of consciousness about "being" in universal union with the rest of humankind, when, faced with their own material and physical limitations, they strove for redemption and transcendence. The axial age that Jaspers speaks about is a period around 500 BC:

> The most extraordinary events are concentrated in this period. Confucius and Lao-tse were living in China, all the schools of Chinese Philosophy came into being, including those of Mo-ti, Chuang-tse, Lieh-tsu and a host of others; India produced the Upanishads and Buddha and, like China, ran the whole gamut of philosophical possibilities down to skepticism, to materialism, sophism, and nihilism; in Iran Zarathustra taught a challenging view of the world as a struggle between good and evil; in Palestine the prophets made their appearance, from Elijah, by way of Isaiah and Jeremiah to Deutero-Isaiah; Greece witnessed the appearance of Homer, of the philosophers—Parmenides, Heraclitus and Plato—, of the tragedians, Thucydides and Archimedes. (Jaspers 1953, 2)

However, this historical construction organized around the human conception of transcendence ignores other major epochal spiritual outbursts that are relevant specifically to the Judeo-Christian tradition. Toynbee criticized Jaspers's conception of an axial age saying that to be able to regard this era as determinant, he had to leave the stories of Moses and of Jesus out (Voegelin 1974, 4–5). Nevertheless, while Jaspers embraces the shape of the Pauline tale and finds a spiritual axis that is common to all humanity (or a good proportion of it), Toynbee points at Judeo-Christian elements that have been displaced by Jaspers's construction and should not be left out for their importance. Both authors are preoccupied with either the form or the content of the Judeo-Christian relationship to historical facticity. In contrast to this, Voegelin's critique conceives Jaspers's axial age as an attempt to force the operations of the spirit into one historical line within what he calls the historiogenetic function of "speculation on the origin and cause of social order" (Voegelin 1974, 60): in this case, a world-social order based on Jaspers's humanism, with Christian shape and ancestry.

We should be able to acknowledge that in all attempts at grounding any kind of chronology (tribal, imperial, or global), the origin and cause are inevitably linked to some form of divine realization, even in the global secular realm. Jaspers's type of historiogenetic speculation ignores the symbolic importance of the Pauline projection of the cycle of spiritual realization onto the historical cycle of collective humanity. "Both Jaspers and Toynbee," says Voegelin, "treated hierophantic [*sic*] events on the level of phenomena in time, not letting their argument reach into the structure of experiencing consciousness" (1974, 5). Therefore, in this work, I refer to the consequences of an axial age in order to highlight the importance of hierophany in the construction of universal forms of social interaction, eventhough the shape of the tale of an axial age is already determined by the historical ideal-type symbolization of an essential division between "world" and "transcendence." The relevance of the axial age in human history and the relative simultaneity of the hierophanic events that comprise it— which Jaspers highlights—lies in the discovery (or invention) of transcendence in its original sacred relationship to human beings.

Nevertheless, experiencing consciousness is an activity that remains in the synchronic realm of human life; we can relate to diachronic representations only from the fleeting present instant of meaningful experience. For example, the story of the life cycle of the spiritual master is generally raised as a universal example in religion, because of living interaction with divine experience in hierophany. In it, historical time, or any kind of chronology, is suspended for reality to be reinterpreted in various symbological efforts that will generally promise to inaugurate new eras of wider consciousness of the spirit through discipline, as explained by the master and the followers. It is important to bear in mind, though, both the mythopoietic potential of symbolic systems, and also the universal possibilities of the hierophanies that ground them for teaching transcendence. Myths, stories, and explanations may create doctrinal enslavement, but the symbol of transcendence gives grounds to civilized social interaction through the creation of what Voegelin calls a "language of truth" that tends to universality. As will be discussed below, this language takes various shapes in its prevalent verbal structures.

Voegelin warns us to take "meditative precautions" in order for a "doctrinization of symbols" not to "interrupt the process of experiential reactivation and linguistic renewal" (Voegelin 1974, 56). Our tradition of scientific knowledge has the mechanism of constantly doubting itself as an in-built defense against such doctrinization, but one of its effects is that it constantly breaks the intellectual disciplines down into a wide range of specialties. This produces a centrifugal movement of scientific "progress," which is already part of the scientific discipline itself, whose explanations of "aspects" of reality become diluted in the atomization of a cosmos that is supposed to work along perfectly universal lines. "When the symbol separates from its source in the experiential Metaxy, the Word of God can degenerate into a word of man that one can believe or not" (Voegelin 1974, 56). Universal human history is situated within a language of truth that finds it very difficult to question its own grounds because they are veiled by the European Enlightenment's drive to reinvent social collective reality rejecting the doctrinal symbolic assumptions of Christianity, but inadvertently also embracing the divided cosmology that was its source.

Nevertheless, a "language of truth" in consciousness of transcendence is at the basis of the development of creeds, which in social interaction bring about religions, disciplines, and institutions as stable sets of rules with general, and so, ideal applicability. In a pragmatic sense, though, the universalistic or otherwise spiritual institutions (rituals and religions) and their practices produce a common material *milieu* within which they can flourish, this *milieu* is the material organization, experienced within the spontaneity of everyday life. The major transformation in various societies that underwent spiritual outbursts of the kind described in the Jasperian axial age is related to "the emergence, conceptualization and institutionalization of a basic tension between the transcendental and mundane orders" (Eisenstadt 1982, 294). The relevance of the hierophanic events in human experience is revealed by their effects on the immediate institutional and organizational settings of several major civilizations.

Modern civilization, with its love of intellectual knowledge, has produced a diachronic cosmology that describes, or attempts the description, of our origin, our nature, our history and evolution, and in some constructions, the fate of humanity. Modern cosmology, though, organizes ideal aspirations of truth that can never be achieved because the structure of scientific enquiry leaves space to infinite speculation for its own progress and advancement. This realization may strike us as the positive consequence of an infinite openness of society, but as Erikson says, "the values associated with indefinite progress, just because it strains orientation as well as imagination, are often tied to unbelievably old-fashioned ideas" (1968, 33–34). An infinite type of openness renders nihilistic consequences when it is dissociated from transcendence and is associated with our bodily and finite existence. According to Nishitani, "to be infinitely finite, or in other words, for the finite to continue on infinitely, is 'bad infinity' (*schlechte Unendlichkeit*, as Hegel calls it), a concept that logic usually treats as a stepchild" (1982, 170), but this type of infinity is often resorted to when imagining the size of the sidereal space (see Block et al. 1997). The linear diachronic time of modern cosmology was produced by assuming the universe to be a mechanical whole with interconnected laws. This is a cosmology that is relevant to the way in which we interact today and, even if it has been questioned by academic intelligentsia, its nihilist doubts have only marginally reached the functional realm of world interaction, if at all. Modern notions about evolution and historical and economic progress are embedded in the culture and cosmology of contemporary global interaction.

From a contemporary perspective of world interaction then, the elements of progressive betterment have already been transformed from being laws of nature, to being purposive goals of humanity. The latter assumption is inscribed in the structures and practice of science and of economic and moral interaction in the world. While situating ourselves in the cosmology of our own tradition, and assuming the deepest concerns of our academic discipline, one can only evade the importance of these issues either through naive optimism or cynicism. This is one of the reasons for pointing at other two possible views of reality from our own cultural perspective in order to expand it toward awareness of a wider spectrum of human experience. In this work, these issues are taken on board as a matter of balance: Progress as a law of nature is already regarded as a myth in the sense of it not being factually real to an informed observer, yet it is a myth that defines what is important for the modern mind in global interaction as a culture, and should not be regarded as "not real" in the same sense as "not objectively real." Progress is a myth and also already objectively real in our experience, because we have structured our interaction and disciplined practice around this notion, and reproduced it socially for ourselves. Nevertheless, it is important to bear in mind that this grand modern cosmology also rationalizes primitivism as its own past—present today either in *unconscious* and (dark-wrong) psychological fixations or in distant lands—and spirituality as a private business. If we look at it from a synchronic perspective, the modern perspective fails to grasp that primitivism and spirituality are also alive in contemporary human life, and in the embodiment and personal development of the disciplined observer herself.

However, the notions of progress and diachronic movement in time that we can record as human history are part and parcel of the way in which the world interacts currently. In the scientific tradition itself, it is next to impossible to escape them, basically due to the way in which this tradition is structured. We "stand on the shoulders of giants" to borrow one of Sir Isaac Newton's favorite quotations. This means that, while we refute some aspect of this tradition's vast assumptions, we must also take on board everything else that it considers as knowledge. This knowledge in our tradition is intellectual knowledge and is, therefore, faithfully described by conceptual language as a requisite of the discipline. This product is essentially diachronic, even if in producing it there are essential synchronic elements. This is the reason why, throughout this work, I resort to historical accounts of the way *universal humanity* has developed and "progressed" in consciousness. However, this does not mean that this is the direction that it necessarily followed in its original synchronicity, but that it is the direction for the present order of things that it was important to realize that it followed. Synchronic interaction is a boundless maze of happenings that history orders in sequence not only according to their order of relevance in the observer's conscious subjectivity, but also according to the order of relevance of the happenings in the observed society. The historian's evidence is tied to this autonomous order and it therefore describes something that is relevant to our discipline. On the grounds that they are relevant to our present construction of reality, I therefore use diachronic accounts of "what happened" under the light of the above considerations, also taking into account that both synchrony and diachrony may be regarded as separate legitimate bases for institutional discipline, but their distinction depends on each other and therefore they are inseparable in any type of reality that we may construe and experience.

The three ideal types of views of reality outlined in the first section of this chapter manifest themselves empirically in both immensely diverse and converging ways of representing the experience of time in its simultaneity and its sequentiality. However, for the sake of construing useful analytical tools, we will say that both synchrony and diachrony are *organizational* aspects of *any* belief system, while the *institution* and disciplined practice is legitimized in only one of the two orders of events in time identified here (either synchrony or diachrony): The *primitive* legitimate type of time contemplates the cyclical essence of natural environment, tied to the earth's fertility, human calendars, and the myths that produced various versions of ritual repetition of the act of creation in *illo tempore* (Eliade 1955), at the origin of the world. This type of time frames the experience of duration of human events and their cyclical renewal; duration is sequential and diachronic, renovation is synchronic and the producer of legitimate authority.[9] The *historical* legitimate type of time is progressive, in contemplation of the past, but with a qualitative difference based on an axial event—a transcendental jump in consciousness—which projects the life of humanity as a collective "body" toward its future perfection in history. In Christianity, the synchronic Divine moment is represented as God's presence in Genesis and Apocalypse, and in factual *real* history, as the axial events of Revelation or the coming of the Messiah; time is experienced as a tension between the Creation, the origin of history in sin, one's own deeds, and imminent Judgment, and the legitimate essence of this experience is diachronic. In a secular worldview, the realm of legitimate reality and authority is also diachronic experience as human history; here, individual personality is essential, and creates the disciplined habit of contemplating the history of human personalities as *responsible agents*. The *mystic type* of legitimate time is the eternal present of the "here and now," the moment of Grace or spiritual Enlightenment whence perfect union with the Divine collective mind is accomplished: the synchronic source of authoritative legitimacy. In the practice of the spiritual path, though, diachrony is represented as the duration of the path to Enlightenment, always regarded as an illusion of the world of forms, but nonetheless seen as an important organizational notion in the practice of spiritual discipline. In the mystic view of reality, mundane time is seen as a burden of cosmological debt in an eternal wheel of rebirth that can only be escaped through spiritual Enlightenment.[10] All three types of reality represent both types of time organizationally and cosmologically, but only one of them is legitimate in substantive institutions and the practice of ethical discipline.

LANGUAGE: METAPHOR, METONYMY, AND DESCRIPTION

Besides the embodied and conscious experience of time, human beings also interact in language. Language is structured as an identifiable nexus of references in synchrony, yet in constant change in diachrony. Northrop Frye follows Giambattista Vico in order to attempt a classification of verbal structures that are observed to rise and fall through history—diachronically—which can also be regarded as prevalent in different degrees of cultural ascendancy in different human forms of interaction in the world right now—synchronically. Nevertheless, these verbal structures cannot exist in isolation from each other even as they characterize different historical stages or different present particular cultures. Frye identifies (diachronically) three different stages of cultural ascendancy of specific verbal structures: the hieroglyphic stage, dominated by metaphoric verbal structures; the hieratic stage, dominated by metonymic verbal structures; and the demotic stage where the descriptive verbal structures are dominant. My own perspective concentrates on the synchronic (contemporaneous) aspect of language in the sense that it contemplates all three types of verbal structures as present and relevant for the organization of language in any experienced culture right now. I will argue that each of the types of verbal structures described by Frye (Vico), ideally, corresponds to legitimate language in the three views of reality proposed: metaphoric language is legitimate in the primitive view; metonymic language in the mystic view; and demotic language in the historical view. Empirically, though, they can be observed to be only prevalently legitimate in various cultural settings, as they coexist in mutual complementarity and dependence on each other.

Following Vico's typology of distinct ages in a conception of history that is cyclical, Frye describes a typology of prevalent verbal structures throughout Western history that has already dropped Vico's historicist structure. Nevertheless, while Frye's idea of history is not cyclical in a determinist fashion, he borrows Vico's notion of *ricorso* to describe renewed ascendancy of any of the types of language that he describes:

> According to Vico, there are three ages in a cycle of history: A mythical age, or age of the gods; a heroic age, or age of an aristocracy; and an age of the people, after which there comes a *ricorso* or return that starts the whole process over again. Each age produces its own kind of *language*, giving us three types of verbal expression that Vico calls, respectively, the poetic, the heroic or noble, and the vulgar, and which I shall call the hieroglyphic, the hieratic, and the demotic. (Frye 1982, 5)

What Frye means by the use of this "cyclical" typology of preeminent language is to say that these types of verbal structures are always present in any community of human beings, and that the particular life of the group brings either of them to ascendancy in their cultural relevant exchanges. Eventhough Frye regards progressive accounts of history as the mythical expectation that "contemporary events are proceeding toward their own antitypes in the future, toward a state of human existence that will make what is now happening intelligible as a series of signposts pointing in that direction" (1982, 86), he cannot evade to take on board a view similar to Spencer's on progress as differentiation and complexification when it comes to the issue of the gradual emergence of human consciousness and communication. Even if history and nature cannot be mixed in our tradition, there is a cosmological point in the past when they are supposed to have bifurcated. As I have argued, though, the idea of evolution and progress is so persistent because it is already a constitutive aspect of our conception of how history unfolds, and it is also confirmed in the empirical observation of biological development.

Nevertheless, Frye also assumes that people live in mythology even now and have done so since the beginning of time, or since there has been discernible human interaction and communication. "In its early stages," says Frye, "it is difficult to separate or distinguish the various aspects of mythology, but as society becomes more complex, different areas of culture—literature, religion, philosophy, history, science, art—become increasingly distinct from one another" (1982, 51). From a synchronic standpoint, though, we can say that it is important for our modern culture to separate and record in a discursive and descriptive fashion all these different areas of interaction, and so we look for this differentiated feature in the past, but we do not find it because it might not have been important to our ancestors. Hermeneutics teaches us that when we look at the past to find out what was relevant for people then, we always have to do it through what is relevant for us now. The sense in which Frye refers to mythology, in a generic manner is as *mythos*, narrative, plot, or the general sequential ordering of words, but he also distinguishes the more archaic type of myth (story or tale) from history:

> In our culture, some narratives dealing with personalities run parallel to a sequence of events external to themselves; others are based on a sequence of events that seem to be constructed for its own sake. This distinction is reflected in the difference between the words "history" and "story." The word "myth" . . . has tended to become attached only

to the latter, and hence to mean "not really true." This is a vulgarism for many reasons, apart from the fact that it so often assumes a judgment on factuality long before we are in any position to make one. (1982, 32)

Frye also considers that, in history, the sequence of events is only partly external to the narrative about personalities—its account obeys a factuality sanctioned by disciplined practice—but it is also linked to substantive rationality, to values, to what is important for the discipline to know (see Weber [1904] 1949). Data must be selected and arranged subjectively by a historian and, therefore, the shape of the sequence does not wholly come from outside. According to Frye, to think that it does is "an illusion of projection."

Our particular contemporary modern "mythology" compels us to interact through objective reality. In this reality, the separation of object and subject is relevant to our culture and our discipline in scientific disquisition and it is therefore a relevant category in order to investigate verbal structures in other mythologies (where the factual may have a degree of relevance that may not be preeminent). However, in the synchronic awareness that a complete separation between subject and object is impossible, a clear divide between the two becomes an illusion of abstraction that lacks factuality. This does not make it into a myth in Frye's story-for-its-own-sake sense, but it makes us aware that it is a principle of disciplined observation for the sake of the discipline. The myth of objectivity is an unattainable ideal that sets the whole discipline rolling in its structurally progressive fashion: its progress depends on the human impossibility of achieving complete objectivity. However, the subject/object divide is our cultural inheritance and our cosmological basis to access other types of cultural inheritances. From the present perspective of an observer who stands on uncertainty in the synchronic moment of meaningful interaction, objectivity and subjectivity are entwined experiences that cannot be differentiated at the same time as they are experienced: According to the phenomenological approach, they can only be differentiated one at a time in diachronic sequence.

Nevertheless, sequential signification (diachrony) achieves its meaning through the simultaneous presence of an essential net of references (synchrony) with paradigmatic and syntactic functions. Analog and digital communications are cybernetic terms that illustrate the difference between synchrony and diachrony. Within this Saussurean framework, Anthony Wilden (1972) describes the difference between analog and digital communications: the former conveys the message through an operation of similarity or contiguity, while the latter conveys the message through arbitrary signifiers based on custom and convention. Analog implies a continuum whereas digital involves yes/no computations (conveyed in the binary code of one and zero in computers). In analog communication, the message is concretely "performed," the distinction flows from the center of the meaningful object of communication and, therefore, its borders are not identifiable; in digital communication, the message is "signified," which requires discrete and clearly defined boundaries at the borders of the objects of communication. This is the basis for Wilden's distinction between *meaning* and *signification*: Analog communication is engaged with *meaning* through similarity and contiguity and digital communication is engaged in factual *signification* through abstract identity. Nevertheless, digital communication is useless on its own; signification depends on meaning through similarity and contiguity of signifiers—their paradigmatic and syntactic synchronic functions. Wilden believes that the analog/digital distinction helps us clarify scientifically the difference between meaning and signification: He gives a mathematical example, where $\frac{2}{3}$ and $\frac{4}{6}$ are identical in signification whereas their meaning is necessarily different due to the distinct referents used. Meaning is thus related to concrete interaction between embodied entities in the domain of symbolic exchange, while signification belongs to the realm of pure abstraction. Nevertheless, while the distinction is useful, it is never complete except in imagination or in the abstract world of digital diachronic communication. This is illustrated by the difficulty that Wilden expresses in order to define a line between analog and digital signification; thus, he allows for *signals* and *signs* in analog communication and for *signs* and *signifiers* in digital communication (Wilden 1972, 184). Here, *signals* refer to physical and embodied messages that may be symbolic of concrete referents; *signs* are symbolic, but are related to relevant referents that may be concrete or abstract; *signifiers* are wholly abstract and arbitrary, and correspond to the world described as an image in a mirror corresponds to what is reflected.

Analog and digital communications are similar to the synchronic and diachronic realms of time in that they refer to the distinction between simultaneity and sequentiality; however, this is a convenient distinction for heuristic reasons in abstract explanation. The borders of the objects of communication are clearly defined in abstract explanation, whereas in phenomenological observation, these borders disappear, and we must construct them imaginatively and emotionally. This paradoxical predicament and its substantive consequences will arise all through this work in order to highlight the synchronic realm of experience, and it is a structural feature of the way in which I use Frye's typology of verbal structures, which he means to extend throughout history (diachronically), and I mean to map onto ideal types of contemporary views of reality (synchronically). Frye's hiero-glyphic, hieratic, and demotic periods are relevant in diachronic history, which I identify with my ideal–typical views of reality that are relevant to contemporary synchronic world interaction right now, namely primitive, mystic, and historical.

Frye identifies a clear hieroglyphic (primitive) period in the poetic language of most Greek literature before Plato, in the pre-biblical cultures of the Near East, and in much of the Old Testament. He uses the term "hieroglyphic":

> [N]ot in the sense of sign-writing, but in the sense of using words as particular kinds of signs. In this period there is relatively little emphasis on a clear separation between subject and object: The emphasis falls rather on the feeling that subject and object are linked by a common power or energy. Many "primitive" societies have words expressing this common energy of human personality and natural environment, which are untranslatable into our normal categories of thought but are very pervasive in theirs: The best known is the Melanesian word *mana*. (Frye 1982, 6)

But words refer to concrete things, to physical and emotional involve-ment with them in imaginative production of stories that, on their own, are a human mimicry of relevant experience in connection to embodiment and the world. The relevant feature of this type of verbal structure is the metaphor that we recognize as such from our own cultural perspective:

> As we think of words, it is only metaphor that can express in language the sense of energy common to subject and object. The central expres-sion of metaphor is the "god," the being who, as sun-god, war-god, sea-god, or whatever, identifies a form of personality with an aspect of nature. (Frye 1982, 7)

Metaphors work by similarities and, in factual language, they are anal-ogous to Wilden's linguistic *signals*, where the message is contained in what is physically done and concretely experienced.

Frye's second phase of language is hieratic, whose verbal structures are congenial with those in my mystic ideal type. According to Frye, the hieratic phase starts with Plato and its name comes from the explicit assumption that this language is produced by enlightened elites of the post-axial age type and is therefore given a special authority by its society. Here, subject and object become more clearly separated, not necessarily with respect to factuality, but with respect to a separation between emotion and imagination. In the "Western" philosophical tradition, this gradually leads to the ascendancy of intellectual and rational imagination, tied to observation of the phenomenal world. Nevertheless, hieratic forms of verbal expression are structurally displaced from conceiving the world as a reliable source of evidence, as they look to transcendence with a pressing urgency. Hieratic verbal structures produce the possibility of abstraction through disciplined separation between feelings and imagination. The ordering principle to define this distinction is one of valid and invalid relationships between emotion and imagination:

> What Homeric heroes revolve in their bosoms is an inseparable mixture of thought and feeling; what Socrates demonstrates, more especially in his death, is the superior penetration of thought when it is in command of feeling. (Frye 1982, 7)

This separation is produced by awareness of a reality that lies above and beyond mundane life and that dictates its ethical order; the emergence of hieratic verbal structures is determined by symbolization of transcendence. This symbolization depends on language that is mainly metonymic to define distinction, in contrast to metaphor that defines identity. Words must convey an order that cannot be described through identity of a common energy between things and the inner reality of human, but through a transcendent order that is above and beyond. "Thus," says Frye, "metonymic language is, or tends to become, analogical language, a verbal imitation of a reality beyond itself that can be conveyed most directly by words" (1982, 8). Nevertheless, hieratic language benefits from the use of metaphoric structures, already embedded in people's emotion and imagination, in order to perform relevant metonymic distinctions where the latter have primary authority, as in the use of fables, parables, or allegory, or in syncretic assimilation of local goddesses and gods into a transcendental cosmology. Metonymy is analogous to Wilden's portrayal of *signs*.

The contemporary phase of culturally ascendant demotic language—Frye's third phase—contains the whole development of verbal structures up to our modern present: the paradigmatic and syntactic need of both metaphor and metonymy to describe and demonstrate factual "objective" knowledge. Mathematics, Frye tells us, has obvious metonymic features: When we draw a line, "which necessarily has some breadth" (1982, 9), we are really only putting a drawing in the place of the conceptual line, which cannot "exist" in concrete physical reality because it represents the concept of length without breadth.

> One feels that some of the pre-Socratic and atomic philosophers, such as Anaxagoras or Democritus, were moving more directly from metaphor toward what we should think of as science, from gods to the operations of nature, and that Plato turns away from this direction, toward a transcendent world rather than an objective one. (Frye 1982, 9)

But objectivity is a mixture of both of these sources (metaphorical and metonymic) that only needed the Aristotelian theory of multiple causation to produce a technique "for arranging words to make a conquering march across reality, subjects pursuing objects through all the obstacles of predicates, as the Macedonian phalanxes of his pupil, Alexander, marched across Asia" (Frye 1982, 9). Plato's sense for a superior transcendental order that could only be conveyed by words was identified as *logos* in the later Classical period. In Christianity, *logos* was seen as the means to unite humanity both "spiritually and temporally," which gave shape to its institutional structure. A distinct sense of history in biblical cultures is inherited from the importance of historical interpretation in Judaism, which merged with the power of sequential disquisition based on legitimate evidence of "compelling assent." This is the basis for the legitimacy of diachronic symbols in the historical idea of reality.

In distinguishing symbols phenomenologically, we may say that mystic and primitive symbols have an intrinsic sense of immediateness: metaphor and metonymy work through similarity and contiguity, respectively. The metaphorical function is analogous to that of a *signal*, where what is done is what is meant. The degree of abstraction that the metonymic function acquires is directly related to an ordering of thoughts and emotions through categories of validity; it is analogous to linguistic *signs*: the message itself is what is meant. There are metonymic elements in Habermas's love for perlocutions, where all emotive tendencies to falseness and manipulation should be firmly controlled by rationality (Habermas 1984, 1990), and also in the Buddhist use of contradictory statements (*koans*) that should produce a spontaneous dissolution of emotional attachment to concepts in the pupil. Both metaphor and metonymy imply the involvement of physical, emotional, and imaginary human experience in the conveying meaning; in factual description, the word used has only an imaginary relationship to the denoted thing. Frye tells us that it is important to be careful of associative language in description: "You'll find that analogy, or likeness to something else, is very tricky to handle in description, because the differences are as important as the resemblances" (Frye 1964, 32). Ideally, the degree of abstraction in the descriptive function is complete: The *signifier* is an arbitrary symbol that stands wholly for the signified (Wilden 1972; Merquior 1986). Objectivity depends on the preeminence of this function of language where the absence of emotional involvement is compensated by the factuality rendered by concrete evidence and sequential argumentation. It is less evident, though, that objectivity also depends on metaphoric and metonymic verbal structures to be grounded in anything at all (see Lakoff and Johnson 1980).

Our current responsiveness to factual reality, however, is firmly based on the belief that, in descriptive-demotic language, isolated words are signifiers, or pure arbitrary abstractions that have no *magic* power of their own or a shared substance with the signified. The scientific factual and functional power, to us, lies in the internal coherence of substantiated rational disquisition, where the substance is concrete experience of effective functionality. One of the premises of scientific disquisition is that the isolated word has no power to be anything but a word, but the description that is built scientifically through them must convey the order of nature. The inner coherence in scientific explanation must map onto, or "mirror," what we can experience physically (see Rorty 1980). Its *magic* is the confirmation of the proposed scientific mechanism through repetitive testing. Poetry embraces the emotional role of *magic* in the modern tradition of knowledge, but it is based on novelty, contrary to the repetitive essence of the magic spell. "Poetry," says Frye, "does not really lose its magical power thereby [through novelty], but merely transfers it from an action on nature to an action on the reader or the hearer" (1982, 25). Thus, science is based on systems of words of coherent explanation that may be reproduced, and not on repetition of isolated *magic* words. Frye gives the example that in biblical metonymic language, where we assume that the Word is analogous to God or His power, John's statement "And the *logos* became flesh," according to the internal structure of Christian assumptions, is "an intelligible statement of the type 'And the boy became a man,' or 'And the ice became water.' But within a descriptive framework of language it can be only an unintelligible statement of the type 'And the apple became an orange'" (Frye 1982, 18–19).

Nevertheless, as I have argued above, even if the descriptive type of verbal structure is accorded preeminent objective validity because of effective explanation of sequential diachronic causality, the inner coherence of the scientific account itself depends on the analogical functions of metaphor and metonymy, which are eminently synchronic. In the hieroglyphic phase (primitive type), words and things are entwined by a common powerful "substance" or energy inherent in the natural order; miming that order in ritual produces relevant synchronic enacted events according to which order is "mapped" and produced at the same time. In the hieratic phase (mystic type), the sense for a synchronic experienced awe for divinity becomes part of the cosmological account of a higher reality as transcendence, and how the inner coherence of a verbal structure can convey this reality.

> Hence the medieval fascination with the syllogism and the great medieval dream of deducing all knowledge from the premises of revelation. Later we have the "I think therefore I am" of Descartes, where the operative word is "therefore," because before we can accept the proposition we must accept the cogency and reality of therefores. (Frye 1982, 11)

Nonverbal eastern mysticism and the Western mystic tradition emphasize the inadequacies of any type of verbal account to convey the experience of transcendence in hierophany (Sogyal 1992; Underhill 1995; Kulananda 1997). According to Frye, in the Dawning of European culture, transcendental metonymy, or hieratic language, remained culturally ascendant due to the cultural and political necessity of preserving authority "down to the time of Kant and Hegel, after which it became increasingly specialized and academic.[11] One of its culminating points is the metonymic universe of Kant, where the phenomenal world is 'put for' the world of things in themselves" (Frye 1982, 12). Our sense for descriptive factual reality is rooted in the metaphoric and the metonymic functions of language, and is also rooted in the physical and psychological involvement of the observer.

As described above, the cultural ascendancy of any of the three types of verbal structures—metaphoric, metonymic, descriptive—are shown to coincide not only with Vico's and Frye's three phases of language in history, but also with their preeminence in my three types of ideas of reality—primitive, mystic, historical—in contemporary interaction in the world. Nevertheless, as in the ideas of reality, the verbal structures are complementary with each other and do not exist purely on their own—at least in current world interaction. To say that either of the functions emerged earlier than any other, I believe, is an illusion of the idea of "progress" in its teleological story-myth mode. But this myth is already relevant to our way of knowing and of doing history and, in this factual way of knowing, even if we concede that the other verbal structures were already functionally present in human language from the beginning, their cultural ascendancy is liable to be traced historically. This does not mean that there is necessarily a linear progress, or a cyclical one like in Vico, but to use Vico's figure of *ricorso* as Frye does, shows that they achieve different degrees of importance in different, distinctive time periods and cultures. It also depends on what culture we are analyzing and what the verbal structure expresses in the particular social hierarchy of that culture. On this point, Frye's phases refer to the view of order that emanates from the centers of legitimate authority that both discover and produce knowledge about "reality" at the same time; from my synchronic perspective, these verbal structures refer to the view of order that may emanate from any group of people in the simultaneous process of creating and being created by their culture (family, team, tribal, organizational, national, continental, global).

Legitimation, therefore, is linked to the culturally ascendant idea of reality in that the latter determines the type of verbal structures that produce the authoritative shape of concrete human organization. Institutions (religion, spirituality, ritual, discipline, moral principles) acquire an aura of distance from concrete organization in that institutions dictate a substantive idea about behavior of the human self (human identity). With respect to my three ideal types of reality, the culturally ascendant institutions dictate an experience of self that is ideally collective for the primitive and the mystic types, and one that is ideally individual for the historical type. This is due to the feature that both the primitive and mystic views are based on an idea of reality that is whole: *either* the world *or* transcendence are the locus of holistic reality, respectively, while in the historical view, *both* the world *and* transcendence are real simultaneously and, therefore, reality is conceived as essentially divided and in a quest for unification with a beginning and an end in Christianity, but that becomes linear and indefinite progress in secular Modernity.

The centripetal/synchronic organizational functions are expressed in metaphor and metonymy—the paradigmatic and syntactic functions of language (Jakobson 1956; Wilden 1972)—the centrifugal/diachronic organizational functions are expressed in the descriptive function of language. Frye illustrates the two functions in language through two ways of half-reading or misunderstanding a subject, a technical treatise, or a cultural *Gestalt*. One is through incomplete knowledge of referents, as when reading in a language that we know imperfectly; the other is when the organized effort to unify the referents syntactically is poor: "Failure to grasp centrifugal meaning is incomplete reading; failure to grasp centripetal meaning is incompetent reading" (Frye 1982, 58). This is an example of pure types with heuristic objectives, in experience, incomplete and incompetent readings are obviously linked to each other. Nevertheless, it shows a relevant relationship between linguistic functions that also applies to the centripetal and centrifugal features of synchrony and diachrony in human order, or in the organization of particular ideas of reality.

Institutionally, then, the locus of legitimacy lies on the synchronic realm of time for the primitive and mystic views of reality, while the locus of legitimacy for the historical view lies on the diachronic realm. Nevertheless, *organizationally*, in concrete human experience, both synchrony and diachrony are given sense and representation and are mutually dependent features of concrete human life (even if either of them is seen as irrelevant or illusory in the domain of institutional legitimacy). Organizationally speaking then, I have said that in the historical view of reality there are clear synchronic symbols of centripetal function, such as the life of Jesus or the figure of transfiguration from darkness into light, or a distinctive sense for a human type of consciousness. But it is also true that, in this organizational sense, in the primitive and mystic views, there are also diachronic symbols of centrifugal function, such as the sequence of events in mythical tales and the spiritual progress of the mystic initiate. I will therefore argue that, beyond the institutional legitimacy of either of these kinds of symbols, it is necessary to consider the organizational factuality of both of them in a scientific spirit of enquiry. It would seem like this is an attempt that may be contradictory with the structure of our own discipline, but it will not be so from a present perspective that attempts to give legitimacy to the synchronic symbols that produce a distinct sense of *ethos* in the ideas of reality that are not culturally ascendant in global interaction today.

It is only through an imaginative effort that the above can be achieved in language, and its significance to world interaction lies precisely in highlighting how this distinctive *ethos* may contribute to the contemporary problematic and limitations of the modern sense of morality in global interaction. I believe that this effort is also substantiated by relatively recent scientific evidence (in this century's physics, mainly) that, after all, subject and object are not factually divided.

According to Frye,

> The thought suggests itself that we may have completed a gigantic cycle of language from Homer's time, where the word evokes the thing, to our own day, where the thing evokes the word, and are now about to go around the cycle again, as we seem now to be confronted once again with an energy common to subject and object which can be expressed verbally only through some form of metaphor. (1982, 15)

In the historical view of diachronic collective progress as cycles and "leaps of being," this image is very suggestive, but in the primitive and mystic view of synchronic consciousness that legitimizes itself in an ecstatic continuum of life/death or spiritual Enlightenment, the thought suggests itself that collective progress might be a relevant myth as an illusion of factuality.

3

The Primitive Ideal Type
of Reality

Primitive reality is fettered in the world, in the embodied aspect of our humanity. In this type of reality, time is experienced as cyclical and renovated in synchronic ritual and festivity, and the expression of its cosmology or view of reality takes place in metaphorical language structures. The primitive ideal type of reality contemplates human beings as animals of a species that need to live in conversations and tales, within a network of references and affections. The basic experience for the embodied human animal is her worldly and concrete reality where human *ontogeny* takes place. I am speaking of interaction within domestic spaces, where the human sense of *self* is originally formed for every embodied member of the species as children growing up. The process of becoming an ethically competent member of a human group rests on primitive practices of care, on nourishing, in personal attachment, and an awareness of human frailty and neediness. I argue that a substantive position that lacks an appraisal of *primitivity*'s relevance to the complex experience of modern life is incomplete. This is the reason why this chapter also engages in a discussion of primitivity seen as the animal characteristics and needs of humanity as a species. Modern life encompasses experiences of valuable primitivity right now, even if they are not legitimate realms of experience to the modern sense of self.

An emotional involvement with myth—to the extent to which it is legitimized as actual reality—is an element of what I define here as the primitive view of reality. This view involves not only belief, but also an emotional involvement with the content of particular belief. This content has to do with what is really important to specific social and cultural settings (Warner 1994). Human groups within specific cultural settings will act according to the content of their belief—even with passionate urgency. The modern person's realm of primitive experience is projected either unto Modernity's own past, or unto a realm of *otherness* whose voice is impossible to represent faithfully (as the postcolonial studies debate illustrates). Therefore, in order to conceptually elaborate this ideal type of reality, I resort to the modern conception of primitivity as *archaic*. Nevertheless, primitivity is very much a characteristic of human beings around the world right now. According to Northrop Frye, people are unable to live nakedly in nature like animals, and this does not refer only to the human physical need to dress; he speaks about a mythological universe: "a body of assumptions and beliefs developed from his [human] existential concerns" (Frye 1982, xviii). He believes that the conscious organizing of a cultural tradition is the practical function of criticism, and this should make us more aware of our mythical conditioning. In this ideal type, I consider human emotional primary involvement that allows for the ideal–typical primitive awareness of ecstatic wholeness. This wholeness legitimizes the living authority of a particular cosmology or belief, and in its collective manifestation, it is experienced most clearly during the time of ritual festivity.

According to Paz (1993), the above type of time is congenial with the one in which poetic creativity takes place, as it allows for a kind of knowledge that cannot be articulated except in poetic expression, that is, in metaphoric verbal structures. Emotions play an eminent role in connecting (in a bootstrapped manner) bodily awareness of whatever is going on in the world to whatever is really important *there* in its absolute particularity, and so this is the realm that rules domestic life.[1]

Time lived in the festive ritual celebration of primitive life—human domestic life—is synchronic and celebrates the emotional involvement with myth or narrative. Paz believes that the worshipping festive time is of a different quality from chronological time: it emulates all endings and all beginnings; it conflates the borders of life and death. Human beings can express this awareness linguistically in conversations and narratives, but they can also live it in their animal embodiment as nonhuman animals do. This allows us to contemplate humans as a specific animal species and highlights the importance of our doing so in contemporary modern awareness. In the latter, human life is construed as having an actual and material distance from nature (to the extent to which human and nature may become estranged from each other), while in primitive awareness, nature is enacted as a "container" of human life.

In the first section of this chapter, I describe the elements of the primitive ideal type of reality. This entails that historical consciousness regards primitivity as its own past, and will be seen as such in some parts of the ideal–typical construction. This type of view of reality is therefore a projection of Modernity on primitive otherness. Nevertheless, it does not intend to be a faithful construction of the primitive mind as it was experienced and lived in an archaic irretrievable past. On the contrary, what I propose is a construction of what the modern mind regards as primitive, or as *other* than modern, and I expand on how this type of reality is relevant for human life right now. In the second section of this chapter, I develop the theoretical basis on which to claim that there is in fact a primitive urge to rescue the notion of nature as a "container" of human life. And one can say that this is an ethical, substantive urge. From this perspective, Modernity can be seen as a kind of abstract mythology that has created artificial environments of interaction—abstract and material *systems*—that *process* the cyclical aspect of time and produce a modern linear-time progression. This is based on artificial reliance in descriptive abstraction as the only source of legitimate knowledge, which relegates the organic root of human existence (and the ambiguity of metaphor) to a second-rate kind of reality. The primitive perspective that regards nature as a "container" of human life will consider the biological function of language for the sustenance of our species. This is based in Humberto Maturana and Francisco Varela's idea of self-creating life: *autopoiesis*, and their theory of cognition.[2] Based on their idea, I propose a model of human cognition that contemplates the biological function of language in the production of culture. The third section of this chapter concentrates on the biological need of nurture and care for human beings as children growing up. This is congenial with some feminist portrayals of the kind of ethics that this realm of *being human* conveys. On the one hand, in this chapter, I want to set the theoretical basis of what I mean by an ideal–typical primitive view of reality. And I also want to point at why in contemporary modern life, one should recenter on the importance of seeing humans—ourselves—as animals of a certain species. On the other hand, I want to point out that the realm of our animality as human beings is our domestic life. An inflated emotional involvement with the narrative of "superior" Modernity has discredited this experiential realm of being human, and has left it beyond our appraisal as an important source of knowledge for our ethical life.

PRIMITIVE REALITY

The primitive ideal-type view of reality does not merely refer to archaic cultures and traditional peoples. Rather, it refers to an aspect of being human that emanates from being embodied and needing other human beings to survive while in the world, as a characteristic of the human species. The primitive aspect of human life is thus related to regarding human beings as members of an animal species and the particular way in which our species lives its animality. The primitive view of reality is based on an extended pool of primary knowledge that provides substance and the ability to deal with basic embodied human needs, such as the urgency of everyday logistics to feed, carry out domestic work, reproduce, raise children, and eventually die. This realm of private life is generally sustained with work of female members of the species, and children dwell in it until they reach adulthood; it is also the realm where comprehensive views of reality determine the order of everyday life. All of this happens in the most intimate realm of human life, but in modern ethics, it is given a second-rate kind of importance. However, primitive human reality is sustained by emotional involvement with narratives that are particular in the sense that belief systems (even transcendental ones) are brought to relevance according to the personal involvement of specific people with them and how they are spread into the group (family, community, tribe). In this view of reality, the self is not primarily preoccupied with the *objectivity* of the domestic tale in the same sense as science would be, or with the illusory nature of the world in the tale in the sense mysticism would be. In his *The Educated Imagination* (1964), Northrop Frye refers to the need of literature in an age of "private airplanes" in terms of what I have called the primitivity of human beings:

> The world of literature is human in shape, a world where the sun rises in the east and sets in the west over the edge of a flat earth in three dimensions, where the primary realities are not atoms or electrons but bodies, and the primary forces not energy or gravitation, but love and death, passion and joy. (1964, 28)

The primitive self has a deeper involvement with what she perceives as real and pressing in the intimate world of human relationships, and in that sense, is very close to the emotional world that surrounds this self and her immediate experience. This is not a world where either the values of precision, or those of spiritual Enlightenment rule; it is an ambiguous and intuitive world, where life and death are intimately bound to each other. My primitive ideal type of reality is framed in metaphorical language and in the cycles of human–animal time, the celebration of which is legitimized in the synchrony of ritual mimesis, even if only metaphorically, and this is found also in the midst of modern life.

From my contemporary synchronic perspective, the human being is seen as essentially primitive despite any level of civilization. "[I]t apparently takes social scientists," says Frye, "much longer than poets or critics to realize that every mind is a primitive mind, whatever the varieties of social conditioning" (1982, 37). I am using the concept of primitivity here to point at a human characteristic that never left us humans. Yet, part of the mythical conditioning of our historical mind is to believe that primitivity is left behind in Modernity. Even if we dress, trim, decorate, and perfume our bodies, or deny them, we are still embodied. Sustaining our own embodied condition organizes most of our activities throughout the day, and to abandon this mundane preoccupation is regarded as ascetic practice that seeks some kind of state where the body is not. Also, the modern-scientific tradition assumes a bodiless kind of consciousness—abstraction—that takes the position of the objective *vantage point*, a necessary aspect of our methodology, or ritual practice. But we must never overlook our own embodied animal existence—although this is easy in artificial environments. Our body is the source of our experience in this objective world of ours. Embodiment and the consciousness of self are intricately entwined, as expressed by primitive cosmologies that do not symbolize transcendental reality explicitly.

In the modern world, the quality of our daily life is quite dependent on the functionality of our urban artificial environments. Modern urban life may keep our attention from focusing on the extreme circumstances to which living in nature may produce, unless we observe nature as spectators within an artificial environment on which the modern person's life has come to depend (our cities, offices, houses). This urban lifestyle takes place within a view of reality of diachronic time and material *progress* that modern people relate to as an imperative: prosperity as a measure of success, wealth expansion, modernization, and democratization. This is determined by the creation and maintenance of extreme artificial environments, institutions, and descriptive factuality—which can produce horror stories as well as naively optimistic ones (the Weberian "dark polar night" of the totally administrated world or postmodern mass consumption as emancipation). In contrast to this, in the primitive view of reality, human life is *ideally* closer to the natural world and to embodiment. This closeness is achieved through emotional involvement with particular narratives, mythical tales, and cosmological beliefs whose expression is eminently based on metaphoric verbal structures.

The conception of time in the ideal primitive view of reality is organized here around the notions of duration and renovation, following Mircea Eliade. He has argued that the primitive (he calls it archaic) idea of reality is manifested "as force, effectiveness, and duration. Hence the outstanding reality is the sacred; for only the sacred is in an absolute fashion, acts effectively, creates things, and makes them endure" (1955, 11). This accounts for what has been regarded as the pragmatic character of the primitive mind (see Radin 1953; Mumford 1967). Although the effect of sacred ritual is experienced as finite, its reality is rooted in the constancy of the natural cycles that are symbolized in an enacted renewal and repetition of cosmogony.[3] The temporal duration of experienced effectiveness is made real by the lived and enacted ritual of renovation. In a social context, this acquires the ritual cyclical characteristics of constant renewal of life in the world, which cannot make do without constant representation of death as a necessary step for renovation of life.

The phenomenologists of religion (Eliade, van der Leeuw, Leenhardt) believed that primitivity was an experience of indivisible plenitude where nature and psyche have not yet been separated, where their unity defined an ongoing experience of plenitude. Nevertheless, as Ricoeur (1967a) argued, before symbolization of transcendence, primitivity must also have already been physically conscious of embodied separation. To Ricoeur, their myths signified a plenitude that was only *aimed at* in symbolical intention; to him, unity is only an intuition, "from which man is not separated" (1967a, 167). I agree with Ricoeur because primitivity, as undifferentiated experience, is a kind of "unconsciousness" that is given a romantic essence of continuous harmony and plenitude. However, moving away from Ricoeur's line of argumentation, while collective union in plenitude could not possibly be constantly experienced, it can be experienced occasionally in primitive mimetic ritual. In primitivity, it is transcendence that is only an intuition, plenitude (embodied and enacted awareness of simultaneity) is cyclically lived in mimesis during sacred festivity, and in the experience of magic.

The above aspect of human experience is expressed metaphorically by means of symbols that do not search for precision, but for meaning to the human sense of self. As Frye puts it:

> As for metaphor, where you're really saying "this is that," you're turning your back on logic and reason completely, because logically two things can never be the same thing and still remain two things. The poet, however, uses these two crude, primitive, archaic forms of

thought [simile and metaphor] in the most uninhibited way, because
his job is not to describe nature, but to show you a world completely
absorbed and possessed by the human mind. (1964, 32–33)

Frye considers that the poet's magic is suggestive and that it includes
object and subject at the same time. Nevertheless, we could say that
archaic forms of magic also entail reciprocal involvement of what we
call objectivity and subjectivity in whomever undergoes its experience,
for her to be able to perceive an effect. Magic may be construed as real
only in myth or explained away by an observer as sham or as contingent coincidence of ritual with expected events, but it is experienced
as real by the participants.

The ideal–typical primitive view of reality is legitimated during renovation and unity in the psychological and mimetic effect of natural
cycles in bodily rhythms (life, sex, death), magic, festivities, and sacred
ritual in the participant. According to Paz, the religious festivity is
much more than just a date or an anniversary: "It does not celebrate,
but reproduces an event: it opens up into two the chronometrical time
so that, during some incommensurable hours, the eternal present
reinstates itself. Festivity makes time creative. Repetition becomes
conception" (1993, 228; my translation). He compares this primitive
instant to that of poetic creativity and thus links it to the aesthetic
sphere. Legitimation for this view of reality is in the union of the
human group in meaningful synchronic pauses in the continuum of
time, which produces awareness of each individual's dependence on
other human beings to survive. In primary accounts of reality, life and
death are not as clearly differentiated from each other as in the modern perspective; they are entwined: Life gives rise to death and death
to life. This is one of the most important pragmatic teachings that
modern people can obtain from their own primitive intuition.

In a primary awareness of reality, the individual entity is not
regarded as important as in Modernity. The abstract–ideal individuality of a living human being on her own is not as relevant. Awareness
of the cycles of life and death of the whole group sustains awareness of
the relevance of an extended collective self. But this collective self
emerges from individual consciousness, which is an important side of
the constant creation of culture. According to Anthony Cohen,
individuality (as opposed to individualism) is a biological and psychological fact; it is a pragmatic feature of being alive and embodied.[4] But
in primary awareness of self, individuality is *endured:* Survival of individual entities depends on the survival of the group—and this is a
human fact that often escapes the awareness of the individualistic

modern mind. In ideal primitive reality, a cyclical relationship is established between individual self and collective self, the former providing spontaneity and creativity and the latter providing experience of ecstatic wholeness. The collective life of the human group in celebration of sacred reality compensates for the embodied separation of the living entity. The *primary experience of the cosmos* is aware of an *intangible embracingness* that signals the simultaneous organic union of all things and is also practically aware that the integrity of individual embodiment depends on collective human life. This dependence refers to human–animal characteristics of vulnerability, frailty, and neediness.[5] In this reality, the self that we relate to personally is thus conceived as a collective self, what we are—whatever the size of *we* as a group—and human practical consciousness relates to it emotionally. The inner longing for wholeness of existence is not translated consciously into transcendence, but into ritual worship that brings about awareness of organic union between the members of the human group and of the constant flow of the cycles of life and death.

In the primitive view of reality, there is a relationship between life and death and the discipline of enduring embodiment through a kind of work that crude natural circumstances impose.[6] As Ortegay Gasset expressed in his *The Rebellion of the Masses* (1937), as modern individuals, we enjoy the advantages of artificial environments and can afford to ignore existence in extreme natural circumstances. We can even think that the fruits of Modernity *are* the natural circumstances and forget that this kind of comfortable life is sustained by discipline. The problem for Ortega, as well as for Alisdair MacIntyre, is that one may sustain a functional type of discipline, but it will not be enough to sustain the type of individual substantive self-awareness of Modernity. We have created artificial environments (cities) that help us forget about (or deny) our embodied condition. However, nature catches up with us at the moment of individual death: It reminds us of our own embodied individual existence, our futility in human history. The burden that this creates for the individual consciousness of self is related to her insignificance in universal history, which is related to the *unhappy consciousness* of the modern person:

> In the progressivist intoxication of the eighteenth century Kant raised the sober question what interest a generation of man at any given time could have in the progress of mankind toward a cosmopolitan realm of reason. Even if a man should consider the labors of his life a step of mankind toward perfection, the fruits of his labors would be enjoyed by men of a distant future. Hence, the meaning of history is not the answer to the question of meaning in the life of man. (Voegelin 1954, 4)

The symbolism of personal efforts in Modernity is either framed within the myth of personal success (Berman 1992; Maturana and Verden-Zöler 1995) and diluted in human history, or denied a place in any kind of cultural representation of togetherness beyond the family circle. In these cultural circumstances, a late awareness of death in the moment of personally facing it may be faced with horror after a lifetime of individual assertion.

Death is an essential aspect of primitive human life that Modernity displaces to oblivion. It is an element of this kind of "concrete human world of immediate experience" (Frye 1964, 27). Although Modernity has managed to tame raw nature—to an extent—in daily life, its dependence on the distance of human beings from nature displaces the immediate awareness of death from this way of living. Death becomes a neglected aspect of human reality in everyday modern life, a dreaded ghost standing in the dark that the modern individual's sense of self cannot come to terms with, at least not as a mere individual. Here, I want to emphasize the notion of *death* as an experience that every embodied being can relate to as *certain fate*, which the modern belief system ideally displaces from public life. In contrast to this, primitive human awareness, based on the experience and contemplation of raw nature and embodiment conceives of death as the end of a life cycle of an individually embodied human being. It is one of the clearest situations in which a person must unavoidably face raw nature, and it is important to consider how this human experience produces cultural creations or different kinds of knowledge.

Primitive experience of embodiment organizes social interaction around perception of natural cycles. This applies not only to the cycles of the earth and their relationship to creativity and production in an agricultural system, but also to the cycles of life that organize what is important in the domestic realm of the human self: birth, sex, death. A ritualistic constant in all human cultures is celebration of a newborn baby, marriage, and funerary rites. In this spirit, Frye reminds us that these topics have always preoccupied the mind of humanity; "weddings and deaths and initiation ceremonies have always been points at which the creative imagination came into focus both now and thousands of years ago" (Frye 1964, 42). These cycles are represented in narratives, personal stories, metaphorical symbols, myths, and how the human self is emotionally involved with all of them. These stories portray human experience in an emotional involvement of archetypes that both belong to a human group, and constitute myth legitimized as the "actual state of affairs" (Geertz 1973). The power contained in both greatness and lowliness of human mythical archetypes symbolizes cyclical movements of constant creation, destruction, and renewal, which find their prototypical perfection in the imagined very first act of creation in *illo tempore* (Eliade 1955, 4). Octavio Paz, evoking van der Leeuw (1940), says that this prototypical beginning "contains all beginnings and introduces us in the time that is alive, where everything really begins at every instant. By virtue of the ritual that realizes and reproduces the mythical tale, that of poetry and of fairy tales, man enters a world where all the contraries merge into each other" (Paz 1993, 229). But this kind of power is also contained in human awareness of creativity, of collective life that produces symbols as a means of self-representation. In primitive awareness, this self is collective, and therefore, its power of creation belongs to every embodied entity alike. The link between the unborn, the living, and the dead is an organic and spiritual continuum; therefore, so is the link between mortals and gods. Diachronic (sequential) time is structurally integrated in the duration of the cycles within the cosmology. These cycles, though, are fettered to worldly experience (the weather, the sowing, the harvest), and do not symbolize a "leap in being" toward transcendence. In this view of reality, history—the realm of the past and the future beyond the life–death cycle—is unimportant. As Paz says:

> Mythical time, contrary [to chronometric time], is not a homogeneous succession of equal quantities, rather, it is impregnated with all the particularities of our life: it is as long as eternity or as brief as a sigh, inauspicious or propitious, fertile or barren. This notion admits the existence of a plurality of times. Time and life merge and form a single block, a unity, impossible to split. (1993, 228)

Ritual sacred celebrations—and the mysteries they bring to the fore (sex, life, death)—make it possible in this ideal view to produce human awareness organized around the celebration itself. Human imagination constantly portrays this consciousness emotionally in immensely diverse and particular tales and myths that *stand for* somatic mundane human experience. The preeminent feature of the tales is their metaphoric verbal structure, which expresses synchronic similarities between emotion and imagination in ecstatic ritual and somatic exploration of the mysteries of consciousness. Here, Frye's hieroglyphic language is culturally ascendant.[7] "The intracosmic areas of reality, one may say, provide one another with analogies of being whose cosmological validity derives from the experience of an underlying intangible embracingness, from a something that can provide existence, consubstantiality, and order to all areas of reality eventhough it does not itself belong an existent thing to any one of these areas" (Voegelin 1974, 72). These traditions of knowledge survive quite comfortably within the ambiguous verbal structures of metaphor. Primitive symbols, what Voegelin calls "analogies of being" are represented in metaphoric verbal structures, in compact symbolism, that can be interpreted in various human settings across time and cultures. Metaphor is ambiguous, but its compactness allows for human experience to converse in an aesthetic sphere.[8] The absence of an explicit representation of *universe,* and thus the absence of a universalizing thrust, allows these representations to coexist, merge, and reinvent themselves constantly in what we would call a cross-cultural manner.

Although the principle of universality is not articulated explicitly in the primary experience of the cosmos, the experience of an underlying intangible embracingness accounts for its presence as intuition, even if it is not differentiated and given a unifying symbol to represent it. Only when consciousness of transcendence has become a differentiated experience, is "universe" represented in abstraction:

> Obviously, the metaphysical concepts of the archaic world were not always formulated in theoretical language; but the symbol, the myth, the rite, express, on different planes and through means proper to them, a complex system of coherent affirmations about the ultimate reality of things, a system that can be regarded as constituting a metaphysics. . . . It is useless to search archaic languages for the terms so laboriously created by the great philosophical traditions. . . . But if the word is lacking, the thing is present, only it is "said"—that is, revealed in a coherent fashion—through symbols and myths. (Eliade 1955, 3)

In the absence of an explicit symbol for the human transcendental identity, "universe" is not symbolized discursively but it is lived as an enactment of the organic union of everything that is alive and dies in ritual representations of the cosmos.

The best term that represents this kind of *lived* ritual symbolization is *mimesis*. This has generally been translated as "imitation," but this notion does not wholly convey how emotional involvement, perception, and symbol are unified in experience in primitive ritual. "The term mimesis is chosen by Plato as the one most adequate to describe both re-enactment and also identification, and as one most applicable to the common psychology shared both by artist and by audience" (Havelock 1963, 60). In his book *Preface to Plato* (1963), Eric Havelock explains why it is that Plato in his *Republic* directed such an aggressive attack on the Greek tradition of poetic representation. Plato's axial hierophanic experience made him point the way to transcendent reality and, as discussed in chapter 2, opened the door to what Frye describes as the hieratic phase of a culturally ascendant language dominated by metonymic verbal structures. Their pagan present was being rejected as a means of public education due to its inherent inability to represent universality, its inability to teach the discipline of separating emotion and imagination from lived experience to arrange them in an order that is congenial to the reality of transcendence.

"Changes [in the cosmogony created by the primary experience of the cosmos]," says Voegelin, "can come only through noetic advances which let more compact symbols appear inadequate in the light of more differentiated experiences of reality and their symbolization" (1974, 71). From a contemporary perspective, the disciplined ability to perceive reality through a sophisticated system of differentiated symbols eventually brought about the observer of the scientific tradition: the capacity to appreciate art and religion as subjective aesthetic experience and science as an objective search for truth. This transformed Hesiod and the Homeric classical tales into "literature." Yet, they were produced by an oral and mimetic pagan cosmos of ritual, in the practice of which, the relevant order of time was synchronicity. "Homer," says Auerbach, ". . . knows no background. What he narrates is for the time being the only present, and fills both the stage and the reader's mind completely" (1953, 4–5). What Havelock analytically separates into "artist and audience" who share a "common psychology" in ritual and festive experience is mimetically integrated in synchronic awareness of ecstatic wholeness. Mircea Eliade has argued that this kind of mimetic fusion of symbolization and experience of cosmos is an archaic defense against the irreversibility of historical time:

> Insofar as he allows himself to be influenced by history, modern man feels himself diminished by the possibility of this impersonal survival. But interest in the "irreversible" and the "new" in history is a recent discovery in the life of humanity. On the contrary archaic humanity . . . defended itself to the utmost of its powers against all the novelty and irreversibility which history entails. (Eliade 1955, 48)

Primitive awareness of the close relationship between life and death is sustained in collective synchronicity in mimetic ritual and emotional involvement with persons and myths within an organic and domestic background, and this produces an inarticulate trust in the union of all things. According to Voegelin, in this view of reality, "the cosmos is not a thing among others; it is the background of reality against which all existent things exist; it has reality in the mode of non-existence" (1974, 72). But this trust in cosmology is not articulated as faith, it is an experienced reality that is lived in organic awareness, it is intuitively known as a characteristic of embodied humanity. Voegelin calls this knowledge the "primary experience of the cosmos," which embodied existence is unable to leave behind and which is often rediscovered in the midst of unspoilt nature:

> The cosmos of the primary experience is neither the external world of objects given to a subject of cognition, nor is it the world that has been created by a world-transcendent God. Rather, it is the whole, *to pan*, of an earth below and a heaven above—of celestial bodies and their movements; of seasonal changes; of fertility rhythms in plant and animal life; of human life, birth and death; and above all, as Thales still knew, it is a cosmos full of gods. . . . This togetherness and one-in-anotherness is the primary experience that must be called cosmic in the pregnant sense. (1974, 68–69)

It is quite significant that Voegelin uses the figure of pregnancy to describe the primary experience of the world of conscious humanity. The original human experience of wholeness, although inarticulate, can be described as the life of the fetus in the womb in organic union with the mother. Morris Berman says that "much of what we call today could be no more than a kind of bodily memory [of the time spent in the womb]" (1992, 9).

The primitive view of reality that I propose here conceives of this cyclical wholeness as the sacred provider of existence, and worships it accordingly. The primary experience of the cosmos brings awareness of self as the human community, and the other as what lies outside it. Berman says that the original source of the contrast between the self and the other was animal otherness, and this awareness produced a sacred celebration of this relationship in the form of worshipping of totems (1992, 49–90). The Paleolithic representations that combine hunter's and artist's knowledge united the primary consciousness of those human groups with their whole body of ritual that brought the participant "to an exaltation of the ideal species unattainable by individual experience" (Levy 1948, 42). The relationship with totems expanded and goddesses emerged in their human shape as sacred symbols of the experienced source of birth and embodiment—the mysterious "container" of human life. As Benjamin illustrates in his reflections on archaic primitive humanity,

> We must assume in principle that in the remote past the processes considered imitable included those in the sky. In dance, on other cultic occasions, such imitation could be produced, such similarity manipulated. But if the mimetic genius was really a life determining force for ancients, it is not difficult to imagine that the new-born child was thought to be in full possession of this gift, and in particular to be perfectly molded on the structure of cosmic being. (Benjamin 1979, 161)

While this could be nothing more than imaginative musings, Benjamin's quotation illustrates that primitive imitation of nature could not have been a mere kind of archaic science. Following Frye, myth is constant in human life; its primary role is to function as a multilayered border for the world where the human community lives and then "look inward toward that community" (1982, 37). Embodiment can be seen as endured in awareness of bodily separation from one another, but also lived as organic–collective union with the world and such union experienced in mimetic ritual and domestic order (however small to our cosmopolitan awareness—the family, the group, the community, the tribe—is still all important to a person's life). A primitive type of social order can be seen as a nexus between the unborn, the living, and the dead. In primary awareness, social order and embodiment are inextricably entwined. In the collective consciousness of embodiment in the primary experience of the cosmos, the creative powers of the world and nature itself are acknowledged and lived as exalted characteristics of human experience. In the following section of this chapter, I shall concentrate on why it is important that humanity regards itself as one more animal species living on this planet; and also to appraise a primitive awareness of nature as a "container" of human life.

NATURE AS A "CONTAINER" OF HUMAN LIFE

A kind of experience with various consequences for social order is the experience of being embodied as a specimen of the human race, either male or female, with a cultural personal story attached to embodiment. We differentiate this experience from mere animal experience through an articulate and reflexive consciousness of the self, although there is no intellectual way of knowing the kind of consciousness that other animal species have. It may seem to us that our degree of consciousness about the self is more articulate than that of the rest of the animal kingdom; however, human beings are also animals. The contemplation of the self must take this into account in order to build a model of ethical life than can accommodate and value its own primitivity. The primitive ideal type of reality conceives of nature as a "container" of human life, and as has been outlined, this is legitimized synchronically within the simultaneous rhythms of daily life, and expressed in myth through metaphoric verbal structures as "part of the imaginative insulation that separates us from that [natural] environment" (Frye 1982, 37). As Frye puts it, the interest in myth is not that it inquires about nature itself, but that it uses nature's elements as metaphors to demarcate the borders of the human community, and then looks inward. Here, following Frye, I regard myth or narrative as an artificial border built by human emotion and imagination in order to live in the world in a meaningful manner. Myth expresses what is really important for this world at a domestic as well as at a cultural level. What this means is that myth may involve imaginative stories (cosmologies) about how the world came to be, or how it keeps running, but it also involves imaginative *personal* stories about who one is and how one is related to the world in a meaningful manner: the complex network of references to other people, objects, animals, human space. This is a characteristic of our species and we keep producing it in imaginative language and emotional personal involvement with such cultural creations. That is, language has a biological function to sustain human life.

I argue that this network of references can only be sustained by a very important emotional involvement with the stories that we imagine about ourselves. According to Martha Nussbaum, "emotions always involve thought of an object combined with thought of the object's salience or importance; in that sense, they always involve appraisal or evaluation" (2001, 23). In her *Upheavals of Thought* (2001), Nussbaum shows that to have emotions is a feature that we share with nonhuman animals; their evaluative aspect has to do with how embodied entities relate to the physical world within which they find themselves. In this sense, she stresses that the evaluative aspect of emotion is cognitive–evaluative, not merely motivational—as Jürgen Habermas would have it (Habermas 1990b; see also Benhabib 1992, 178–202). According to Nussbaum, by cognition she does "not mean to imply the presence of elaborate calculation, of computation, or even of reflexive self-awareness" (2001, 23). I call this cognitive–evaluative aspect of emotions "emotional cognition," which will be the object of analysis in the next section of this chapter. Here, I want to stress that both human and nonhuman animals display emotional cognition and this type of cognition takes place as animals (human or nonhuman) display what Tim Ingold refers to as *practical intention*. This type of intention contrasts with *discursive intention* that only humans display by means of complex symbolic systems. In animals though (human and nonhuman), the cognitive essence of emotions is connected or bootstrapped to the biology of living organisms and the knowledge that this cognitive aspect brings to consciousness is the kind of knowledge that nonhuman animals also produce to survive in the world: An embodied awareness about the entwinement of life and death, the need to sustain the former and beware of the latter—which need not be articulated in symbols, yet is present in animal behavior.

Nature as a "container" of human life in the primitive type of reality conceives of human beings as animals of a certain species with its particular biological characteristics. One of these characteristics is how human beings create a meaningful order where they insert themselves and which is sustained in language and emotional involvement. In order to understand how these characteristics ultimately give shape to how human beings live in society, I propose a phenomenological model of cognition with what I call the *present moment of meaningful experience*, at its center. I will keep going back to this model of cognition in later chapters in order to propose a realm of human morality that could be used as the basis for a global ethics. In the primitive type of reality, though, the present moment of meaningful experience is related to how children develop a sense of self as they grow up in an emotional and imaginative involvement with the people who take care of them and their culture—which they also relate to in an imaginative and emotional manner. And so, child development is intimately related to caretakers in the domestic life, who are generally mothers. I agree here with feminist political theory that considers this realm of interaction as essential for the creation of human beings who are able to live a moral life. I will elaborate further on this in the next section of this chapter. My position contrasts with abstract–liberal individualistic characterizations that postulate ready-made adult rational entities engaging in contractual behavior without considering their emotional ties while they do it.

When Humberto Maturana and Francisco Varela say that "to live is to know" (1987, 174), what they refer to is a kind of knowledge congenial with what Tim Ingold describes as practical intention, which they call autopoiesis. For now I follow Maturana and Varela to define autopoiesis as the embodied and biological self-production or production of one self, but this concept will be explained in more detail further below (see Maturana and Varela 1987). Bodily and embodied primary knowledge or autopoiesis, comes simply from being alive, from living in a body carrying out the work needed to survive in the world and interacting with other human and nonhuman animals. While the primitive ideal type of reality must consider this organic aspect of being human, it must also look at how human interaction is different from other kinds of animal interaction by focusing on the particular biological traits of our species, which include an evolutionary specialization on a rather large brain and a complex nervous system. Human autopoiesis, involves language and very intricate imaginative and emotional relations, whose initial manifestation is the domestic world within a particular cultural setting of practices and beliefs (expressed discursively). Nevertheless, every single living organism knows in a practical manner as it is engaged in its own autopoiesis. In order to explain this primary organic source of human interaction, I propose a theoretical construction of human cognition that is related to the development of abilities necessary for human interaction based on the present moment of meaningful experience as a phenomenological center for human interaction. This is congenial with the constructivist position of this work, according to which human interaction is a social construction based on shared references. However, here I go beyond this in arguing that the imaginative and emotional construction of human space is also a biological trait of our species, which starts at childhood for individuals, and is also determined prior to individual ontogeny by the human group where the child grows up. Ontogeny is a concept that I borrow from biology that means: "The course of growth and development of an individual to maturity" (Lincoln et al. 1982, 174).

Maturana and Varela's theory of life and cognition is based on two complementary concepts as aspects of biological order (life): *Structure* and *organization*. In their observation of life, the organization of organisms is the "permanent" aspect of the system, and structure is its changing aspect—as opposed to traditional structuralism. The "permanent" aspect of Maturana and Varela's model of life is within quotes because this is only an indicative permanence, which helps us identify difference between entities, yet the changing structure of the model necessarily produces a changing "permanent" organization. For example, an individual human being will be "organized" as a human being all her life, which is a permanent aspect of this entity, yet her structure is bound to change at the same time; she won't be the same human being all her life. And so organization allows us to identify permanence while structure allows us to observe change. To explain the conceptual difference between these two notions (organization and structure), Maturana uses a nonliving (and therefore *non-autopoietic*) system—a chair—as a straightforward example (1992, 68–69). The variability of chairs in the world depends on the diversity in structures or designs that there can be, and yet the particular form of organization of materials is the one recognized as a chair by an observer. Even if you take the chair and paint it or drill holes in it, the structure is changed, but if the chair is not destroyed—operationally "killed"—its organization remains the same. We can observe the dynamic structural aspect of the entities that we interact with, which is constantly changing, accommodating itself to the environment and to the needs of the moment, moving to satisfy its own needs as well as those that it must satisfy for the other entities that it is related to. But we can also observe the organizational permanent side of this order: A number of qualities that we distinguish as the identity of the organism that we interact with; the organization of a living entity is only permanent during its lifetime. This type of primary organization of human life is sustained at a domestic level, and here, children are brought up to adulthood. This is a universal human characteristic, every human group conceives of human order and interaction, and is emotionally and imaginatively involved with that order at the same time. And yet, all of those conceptions are culturally particular, and even more so at the level of the domestic life.

I have referred to the concepts of structure and organization in Maturana and Varela's theory of autopoiesis. In this model, I propose that interaction includes an animal or *organic*, embodied aspect, as well as a solely human *artificial* aspect (nonhuman animal interaction lacks the latter), and both are organized around the phenomenological center that I call the present moment of meaningful experience. This conscious center represents human awareness of its own embodied condition and of its possibilities to expand consciousness beyond embodiment by the creative and particular use of emotion and imagination, which are central to the model. Therefore, I consider the concepts of imagination, emotion, consciousness of self, and embodiment as *structural organic* aspects of the basis for the unity of the human self to the fellow humans of her species. These elements constitute the organic side of human interaction. On the other hand, to approach *artificial*-human interaction, I use another four *structural* elements whose interplay among them help us see what makes our species' kind of interaction clearly different from any other type of animal interaction: discipline, spontaneity, past path dependencies, and potentiality (see figure 3.1).

I have spoken of organic and artificial *structural* elements of the model—the ones that interact in a constant dynamic interplay—but we

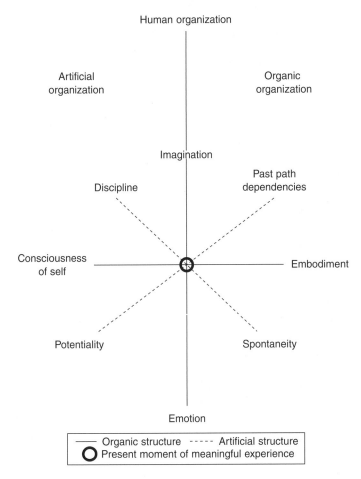

Figure 3.1 A phenomenological model of human cognition

can identify two *organizational* sides to the model, when we look at how these structural elements are arranged within the whole system. Human organization can be said to disclose its permanent or identifiable organic and artificial aspects, separated by its most subjective pole, the central asymptote represented by the dichotomy emotion/ imagination. I will not linger much on the organizational aspect of this model of human cognition, whose consequences cannot be dealt with within the scope of this book on political theory. Suffice it to say now that the organic and artificial types of human organization are complementary; they help us identify how the present and concrete social reality is organized with respect to the past and constant spontaneity, as well as consider present disciplinary habits that will take this social reality into a potential future, all of this arranged around the perspective of the present moment of meaningful interaction, and also taking into account our conscious and embodied condition. The organic and artificial types of organization disclose the fact that human beings are always hybrids of nature and culture at the same time. For the purposes of this book on political theory though, I resort to the structural elements of the model that relate to each other in a dynamic interplay of their characteristics. I do this in order to justify human awareness and cognition as being animal at the same time as they are human. For heuristic purposes, I arrange the structural elements of the model as dichotomies or *poles* that lie in mutual tension and dynamic interplay: Emotion–imagination; embodiment–consciousness of self; discipline–spontaneity; path dependencies–potentiality. This is a synchronic model of human self; it assumes that a human being is a complex mixture of all these aspects at the same time.

Imagination and emotions are just as natural to us in our everyday operational life as is our body and the consciousness of ourselves. People live an operational daily life informed by various disciplines that are culturally learnt as systematic actions. In the daily construction of ourselves, we perform these actions, in combination with the constant irruption of spontaneous manifestations of error, creative intelligence, or mere luck. We do this based on what we have become throughout our lifetime, which determines the potential of what we are yet to become while we remain alive and embodied. In this theoretical formulation, I consider the realms of imagination and emotion as the distinctly human innate creative aspects of consciousness—the depth of our subjectivity in Modernity—and it is through them, in an organic interaction between consciousness and embodiment, that humans naturally build an imaginary shelter, or "integument of culture," that protects them from the environment, which in turn serves as a self-referential environment for the human self to produce her own identity. As Tim Ingold puts it, "human beings are *not* simply instruments for the replication of culture; rather they *use* their culture (including architecture, costume, and language) as a vehicle for living, for the mutual creation of themselves" (1986, 319). As I have said, it is important to recenter our attention to human beings as animals that belong to a specific species.

The dichotomy emotion/imagination can be regarded as a metaphor for human subjectivity, and organizes a perfectly particular perspective. Only through this subjectivity does a person have access to experience and perception of any kind of order. The axis imagination/emotion can be seen as the basic ingredients of human creativity: imaginative visualization of possible outcomes and the driving emotional force to bring them into existence. This highlights the need to include at this point the other axis in the organic life of the human species: embodiment/consciousness of self. The embodied human animal is related in a very complex way to her consciousness of self. On the one hand, we could say that consciousness of self is structured imaginatively as an emotional involvement with narrative or myth, yet this is not necessarily the case during infancy and early childhood, when there is only inarticulate practical consciousness. On the other hand, we could say that embodiment is structured only in physical phenomena, but we would fail to achieve understanding of how the latter interacts with human emotion and imagination. And so, in order to attempt a first approximation to how these two dichotomies interact in the creation of human selves, it is useful to visualize the dichotomy embodiment/consciousness of self as two moving concentric circles that grow according to the rhythms of the biological development of the body and the cultural production of the people where one grows up. Of course, the body grows old in a different way as compared to how consciousness of self grows old. In spite of this difference, they are bootstrapped to each other and so codetermine each other. This phenomenological perspective to visualize a person growing up conceives of the development of a consciousness of self as moving horizons that expand.

Consciousness of self, seen as how one orientates oneself within the human group where one grows up, is also shaped by shared references and the importance of comprehensive conceptions of the good in that same group. I have spoken of emotional and imaginative cognition for the *co-ontogeny* of embodiment and consciousness of self. Here, the axis emotion/imagination supports such cognition in providing imaginative symbolic representation and an emotional attachment to such representations. At birth, the circle of human consciousness is already at work in a practical unreflective manner, but during her infancy and early childhood, the child learns to differentiate her own embodied self with respect to the realm of social collective human interaction where she develops and becomes discursive and reflexive. To an observer, it takes the child's development into her own consciousness of self and bodily functionality to become an adult—according to the particular culture in which she grows up. In order for this to happen, human consciousness constantly *spills* beyond the confines of the physical body through imagination—while staying with it at the same time. But this is not necessarily a purely random spilling, it is more generally experienced in everyday life as guided by our emotional involvement with the objects that entertain our imagination (spontaneously induced *and* chosen by disciplined practice).

The difference between embodiment and consciousness of self can only be construed in terms of language, the aspect of interaction that is characteristic of the human species. As the model I have outlined above conveys, when considering how human animal life is different from nonhuman animal life, one refers to the artificial aspect of human interaction. The four structural artificial concepts I have referred to— discipline, spontaneity, path dependencies, and potentiality—create the basis for the difference between the human self and the rest of the living entities that we can objectively distinguish as such. Following Tim Ingold (1986), in order to differentiate the pair spontaneity/ discipline, I suggest a phenomenological distinction between practical and discursive intention. The concepts of path dependencies/potentiality are differentiated as past and future interaction within a present contemplation of the flow of time. In other words, from the present phenomenological perspective, spontaneity and discipline (practice) are manifested and observed in a synchronic plane of interaction while path dependencies and potentiality are construed in a diachronic plane (as myth or narrative), which nevertheless has the present moment of meaningful experience at its phenomenological center. While it is fairly straightforward to deal with past (path dependencies), present (observation), and future (potentiality) diachronically, the synchronic relationship between spontaneity and discipline is not so clearly defined. This brings the need to discuss the relationship between time and experience as it is conceived in this work. After considering the synchronic relationship between spontaneity and discipline, I go back to that between past path dependencies and potentiality. The following discussion derives mainly from a perspectival disagreement with Tim Ingold, whose analysis is framed in a strictly diachronic view of time in his book *Evolution and Social Life* (1986). I find his notions of practical and discursive intentionality very useful in order to differentiate spontaneous from disciplined behavior synchronically, and will therefore integrate them to my model: The dichotomy spontaneity/discipline can be dealt with by the observation of Ingold's practical (spontaneous) and discursive (disciplined) intentionality.

Tim Ingold situates his analysis temporally in what he calls "real time," or Bergsonian *duration*, to escape the complications of structuralist analysis.[9] The problem of temporality in Ingold's analysis is linked to the perspective of a second-order observer. As he does not propose a phenomenological perspective, he situates himself outside the phenomenon of the flow of consciousness, and so, in observing a perpetual natural continuum, the difference between synchrony and diachrony becomes irrelevant:

> [R]eal time—Bergsonian duration—inheres in practical consciousness, which is one reason why this form of consciousness cannot be comprehended within the structuralist paradigm, constructed as it is on the abstract axes of synchrony and diachrony. Discursive consciousness, revelatory of synchronic structure, is played out in a motionless, extended present and has no essential time component. (Ingold 1986, 301–02)

However, in situating himself outside the flow of consciousness, in the position of a second-order observer, Ingold ceases to contemplate himself within his own intellectual discursive awareness of his argumentation, one that is sequential and necessarily flows. From the perspective of the present moment of meaningful experience, discursiveness is inherently diachronic in that it needs the sequence of explanation or narrative in order to be reified. But from Ingold's outside perspective and structuralist frame of mind, the synchronic aspect of experience in discourse is comparable to a static vessel "a mapping of the regions of the mind as though it were a container, private to each individual" (1986, 301).

In contrast to this, inside the experience of consciousness, from a phenomenological perspective of present observation, discursive (disciplined) consciousness becomes diachronic while practical (spontaneous) consciousness is synchronic. From this perspective, the realm of synchronicity is given symbols of a permanent essence that mark relevant simultaneity (spiritual unity, understanding, trust, empathy, relevant borders in relationships or functional coordination, autopoiesis, structural coupling . . .), but discursiveness is experienced the same way as the flow of time is experienced, as movement and sequence—it could even be said that it is our discursive consciousness that organizes this flow as sequentiality. From Ingold's perspective, one cannot see that a human discursive (disciplined) aspect is already embedded in the description of practical (spontaneous) consciousness, which from his second-order observer—outside—perspective, is conceived of essentially as a perpetually unfolding continuum (of diachronic essence). But in the present instant of the consciousness of being alive, there is a synchronic realm of simultaneity that was the one Bergson was trying to point to, but to an extent failed due to the diachronic nature of the conceptual and argumentative tools that he was using—necessarily coherent and sequential. The present instant cannot be symbolized discursively because it loses its practical (spontaneous) synchronic quality and becomes absorbed by the sequence of narrative, tale, or description.

The problem of a second-order observer perspective is solved by Ingold in synthesizing synchrony and diachrony in a Bergsonian construction of time as a continuum of the flow of experience, and so favoring indirectly a representation of time that is strictly diachronic. However, Bergson himself is opposed to this kind of characterization in his book *Duration and Simultaneity* (1965), where, according to Moore, he celebrates Einstein's theory of general relativity where the abolition of absolute properties should be "complemented by the kind of absolute awareness of simultaneity which could flow from [Bergson's] earlier work" (Moore 1996, 11). Bergson's *durée* was a reaction against abstract constructions of reality that were "not sensitive enough to that vital substratum of concrete, lived reality available only to the holistic understanding of the intuition" (Jay 1993, 194). His main claim was that the discreteness of events—somehow "threaded together like beads on a string of consciousness" (Moore 1996, 55)—is not real, that time is a continuing flow of experience. However, even if one would feel inclined to agree with Bergson's view of time as a synthesis of synchronic perception, in observation of complex simultaneity where everything is related to everything else, we should have a look at just how this view is constructed.

As a reaction against abstract absolutism, Bergson opposes a perceptual absolutism and condemns the relevant symbols of his tradition to unreality because they deny embodied perception. Eventhough his philosophy has been heavily criticized due to its lack of formal precision, Bergson contended that his notion of precision rooted philosophy in the concrete experienced world, otherwise the formal trappings of precision were vain (Moore 1996, 17). The philosophical trap for Bergson was that intellectual knowledge relies on abstraction and so does his own philosophical project; thus, through abstraction, an absolutism of perception is not wholly apprehensible. In the representation of time as *durée*, Bergson opted for a representation of time beyond human history, the bodily animal, the one that Darwin gave to nature in general but not to human beings. In this construction of time, he seems to regard the domain of relevant human events (historical, cultural, mythical, or otherwise) as unreal. My contention is that, in the realm of relevant social events, we are emotionally and imaginatively linked to—created and creating—historical and cultural domains, or the "beads" on the string of consciousness. However, one could argue that these realms are unreal in as much as they are emotionally imagined, and that discrete events may disappear once they become trivial for cosmology, but they are real to the social sciences as they constitute relevant domains for concrete experience of interaction among human beings. Events become symbolized in different types of language in personal and collective imagination, even if they are illusory, emotionally sustained, non-concrete ideological, or abstract "things." Nevertheless, for human beings as animals, Bergson's construction of time as *durée* is a legitimate aspect of experience that traditional philosophy until then had chosen to ignore.

It is posed by Ingold, and convincingly sustained by empirical evidence (see Ingold 1986), that human and nonhuman animals share this "animal" aspect of time in practical (spontaneous) consciousness that, until Bergson, was not considered as a realm of legitimate experience for human beings. Ingold regards the spontaneity of practical consciousness as "a process, a creative good, which works through a whole series of fabrications and observations in the course of its unfolding" (1986, 298). However, as I have argued, Ingold's perspective stands outside the flow of time and consciousness. The perspective I propose—the present moment of meaningful experience—lies within the lived experience of practical consciousness. The notion of simultaneity is always present and this amounts to Ingold's own characterization of practical consciousness as "the notion of mind as the enfolding of an intersubjective process" (1986, 301). Beyond the problem of perspective, however, Ingold is engaged in differentiating discursive (disciplined) consciousness from a practical (spontaneous) one that is nonreflective. In doing so, he surprisingly finds the locus of creativity in the latter, which we share with nonhuman animals, thus regarding them as co-creators with nature of their own business of living and not just as mere Cartesian "automatons."

In order to see this, Ingold deals with the intrusion of the contrastive term "the unconscious" that, he notices, is rarely referred to as "unconsciousness" (Ingold 1986, 298); it denotes passivity and is therefore essentially noncreative. In order to clarify the ambiguity that the unconscious introduces in any discussion about consciousness, he contrasts Ricoeur's notion of the unconscious to that of Levi-Strauss's: The former sees the unconscious as pulling us back to "the order of the primordial"—the Christian inheritance of the tradition of consciousness as a struggle for light—and the latter as "the task that cultural human beings live to execute [which] is itself inscribed in the unconscious" (Ingold 1986, 299). This is a very useful contrast in order to illustrate how the unconscious can become a catchall principle of explanation when it comes to find a place for the spontaneous manifestations of human life, seen as either negative or positive. Francisco Varela criticizes a similar idea, according to which intelligence resembles computation and the brain is seen as an information-processing device not only as a metaphor but also in a literal sense, with no direct access to its own mental or cognitive processes. Varela calls this the "cognitivist paradigm": "[I]n addition to the levels of physics and neurobiology, cognitivism postulates a distinct, irreducible symbolic level in the explanation of cognition" (Varela et al. 1991, 41). And this symbolic level is supposed to be both unconscious and get its meaning from the syntactic logic within the system that can be accessed from an outside mathematical formal modeling. This is the reason why, following Ingold, I reject the notion of *the unconscious* as a realm of explanation for cognition because it either gets the shape of a deterministic "black box" or that of a structural model that holds the keys to conscious life. As Nishitani says:

> The realm of the unconscious, no matter how deeply it reaches into the strata underlying consciousness, remains after all continuous with the realm of consciousness and on a dimension where, together with consciousness, it can become the subject matter of psychology. (1982, 153)

I find it more useful to consider the two notions of practical (spontaneous) and discursive (disciplined) consciousness as complementary realms of the human conscious life.

Ingold poses the difference between practical and discursive consciousness as the difference between "knowing *how*," and "knowing *that*." A practical kind of consciousness is clearly shared by human and nonhuman animals, but even if nonhuman animals may know *that*, they cannot reflect on their knowing *that*—and we might not always do. "Knowing how" is the kind of knowing that Maturana and Varela refer to when they say that "to live is to know" in organic *autopoietic* interaction with the environment. The basis of the difference between the two kinds of consciousness is generally seen as as the distinctively human capacity for symbolic thought. However, Ingold reviews various studies of nonhuman animal communicative behavior and arrives at the conclusion that symbolic thought is no absolute difference between animals and humans and that whether intermediate stages cannot be admitted "remains a legitimate subject of speculation" (Ingold 1986, 303).

However, he goes on to describe how the identifiably distinctive human symbolic ability is different from an animal kind of communicative behavior. Verbal symbols, Ingold argues, do not only "announce" an object but also rather lead the subject to "conceive" it (1986, 304). Animals continually emit and receive a dense amount of signals that "correspond to bodily states and not to concepts" (Ingold 1986, 309). In contrast to this, the human kind of symbolic imagination enables us to speak and think about remote things in space and time, and also about deception, fantasy, speculation, and hypothetical thought. However, this ability does not guide our behavior all the time; we also act spontaneously, in impulsive, systematic, or unpremeditated manners—and this, according to Ingold, is the main source of creativity. This is illustrated by Ingold's examples that portray practical consciousness as the one that interacts and has the ability to disclose disciplined action without discursive deliberation:

> Anyone who has learned to speak a foreign language or to ride a bicycle knows that in the former case, complete fluency comes when the application of syntactical rules becomes as automatic as for a native speaker, and that in the latter case, a perfect balance is achieved only when one ceases to deliberate on the correct way to go about it. (Ingold 1986, 300)

These examples serve to illustrate how practical human consciousness has already assimilated the discursive intention of discipline and has become fluent practice. But there are also preeminently spontaneous human behaviors that are disclosed without the need for prior articulation of discursive intention and rules, like baby play, sex, or intimate and emotional interaction, and learning to speak one's native tongue, or to walk.[10]

The above rationale leads Ingold to consider practical intention as a legitimate aspect of human interaction, which traditionally has been seen as located in the discursive realm of rational deliberation and only present as articulated thought before action. Following Searle (1979), Ingold distinguishes between prior intention and intention in action. "A prior intention," says Ingold, "is an imaginative *re*presentation of a future state that it is desired to bring about, and differs from memory only in that it precedes rather than succeeds the objective realization of that state. . . . The intention in action, by contrast, corresponds to the experience of actually doing; in that sense it is *presentational* rather that *re*presentational" (1986, 312). According to this, then, intention in action is not necessarily discursive, nor is it necessarily only human; nonhuman animals have a spontaneous presentational intention in the realization of the acts of living; even if they do not construct a stable representational notion of self that is aware of realizing them, one that is taken to be only a human experience based on our discursive ability. The confusion of the categories practical and discursive in consciousness may lead to denying both consciousness and intention to animals, while at the same time, it ascribes them a representational quality built inside the mechanics of their brain about which they are supposed to be unaware of or *unconscious.*

The axis *discipline/spontaneity* of the artificial structure of my model represents the discussed duality of discursive intention and practical intention in human interaction, which in the present moment, is experienced at the same time—in synchrony. In phenomenological observation, this axis is divided into their synchronic and diachronic consequences for human behavior and interaction. Speaking from the point of view of discipline, intention is always construed discursively either before or after the action, and it therefore has an inbuilt diachronic quality. Yet, in practice, discipline is a manifest aspect of the present moment of consciousness, which is also ruled by spontaneity. In human experience, the present moment is neither mere spontaneity nor only discipline; it is the immediate human life world that needs both to be produced and to produce human identity at the same time. This is an important consideration in order to attempt an explanation of how the domestic life of children and caretakers, their emotional and imaginative involvement with their particular stories, eventually produces ethically functional adults (or not).

Humberto Maturana and the psychologist Gerda Verden-Zöler in their book *Amor y juego* (1995) locate the emotional construction of the imaginary realm of culture in the spontaneous process of development of the child, and in the importance of *love and play* while she grows up. However, during her development, the child is also simultaneously disciplined by her interpersonal relationships and emotional ties to move adequately in the social imaginary particular world in which she develops. As she grows up, the child learns to master disciplined behaviors as well as physiologically determined ones. The disciplinary training involves bodily behavior as well as learning the language used for communication in her particular cultural environment—and it may involve training in many languages. This training takes place both spontaneously and in a disciplined manner at the same time, and these two kinds of behaviors are indistinguishable from each other in the present moment of experience. But in phenomenological observation and description, spontaneity can be seen as the familiarization of the child with its own organic structural sounds and bodily rhythms in play, and discipline is observed as the learnt patterns of behavior in language and culture. It is clear that knowledge is constantly produced by discipline, but it is not always apparent to us that spontaneity plays an equally important role in the production of human knowledge. It seems like discipline is easier to pin down because it is set out sequentially in the formal descriptions of its methodology and in the principles of its systematic application in practice. Yet, the synchronic works of spontaneity are already as embedded in the formal description of the discipline, as in the actual application of the principles of order.

We are now in a position to go back to the diachronic structural axis of the model (*path dependencies/potentiality*), which is disclosed in the relationship that takes place between the present moment of experience and the diachronic aspect of time that continually shapes interaction. According to Maturana and Verden-Zöler, the organic unity between consciousness and embodiment produces an imaginary and enacted "social relational space" grounded in emotional ties (1995, 94). In the development of the individual human being, her relational space keeps growing and producing both a personal identity and a story with respect to the relationships that she gets involved with throughout her lifetime (personal, functional, and cultural).[11] This relevant personal story includes the development of our own embodiment, and is also embedded in a series of relationships with concrete objects and embodied people (or disembodied personalities who either have died or were never born but in human mythical imagination) as well as distinctive collective practices in constant transformation that have a degree of permanence in their systematicity and in collective belief in them.

Path dependencies are construed as the structure of past interactions that has formed the present organization of embodiment. Nonhuman and human animals' perception of the world is structurally determined by their actual embodiment, even as it engages in its own conscious production through practical intention. But humans also produce a notion of self attached both to embodiment (physical development) and to the cultural groups where they belong to (families, tribes, nations, governments, clans, empires, organizations). Human path dependencies are built from a present perspective that has been determined by past interactions. It looks on the past to organize its relevant features according to present necessities, which for humans, are both organic and artificial. Here is where the human identity that is produced by our relational space is able to consider its own potentiality as well as that of the relevant group that it belongs to. Potentiality takes over to organize present discursive intention that is projected into the future. The conceptual pair path dependencies/ potentiality is therefore essentially diachronic, but it is built on the basis of present meaningful experience and their meaning is reified symbolically and sequentially.

Human identity is discursively involved both in creating and in being created by the "conversation" (Maturana 1997) or the meaningful and legitimate present order, which can then be projected unto past and future. Language is then a characteristic of the human species that is essential in the production of persons, and this refers to its biological importance. I have said that human beings are able to sustain their ontogeny in connection with other individual human ontogenies by means of language, as the human world is construed in conversation and relevant shared references. We are left with the idea that human beings or persons are both producers and products of our environment in discursive consciousness, but it is also important to consider that at the same time, in practical consciousness, we are engaged in the process of producing ourselves and are already the embodied organic product of this process simultaneously. In this type of immediate synchronic practical intentionality, the diachronic discursive one intervenes only through the conscious practice of a meaningful discipline—a human trait. This is the business of sustaining human life autopoietically. I have tried to illustrate how our practical intention is entwined with our discursive intention in the creation of persons through language and the emotional and imaginative production of the human spaces where persons live. The model of cognition with the present moment of meaningful experience at its center that I propose, basically puts this moment as the one that can accommodate in synchronicity the four axes I have referred to as a nexus that gives rise to cognition: embodiment–consciousness of self, emotion–imagination, spontaneity–discipline, and path dependencies– potentialities. This is the basis to see that human life produces a vast diversity of conversations, imaginative representations of what is important in domestic personal narratives, stories, and myths. They are creative products of our species and also have the biological function of keeping human groups together in order for the young to grow into functional adults who can eventually perpetuate the species and tell the relevant tales. In this sense, the human species is biologically equipped to keep its own autopoiesis going through the reproduction of persons, relationships, and conversations. One can contemplate nature as a "container" of human life and the fine line that allows for such a differentiation and the definition of our identity as humans is our cultural insulation that we produce and of which we are products. I will concentrate in the next section on a closer description of autopoiesis in order to get a better look at the neglected aspect of emotional cognition in the production of persons. This is based on how Maturana and Verden-Zöler portray the essential role of love and play while children grow up, which leads to the all-important role of the caretaker in this process and her ethical standing as she sustains and enables human autopoiesis. In this way, I hope to clarify how an ethics of care cannot possibly be seen as marginal in moral philosophy, it should be given a central place in the imaginative and emotional production of persons.

EMOTIONAL COGNITION AND THE
FEMINIST "ETHICS OF CARE"

For the purposes of defining the primitive type of reality, a fundamental emotional bond between the child and her caretakers ought to be considered as a realm of human (and moral) development into adulthood. We have said that an essential characteristic of this type of reality is an emotional involvement with collective myths and personal narratives at a domestic level, which we can separate analytically, but which are inextricably entwined in human ontogeny. It is important to contemplate how infants and children develop a distinct notion of self, how this is simultaneously related to their emotional involvement with this self, and also how the role of the caretaker is involved at that level of intimacy in domestic interaction. All this is immersed in what I call *emotional cognition* and has an essential connection with domestic and particular "ethics of care." The relation between these two notions can be posed in terms of how it is that trust is built in the midst of a human group. Trust can be said to be developed organically within the most vulnerable situation of the human baby and can also be said to expand the circle of consciousness in the human self as she grows up. We can identify a trusting behavior in the present moment of experience, even if displayed by an animal. Newborn babies trust completely in a way in which only a human kind of environment allows them to; they are born from the organic womb into the "womb" of relationships and culture that allows the baby to produce a notion of self. The process of creation of this notion of self is far from safe in the same sense as a womb is to the fetus. The human baby faces both the hardship and the comfort of dependence at the same time: From the moment that it leaves the womb, it is immersed in a psychological relationship with its environment and the people in it; if there are no people in its environment, the baby dies (as it is born as an "embryo," see Gould 1977).

Barbara Misztal refers to Giddens's (1990) notion of "basic trust" "which illustrates how the development of trust in infancy determines the core of our ego identity" (Misztal 1996, 91). This brings about the psychological need of security that is based on the formation of trust in human relationships. In human interaction, from the present perspective, the experience of successful social coordination is based on trust, and even if we may refer to it in diachronic accounts of human life, its experiential substance lies in synchrony. Misztal also refers to a variation of trust in Giddens's discussion that seems to suggest that this variation, "elementary trust," is more related to security in the social environments. While one can see the difference between basic and elementary trust analytically, it is not clear just how these two realms of trust can separate in the ontogeny of living human beings. This difficulty of separating in actual lived experience concepts that can only be separated analytically lies at the center of the communitarian objection to separate the good and the right, and give the former to the private realm of interaction and the latter to the public one. I will engage with these issues in chapter 4; here, I want to emphasize that the production of either basic or elementary trust is related to the extended practice of an ethics of care that, on the one hand, is the biological environment necessary for the species to survive and, on the other hand, is the initial approximation to human relationships and a meaningful ethical life. The caretaker is the one who embodies such ethics for the growing infant:

> Developing habits of conversational reflection depends on ongoing mutual trust. When training is a work of conscience, proper trust is a virtue of which unquestioning obedience or blind trust are degenerative forms. Proper trust is a relation between mothers and children for which, in the first instance, a mother is responsible. (Ruddick 1990, 118)

I resort to Maturana and Verden-Zöler's account of the role of human "conversations" as the basis to understand the biological relevance of an emotional involvement with the child's environment for her development. At the same time, I will also resort to Sarah Ruddick's *Maternal Thinking* (1990), in order to consider the ethical perspective of those who take care of children, those in the business of producing functional adults.[12]

In spite of the analytical differences in types of trust that one can concede, human trust depends on the production of what Frye calls an "integument of culture," carved in language and human action by imaginative and emotional involvement. This cultural integument is an emanation of the daily business of human beings preserving their autopoiesis—the organic production of themselves. Maturana and Varela call this *emanation* the domain of "language and self-consciousness" (1987, 176) and they believe it takes place in the form of "conversations." Before engaging on how Maturana and Verden-Zöler explain the complex relationship of consciousness and embodiment in love and play while children grow up, it is necessary to give an outline of Maturana and Varela's theory of autopoiesis in living organisms. From this theory, one can deduce that embodiment and organization are both simultaneously passive creations and active producers of actuality in an organic "dance." This interplay of elements that produces human order can only be spoken of by stopping it provisionally by artificial discipline and its human marks on time. I have said that autopoiesis is a term that contemplates all living entities as conscious and creative in experiential practical (spontaneous) intention—the production of themselves in an intelligent manner. But we would forget to look at ourselves if we did not consider that as we speak of organic autopoiesis, we are also living in a discursive, very human, integument or cultural protection that other animals cannot perceive in the same way, even as they might be involved in the disciplinary human order (like domestic animals).

I have said that the theory about life and cognition of Maturana and Varela is couched in a synchronic perspective of time, and therefore, the observer identifies with her animal object of study: a living entity like oneself. This refers to the organic organization of an ideal human entity that is ideal because—following Tim Ingold's discussion about intentionality—we will only consider its practical intention. This allows us to contemplate the human animal at the same level of consciousness as the nonhuman animal, and realize that language has a systematic everyday life coordinatory use that, even in a discursive mode, displays practical (spontaneous) intention. For example, when one learns to speak fluently as a child, the discursive intention of speaking is not part of that learning. But, through conversation, one may unwittingly either inflict emotional pain as a consequence of careless speech, or provide emotional support without this being the explicit subject of the conversation, which are all practical intentionalities that may become discursive only a posteriori. As observers, we might distinguish practical from discursive elements in the living entity or in the environment, but they cannot be distinguished presently from the perspective of the embodied human that lives them. And so, the purely organic human ideal type does not represent the world discursively to itself, it already knows it structurally (by the embodied history of its past interactions, its present structure); it acts its practical intention and lives.

This is a kind of *embodied knowledge* present in the synchronic theory about life that Humberto Maturana and Francisco Varela have produced: It is a description of how living beings are constituted that defies the traditional assumptions of the biological discipline. In this theory, even if they themselves do not formulate it in these terms, there is a symbological interplay of a dichotomy that describes the essential need of life to constantly move and constantly rest. In sequential diachronic time as movement, this is experienced as the unavoidable need of sleeping and waking, breathing in and out, living and dying; but in the perpetual present time—here and now—there is a world-overall living mixture of individual particular events, which can only be seen as being constituted by discrete events in description. The simultaneity of life on earth is seen as sustained spontaneously with astounding intelligence by an immense variety of living organisms and a changing environment right now. Autopoiesis describes how living beings are organized to engage in the process of the biological production of themselves.

The order of things that the authors of this theory want to describe is framed in a basic conceptual dichotomy that I have already explained above, which refers to two aspects of the same holistic phenomenon. In living organisms, their organization is permanent, while structure is in constant movement. The organization of a living being is accompanied by its structure that engages in the constant dynamics of the processes that produce its integrity as a living entity. In explaining this kind of constitution in the cell, they speak of the relations that are established through chemical transformations:

> On the one hand, we see a network of dynamic transformations that produces its own components and that is essential for a boundary; on the other hand, we see a boundary that is essential for the operation of the network of transformations which produced it as a unity. Note that these are not sequential processes, but two different aspects of a unitary phenomenon. (Maturana and Varela 1987, 46)

The integrity of these processes is sustained in living organisms as operationally closed systems, that is, their *organization is closed* to the environment, but their *structure is coupled* to it. We could still see them as "open" in that they do interact with the environment, but their *closure* entails that they can only do it in their own particular structural ways. The simplicity of the unitary cell allows us to identify organization directly with a boundary that "contains" life. But in multicellular living beings, organization is not simply a boundary, it is the *form* of the structural relations in constant change that makes it possible for observers to distinguish living entities and classify them as diverse species.[13] Living beings differ from each other in their structure (which is always individual, a unique event) and they are alike and can be classified by their organization; their structure is characterized by their constant dynamic processes.

The above incessant movement, what Maturana and Varela call "the throbbing of all life" (1987, 100), is the constant autopoiesis of living beings (without forgetting the equally constant presence of death or disintegration). Autopoiesis can be imagined as happening not only as sequential (discrete and ordered in time past and future), but also as simultaneous in living beings at this present moment in world synchrony. However, what Maturana and Varela want to emphasize is that the production of life and autopoiesis is most importantly situated in present synchrony, and that sequence is essential only to the present description of that condition of life:

> The fact remains that we are continuously immersed in this network of interactions, the results of which depend on history. Effective action leads to effective action: It is the cognitive circle that characterizes our becoming, as an expression of our manner of being autonomous living systems. Through this ongoing recursiveness, every world brought forth necessarily hides its origins. We exist in the present; past and future are manners of being now. Biologically there is no way we can put in front of us what happened to us in obtaining the regularities we have grown accustomed to: From values or preferences to color qualities and smells. The biologic mechanism tells us that an operational stabilization in the dynamics of the organism does not embody the manner in which it originated. The business of living keeps no records concerning origins. All we can do is generate explanations, through language, that reveal the mechanism of bringing forth a world. (Maturana and Varela 1987, 241–42)

History is "hidden" in the organism, yet present in our form of explanation of the living phenomena. But the latter explanation is part of the discursive human dimension as a dimension of interaction that nonhuman animals do not display; what any living organism does display presently (including humans) is its actual structure acquired throughout its development from being born, and this structure has its own particular past path dependencies. The epistemological consequence of this assertion is to say that the present moment of life is all there is, past and future are structural characteristics of our way of explaining phenomena, of our way of knowing now (and of living in that explanation, using it as an imaginary shelter or an "integument"). Explanations are only symbological human dimensions; they are not actual characteristics of experience *qua* explanations, only *qua* acquired structures through path dependencies. This predicament arises especially when the living being under inspection is the human being:

> If everything is ultimately specified through its appearance to us, then so is the knowing subject. Since the subject can represent itself to itself, it becomes an object for representation but is different from all other objects. Thus in the end the self becomes both an objectified subject and a subjectified object. This predicament discloses the shiftiness, the instability of the entire subjective/objective polarity. (Varela et al. 1991, 242)

In this perspective, the living entity is no longer considered just as a passive object that "lives" and that the scientist describes as a structure of sequential processes that "happen" and give its object of study the quality of being alive. Rather, in autopoiesis, the living being is described as the producer and the product of such processes at the same time.

By differentiating the synchronic-present *time logistics*, as it were, of all living entities from our human observer-like need to exist in sequential explanation, Maturana and Varela point at what makes human beings different from the rest of living organisms (the need for explanations):

> [O]ur experience is moored to our structure in a binding way. We do not see the "space" of the world; we live our field of vision. We do not see the "colors" of the world; we live our chromatic space. Doubtless . . . we are experiencing a world. But when we examine more closely how we get to know this world, we invariably find that we cannot separate our history of actions—biological and social—from how this world appears to us. It is so obvious and close that it is very hard to see. (Maturana and Varela 1987, 23)

The living system is identified as an autopoietic embodied entity with a history of past path dependencies that constitute its structural actuality, and this means that its consciousness will give this entity the practical (spontaneous) intention to live its ontogeny.

This brings us back to the present moment of interaction and to the ontogeny of organisms, including us. Maturana and Varela see the relevance of speaking about *phylogenetic* evolution to explain the emergence of different lineages of living beings and their history of structural drift (evolution), their path dependencies. But this is an explanation that is relevant to the observer, in living experience: phylogeny takes place at the same time as ontogeny, and the latter is currently taken to be as unimportant to biology as particular personal life-stories are unimportant to universal history. "The classical approach that is still alive in most textbooks," say Varela et al., "simply jumps from genes and gene frequencies to phenotypes and reproductively able organisms" (1991, 189).[14] According to Sober, the area of ontogeny or development poses various problems that remain unsolved in biology (1993, 22). As has been said before, Maturana and Varela's theory addresses just this area by highlighting ontogeny instead of phylogeny. Susan Oyama also engages with the problem of the implied biological assumption according to which some development follows genetic rules and some does not, an assumption that, Oyama tells us "undergrids the opposition of biological to cultural processes, the mare's nest of biological determinism and the whole nature–nurture complex" (1985, 11). According to Oyama, then, the form of the organism is not transmitted through genes or contained in the environment; it is constructed in developmental processes, in ontogeny.

There is an important commonality between ontogeny and phylogeny: the primeval unicellular point of origin, for phylogenetic evolution is also the point of origin for the ontogeny of all multicellular living entities. The individual ontogenetic history of an autopoietic organism takes place as an epigenetic process:

> In spite of their amazing and apparent diversity, they all [multicellulars] conserve reproduction through a unicellular stage as a central feature of their identity as biologic systems [epigenesis]. This common element in their organization does not interfere with their great diversity, because this takes place in structural variation. This situation does permit us, however, to see that all this variation is a variation around a fundamental type, which results in different ways of being in the world, because it is the structure of the unity that determines its interaction in the environment and the world it lives in. (Maturana and Varela 1987, 83–86)

Eventhough multicellularity represents variation around one type, it is a vast kind of variation. Multicellularity as a past path dependency opened the possibility of many different lineages, much more diverse than the unicellular ones. In the animal kingdom, the one that humanity belongs to, this variation is based on the organism's natural drift to acquiring motility (on which feeding and reproduction are based) and a nervous system.[15]

Taking into account cognitive involvement in autopoiesis, new sources of variation are discovered in the synchronic dimension that Maturana and Varela want to emphasize:

> [T]he behavior of living beings is not an invention of the nervous system and it is not exclusively associated with it. . . . What the nervous system does is *expand* the realm of possible behaviors by endowing the organism with a tremendously versatile and plastic structure. (Maturana and Varela 1987, 138)

This versatile structure is related to movement and to a notion of behavior that, in the more general use of cognition, is "assumed to be limited to organisms with a (fairly *advanced*) nervous system" (Mingers 1991, 321; emphasis added).[16] Here, "advanced" is used in the sense of resembling the human nervous system in a closer manner. What makes the nervous system so versatile is the physical nature of the connections that it establishes. On the one hand, the latter connect cells that are often distant from each other. According to Maturana and Varela,

> What distinguishes neurons is their cytoplasmatic ramifications in specific forms which extend for enormous distances, reaching tens of millimeters in the largest ones. This universal neuronal characteristic, present in all organisms with a nervous system, determines the specific way in which the nervous system participates in the second-order unities that it integrates by placing in contact cellular elements located in different parts of the body. (1987, 153)

On the other hand, neurons are seen as special cells that put in contact sensory and motor surfaces and, therefore, the nervous system is associated to movement and to behavior in an animal sense.[17] The neuronal system is embedded in the organism and it works as a network of electric neuronal interactions with the cells of the surfaces of perception and movement. "Neurons couple, in many different ways, cellular groups which otherwise could be coupled only through the general circulation of internal substances of the organism" (Maturana and Varela 1987, 153). Eventhough neurons are still affected by chemical changes, their universal means of interaction to establish connections with each other and with other cells is through electric impulses (Mingers 1991, 322). Through this simple mechanism of distant coupling between sensory cell surfaces and motile effects, Maturana has found an extended source for possible diversity of behaviors according to the varied patterns of the impulses generated in relative neuronal states of activity that can be observed. However, it is important to stress that nerve cells in constant change respond with definite "transfer functions," that arise synchronically and spontaneously within this continuous change, to classes of spatiotemporal configurations of impulses that also keep arising.[18] These impulses are not recorded or engraved patterns in any part of the cell anatomy (Maturana 1970, 23–24).

Another important characteristic of neurons must be outlined at this point, which has to do with the autopoietic closure of the nervous system and its plasticity. The nervous system itself is engaged in its constant autopoiesis and this means that it is not a static highway of connections, but an active producer of itself. The body in which it is embedded is its environment and it responds to its "triggers" by modulating its internal structural dynamics. "[T]he nervous system does not 'pick up information' from the environment as we often hear. On the contrary, it brings forth a world by specifying what patterns of the environment are perturbations and what changes trigger them in the organism" (Maturana and Varela 1987, 169). As the neuronal system is in constant autopoietic activity, its collector and effector surfaces are coupled to its environment in interaction, this produces a structure of behavior that we can observe, but the nervous system is not really connected to the environment organizationally (only coupled to it structurally and dynamically):

> The plasticity of the nervous system lies in the fact that neurons are not connected as though they were cables with their respective plugs. The points of interaction between the cells are zones of delicate dynamic balance modulated by a great number of elements that trigger local structural changes, and that are produced as a result of the activity of those cells and of other cells whose products are released into the blood flow and wash the neurons. (Maturana and Varela 1987, 168)

These zones are the synapses, very small gaps "across which chemicals called neurotransmitters can flow, triggering an electrical exchange" (Mingers 1991, 322). This characterization of the nervous system will lead us to language and self-consciousness as the domains of interaction that are characteristic of human beings (Maturana 1997).

This supports what I have pointed out before, that language has a biological dimension for human beings as embodied animals and autopoietic systems.

Mingers (1991) explains how, in the theory of Maturana and Varela, our practical interaction and our human type of language is a product of the continual structural change (plasticity) of the nervous system, its autopoiesis, and its internal structure. The nervous system's generalized response to electrical impulses leads to the development of internal neurons that connect only to other neurons. "These interneurons are particularly important as they sever the direct relationship between sensor and effector and vastly expand the realm of possible behaviors of an organism" (Mingers 1991, 322). As the child grows up, the relations that take place in experience at the collector surface of its nervous system, are transferred by classes of spatiotemporal configurations of nervous activity that we can observe. However, inter-neurons grow and so, eventually, these configurations do not have a direct effect on the motor surface, but are already parts of the organism as perturbations for the internal structure of the nervous system itself. It is important to stress, though, that these configurations of nervous activity are not "instructions" for the patterns of behavior themselves as this would entail a "cognitivist" view of how we know the world, which Maturana and Varela reject. Instead, they are configurations of electric impulses that emerge as classes of behavior that arise at every moment in a constantly changing environment. They describe the structural characteristic of the nervous system as expanding the system's domain of its changes of state. In synchrony, these changes follow a course contingent upon both its structure and the environmental triggers. As the nervous system puts in touch cells that are physically separate in the organism, the organism's changing structure displays behaviors that are coupled with the autopoietic nervous activity, one that is structurally able to establish relations between events.[19]

When behavior symbolizes something other than itself, organisms "orient" each other's behavior in co-ontogeny, which is what Maturana calls "languaging" that social animals (human and nonhuman) display. The success of orientating behavior depends on the common cognitive domain of the organisms that can be either physiologically specified, or sustained by common experience, or by a separate domain of language. Nonhuman animals only "language" by means of physiologically determined traits or through common cognitive domains based on experience. Human beings not only use both the latter domains of communication and coordination of behavior, but also a separate domain of complex language as a characteristic of the species. In us, inter-neurons outnumber sensory/motor neurons by a factor of 100,000 (Mingers 1991, 322). According to Mingers, "The human brain is vastly more responsive to its own internal structures than it is to its sensory/effect surfaces" (1991, 325). It is important to realize that the expanded domains of possible behaviors for human beings are seen as relative relations between configurations of neuronal activity and not as the patterns themselves as if they were static representations of the world, such as "pictures" or "engrams" (Varela et al. 1991).

The human nervous system interacts synchronically with vast different states of neuronal activity, and this in turn produces more relative patterns of neuronal activity to be considered independently. The recursiveness achieved by this eventually leaves us with vast domains of possible co-relations within the plasticity of the human nervous system. As Maturana puts it, "although language does not take place within the bodyhood of the living system, the structure of the living system must provide the diversity and plasticity of states required for it to take place" (Maturana 1997, 100–01). But this immense diversity of states take place simultaneously, and they are all present at the same time as we produce language. The latter is not "embedded in our brains" physically, as it has an autonomy that can only be sustained collectively. And this is the essence of the organic nature of language; its autonomy depends on the creative involvement of a group of organisms bringing forth the world in which they interact: one that they create and that creates their sense of self back. The human species sustains its autopoiesis by means of three types of common cognitive domain or "languaging": a physiologically speci-fied one (we are equipped to speak, point, mimic, signal), a common ground of experience (the network of relationships, emotional cognition), and an autonomous realm of complex communication (language, culture, imaginative cognition). We share the first two types with social animals and these first two types of communication are essential in human ontogeny.

Thus, while children grow up, language is a product of human co-ontogeny originally based on physiological communication and a common domain of experience. In every individual, our commu-nicative abilities eventually grow beyond our physiology and direct-experience cognitive grounds, toward interaction through the separate realm of language, which can be regarded as an autonomous domain of interaction. We can then "language" about imaginary behaviors that are supposed to be enacted, that may never be enacted, that were never enacted, or that cannot possibly be enacted, but we also definitely "language" through physiological and experiential common cognitive grounds as the basis for the autonomous domain of language to emerge in our consciousness. Language is part of the organic autopoiesis of human beings and is itself autopoietic in that linguistic symbols are self-referential.[20] Maturana says that we find ourselves, as living systems, immersed in language:

> In the explanation of language as a biological phenomenon, it becomes apparent that languaging arises, when it arises, as a manner of coexistence of living systems. As such, languaging takes place as a consequence of co-ontogenic structural drift under recurrent consensual interactions. For this reason language takes place as a system of recurrent interactions in a domain of structural coupling. Interactions in language do not take place in a domain of abstractions; on the contrary, they take place in the corporality of the participants. Interactions in language are structural interactions. (Maturana 1997, 94)

When Maturana refers to corporality here, he is not referring to abstract engrams embedded in our brains as pictures or representations of reality; he is speaking of our embodied involvement in the action (or nonaction) of interaction:

> The higher human functions do not take place in the brain: Language, abstract thinking, love, devotion, reflection, rationality, altruism, etc. are not features of the dynamics of states of the human being as a living system, nor of its nervous system as a neuronal network, they are sociohistorical phenomena. At the same time, history is not part of the dynamics of states of a living system because this takes place only in the present, instant after instant, in the operation of its structure in changes that occur out of time. History, time, future, past or space, exist in language as forms of explaining the happening of living of the observer, and thereby partake of the involvement of language in this. (Maturana 1997, 100)

According to Maturana, in the realm of simultaneity of embodied interaction through language, cognition has no abstract content as a biological phenomenon. The observer creates this content, as the observer sees it embodied structurally by our physical involvement in interaction, or what Varela calls "enaction" (1991).

However, to Maturana, this physical embodied involvement also unavoidably involves a psychology: the emotional standing of the human animal that interacts. The human animal is necessarily involved in an emotional manner with social behavior in order to enact it. In Maturana and Varela's account of human life, imagination and emotions are not seen as a product of the brain itself, but of the dynamic and plastic structural coupling of the brain and nervous system with the social domain of interaction. Tim Ingold clarifies the link between embodiment and consciousness in the human domain by distinguishing between interactions and relationships: "To dissolve a relationship into its constituent interactions is to drain it of the very current of sociality that binds them as moments of a process, and that is of its essence. The creative unfolding of relationships, however, is also a becoming of the persons joined by it" (1989, 222). The human co-ontogeny that Maturana sees in language is emotionally sustained in what he calls "conversations" that are analogous to Ingold's relationships, and from an even wider perspective are analogous to cultures or worldviews. "Conversations," cultures, or worldviews are analogous to comprehensive conceptions of the good, which are tied to human practices that have specific standards, rules, and ethics. The child relates to these through emotional cognition, and so this type of cognition can be regarded as an essential aspect of the ethical training of children.

During childhood, cognitive abilities are developed to grow into adulthood. In the modern world, this includes the ability to behave in a rational way, a behavior that must be functional at least. The development of such abilities is founded on conventional ethics, which are taught to children as they grow up. Conventional ethics might have universal and transcendental aspirations, but they are always conventional (and this also applies to the liberal tradition). In the discussion of the primitive ideal type of reality, I argue that the development of cognitive abilities to support conventional ethics in any human culture is determined by emotional and imaginative involvement with the prevalent narrative in the human group where one grows up. While in our species doing this takes the form of narrative (imagination), emotions determine the development of the cognitive abilities to grasp conventional ethics and act according to them. That is, the development of such abilities is related to emotions in a very basic and human–animal way.

Humberto Maturana and the psychologist Gerda Verden-Zöler explain the idea that worldviews, cultures, comprehensive conceptions, or what they call "conversations," are sustained emotionally within human co-ontogeny in their book on child development *Amor y juego* (1995). Their ideas are congenial with Ingold's (1986) view that persons exist as embodiments of relationships. From the perspective of the observer, they say that,

> [W]hat we see when we distinguish emotions in us and in other animals are domains of actions, classes of behaviors, and in our living we flow from one domain of action to another in a continual emotioning that is entwined with our languaging. To this entwining of languaging and emotioning we call conversing and we hold that all human life takes place in networks of conversations. (Maturana and Verden-Zöler 1995, 9; my translation)

This representation of the biological function of human language supports the feminist and communitarian view that only in abstraction can individuals be seen as ready made entities that interact through the impulsion of their separate natures. I believe that their critique has very strong grounds in the biological characteristics of the human species, as described by Maturana and Varela. In the following chapters, I also argue that the abstract individual of the liberal tradition is an important product of culture for the way the world is organized in contemporary globality. However, as will become clearer throughout this book, I oppose the view of rational individuality as a "natural" characteristic of all human beings. When I speak of rational individuality, I refer to a much finer product of culture than mere rational instrumentality. The latter can be observed to operate in all cultural settings. Nevertheless, modern individuality is based on a metaphysics that produces categorical force, Kantian practical reason, and the substantive value of the individual self as an end in itself. Nevertheless, on the basis of the discussion of autopoiesis, the abstract liberal idea of "unencumbered" or "asocial" individual human beings breaks down in considering human beings as animals that must develop organically within networks of emotioning and languaging, or within psychological relationships. As Ingold puts it, "[w]e rather *start* with social life, as progressive 'building up' of relationships into the structures of consciousness. This 'building up' . . . is equivalent to the generation of persons" (1989, 222). Individuality may itself be seen as the product of an emotional relationship with a culturally produced idea of self; nevertheless, this *product of culture* cannot be renounced in the midst of global interaction—itself a product of culture (I will discuss this idea at length in chapter 4 of this book).

According to Maturana and Verden-Zöler, the first stage in human development and ontogeny is dominated by spontaneity in play, while the child grows up. In order to highlight the spontaneous side of growing up, Maturana and Verden-Zöler heavily criticize the instrumentality of modern discipline and its detrimental consequences for the self-respect of a growing child, and they argue for letting children live the full spontaneity of play. While I can see the point of their critique of instrumentality and the stress-related problems of modern society's extreme functionalism, a purely organic infancy and childhood could hardly be regarded as human at all. The artificial side of being human does not take place within our embodiment, as Maturana has pointed out, but this embodiment must provide the kind of structural plasticity required for it to interact by means of its artifices. Therefore, while artificiality is not produced by organic processes, the environment where it develops is necessarily organically based human life. Infancy and childhood are elementary aspects of human development that I consider here as only *mostly* spontaneous during infancy because the disciplinary side of social interaction is already present in the background from birth, and is already an aspect of human ontogeny. The caretakers are the prime sources of such disciplinary background, and their role is entwined with the ontogeny of the growing child.

The relevance of discipline to the shaping of practical (spontaneous) consciousness through practice grows as the child grows into adulthood and this relevance is "visualized" and "fueled" by what I've represented as concentric circles of imagination and emotion, respectively. Further, one can differentiate emotion and imagination analytically, and for the purposes of ethical discipline, yet in experience, they are connected to each other in very subtle ways:

> Emotions are not just the fuel that powers the psychological mechanism of a reasoning creature, they are parts, highly complex and messy parts, of this creature's reasoning itself. (Nussbaum 2001, 3)

In this view, discipline is as relevant to the nurturing of the child as spontaneity is relevant during full adult operative disciplined interaction. Awareness expands not only through disciplined practice, but also through the spontaneity of discovery. And so, the process of growing up is never really finished in the practice of any kind of discipline. Our early ontogeny, as part of our history of interactions, shapes spontaneously the initial practical production of ourselves with respect to the world in which we live, but the relevant discipline(s) in the culture where one grows up are also taught during ontogeny, and what is learnt transcends the family circle—the rest of society also contributes through the caretaker—and this is already an aspect of living in society during infancy and childhood.

In her *Maternal Thinking* (1990), Sarah Ruddick approaches the world of the caretaker and her specific mindset as she provides an environment where she raises and nurtures children. Ruddick insists in using vocabulary that refers to this activity as maternal, because she wants to recognize that throughout history and cultures, even now, women take care of children: it has generally been a feminine practice and occupied feminine imagination; gender has not been transcended (and to act as if it has, is dangerous in her view); and the practice she refers to should not be confused with tending to the sick or the elderly (Ruddick 1990, 45–47). Nevertheless, in spite of her insistence on referring to parenting or caretaking as "mothering," I would rather use words that are not gendered, as it is in fact irrelevant to the growing up of the child whether this work is done by men or women. It is sufficient to say that it is an essential aspect in the production of ethical adults. Ruddick refers, however, to three "demands" of mothering, or taking care of children: "preservation," "growth," and "social acceptability." I resort to them in order to highlight the requirements of the specific kind of work that taking care of children implies, which is imposed by the natural and social environment of the child and her caretaker(s):

> Conceptually and historically, the preeminent of these demands is that of preservation. . . . This universal need of human children creates and defines a category of human work. . . .
> When you *see* children as demanding care, the reality of their vulnerability and the necessity of a caring response seem unshakable. . . . Maternal responses are complicated acts that social beings make to biological beings whose existence is inseparable from social interpretation. Maternal practice begins with a double vision—seeing the fact of biological vulnerability as socially significant and as demanding care. (1990, 18)

Ruddick tells us that nurturing the emotional and intellectual growth of children supplements the basic one of preservation. "This demand to foster children's growth appears to be historically and culturally specific to a degree that the demand for preservation is not" (1990, 19). This "fostering" is culture specific and related to the relevant myths or histories in an intricate mix of personal and emotional involvement with the comprehensive conception of reality, the realm of the sacred and/or the transcendental. And this is also supplemented by the third demand imposed on the caretaker, which is made not by the child or her needs, but by the human group that the mother belongs to. The demand of social acceptability makes it important for the caretaker to train the child within the rules (formal, informal, and subtle) of the society where this growing child as a person will live:

> A mother's group is that set of people with whom she identifies to the degree that she would count failure to meet their criteria of acceptability as her failure. The criteria of acceptability consist of the group values that a mother has internalized as well as the values of group members whom she feels she must please. . . . Indeed, mothers themselves as part of the larger social group formulate its ideals and are usually governed by an especially stringent form of acceptability. (1990, 21)

The three demands of taking care of children are essentially connected to the creation of persons and relationships, and of ethical education. This is where the basic elements are taught of how it is appropriate and ethical to behave in a specific social group.

According to Maturana and Verden-Zöler, in order for the child to become socially competent, she must develop the capacity to relate to the world emotionally. The spontaneity of growing up is linked to the simultaneous structural coupling and autopoietic closure of the nervous system with respect to the rest of our embodiment. This brings us back to the mechanisms through which human beings engage in the business of "bringing forth" their world in ontogeny. While the child gets to know the world, she must simultaneously create and expand her own "psychic space" that enables her to relate emotionally to people, to things, and to ideas or ideals. According to Maturana and Verden-Zöler,

> In this process the boy or girl learns the emotioning and the fundamental relational dynamics which will constitute the relational space that he or she will generate in their living, that is, what he or she will do, hear, smell, touch, see, think, fear, want, and reject, as obvious aspects of individual and social living as a member of a family and a culture. (1995, 10)

Maturana and Verden-Zöler argue that the basic emotional referentiality is built as a relational space in the intimate life of the baby's bodily contact with the caretaker. They believe that this intimacy is related to the bodily rhythms that the fetus is used to during the time of pregnancy. To them, intimacy is an innate side of being human that springs in complete trust and acceptance of the natural relationship between the child and its parents or caretakers: people who feed, caress, rock, speak, lull, and put the baby to sleep (1995, 93).

As has been explained, according to Maturana and Varela's theory of life, human embodiment lives in a continuous transformation of its structure, which is determined by past interactions of this present structure, but which is contingent to its coupling with the environment.

As observers, we can speak of its history of transformation that takes place in ontogeny from its embodied point of origin: the undifferentiated stage of unicellularity in the epigenesis of the fetus. Verden-Zöler uses this notion to illustrate how the baby's consciousness is in a similar state of undifferentiated awareness at the moment of being born, and how, in the spontaneity of play, she begins an analogous process of differentiation that will enable her to develop her full conscious human potentiality. And yet, this differentiation is complemented by the balancing side of unification that brings the child back to her own intimate relationships, to whoever takes care of her, who will train this child in the particularities of an ethical life through protective love. This kind of practice must be embodied in concrete relationships and is displaced from being conceived in abstraction:

> In protective love, the natural is, before any moral judgment of it, what is given. The bodies of children are, in this sense, given. . . . In myriad ways, they assert themselves: The physical being is here; whoever deals with me deals with my body. . . .
> To identify the natural with the given does not mean that protecting mothers accept whatever is natural. . . . Yet cannot . . . deny what is natural (e.g. the growing of their children). (Ruddick 1990, 76)

This practice is displaced from abstraction as it happens, it is enacted through a "languaging" of the kind that we share with nonhuman animals in spontaneous physiological and experienced common cognitive grounds, in touch, gestures, and the fulfillment of primary needs, not only physiological, but also—and most importantly to the ulterior conservation of autopoiesis—emotional needs. According to Maturana and Verden-Zöler,

> What in daily life we recognize as emotions when we observe animal behavior (human or non-human) are, as biological phenomena, bodily dynamic configurations that by specifying every instant the possible course of changes of states in an organism, they specify in it a domain of possible actions. (1995, 91)

And so, they propose that human consciousness arises from bodily rhythms and the flow of the sensory-motor configurations of coordinations in the close bodily contact that the child must undergo with whoever raises her not only during her infancy, but also during childhood in spontaneous play with adults and other children:

> Soon children's bodily lives reveal elaborate, imaginative play. Genitals, limbs, toes, and fingers may acquire distinctive personalities and

names. . . . Mothers in turn, respond to these bodies, cleaning, feeding, soothing, exciting, doting. Neither children nor their mothers could distinguish in their bodily lives between rich elaborate mental play and the "merely physical." (Ruddick 1990, 206)

Play and a close emotional relationship with caretakers allows for the development of such sensory-motor configurations. According to Maturana and Verden-Zöler's research, they are simple and basic rhythmic abilities of balancing in order to produce symmetry and movements of equilibrium about a central point. These movements arise in the child "as a process of orientation and spontaneous bodily handling in the freedom of play" (1995, 94).

Maturana and Verden-Zöler consider that before language, in human ontogeny, the child must develop the cognitive configurations of sensory-motor coordinations that will enable her to distinguish practically her own embodiment from other similar embodiments that surround her. The biological role of discursivity in this context would be to help the child locate her own embodied presence within the ongoing "conversation," culture or comprehensive conception that she is born into, and also to sustain her own sense of self, and this is a social activity. Ruddick supports this idea:

> As children try on shifting identities, their ability to create a self is inextricably and often painfully mixed with others' ability to recognize the self they are creating. A "self," however fixed and personal it may seem, is always in the process of being socially constituted. (1990, 92)

And the parent or caretaker is involved in reassuring this construction of self by means of attention, which can be excessive or poor, but there, nonetheless, in the ethics of care that parenting entails. "Attention," Ruddick tells us, "is akin to the capacity for empathy, the ability to suffer or celebrate with another as if in the other's experience you know and find yourself. However, the idea of empathy, as it is popularly understood, underestimates the importance of knowing another *without* finding yourself in her" (1990, 121). Or, in the process of acknowledging another's distinct presence in the social setting where the child grows up. This kind of consciousness is developed practically at first; it provides the matter-of-factual certainties on which practical human life and consciousness depends. It is not unconscious but received and it is enacted in infancy, in the absence of the discipline of self-awareness, which can only be practiced after a sense of self is achieved by the growing child. This is why they say that: "When the baby is born it is only an embryonic possibility of consciousness and of reflection about itself" (Maturana and Verden-Zöler 1995, 102). For this consciousness of self to unfold, the infant must first detach her first notion of self from the embodiment of the adult (or adults) who she uses as her initial points of reference in life. This is an embodied as well as a psychological detachment, when the child has "constructed" her surrounding world as coherent and operative sensory-motor correlations:

> The child at this point in the process of growing up has already lived the sensory-motor experiences that are a pre-requisite of the constitution of human consciousness: Free movement in a social domain as a realm of spatio-temporal relations in the acceptance of herself and of others. (Maturana and Verden-Zöler 1995, 103)

The result of this detachment is an imaginary world that the child uses as her first approach to reality. But this is not a "picture-like" imaginary world, it is a non-static approach made of structural dynamic correlations that allow the child to interact at the simplest level of social coordination, in constant structural transformation and expansion. This transformation and expansion is never finished in the individual ontogeny of the growing child, not even in adulthood. It is an aspect of her human autopoiesis and it is contingent to her constant interactions and her coupling with her environment. At a particular point in ontogeny, this imaginary world achieves a degree of stability that gives grounds for the child to orient herself and "live" in it as an organic individual. This stable imaginary world is part of the child's "inner mind" or an initial sense of reality in ontogeny, which according to Maturana and Verden-Zöler, is one where the social space is essential and far more important than the physical space. In that inner mind, the child manages her domain of relationships with entities that appear to be permanent and separable from the child, who the child imagines in emotional and experiential correlations. "In other words," say Maturana and Verden-Zöler, "the child has become able to see in its mind the *Gestalt* (configuration) of human life as its own life in the cyclical movement of advancement and regress that space and time constitute" (1995, 103). But just as the age of the child when this happens is particular to the person's ontogeny, this configuration or Gestalt is also particular to the "conversation" or comprehensive conception of reality where the child is born and grows up, always within the structural possibilities of human embodiment.

And it is here that the biological relevance of language acquires a new level of complexity in the correlations that start detaching themselves from the individual ontogeny of particular human autopoiesis. As we grow up, we realize that the conversations we hold can be brought outside the domain of family life to wider realms of interaction. In those realms, the group might be related by kin, but it can also be related by the (relevant) stories of interactions and history that produce collective identity and ideas of reality. These may be expanded through empire to become vast imaginary realms of correlations that human life sustains and creates and that end up creating and sustaining human life back. Language is an important aspect of not only them, but also religion and belief system. At the point in human ontogeny when one becomes an adult, the wider realms of interaction become relevant for the growing person who determines and is determined by them. This is because this person, in every case, had to be a child and grow up in a particular culture and discipline. Living in society implies some form of learnt discipline that is not organically produced and yet is based on the organic integrity of people. In order to preserve this integrity, there are basic ethics of care that are never detached from the cultural milieu of the caretaker, and this is a constant practice all over the world as long as there are children to be taken care of. This practice has to do with the personal commitment to create a space of peace and safety, however this is conceived, where children can grow up into adults. According to Ruddick,

> In maternal thinking, feelings are at best complex but sturdy instruments of work quite unlike the simple and separate hates, fears that are usually put aside in philosophical analysis. . . . In protective love, . . . feelings demand reflection, which is in turn tested by action, which is in turn tested by the feelings it provokes, [but] protective love can never be reduced to the sum of its feelings. . . . Mothering is an activity governed by a *commitment* that perseveres through feeling and structures the activity. (1990, 70)

The ethical orientation of care though, can be seen to go beyond this intimate domestic realm, as it accompanies human beings throughout their ethical lives. I agree with Carol Gilligan, who has argued convincingly in my opinion, that an ethics of care is a legitimate orientation in the moral life of persons (1982). Her work critically questions Lawrence Kohlberg's (1981, 1984) claims of universality for his model of human moral development, as it fails to account for women's ethical experience. Kohlberg's highest point of moral development basically enshrines the abstract ability to universalize principles that rule human action. However, it is counterintuitive to conceive of such capacity for abstraction as the sole basis for moral principles. When Ruddick refers to the type of thought that those who take care of children display, one can get a hint of the complexity that an ethics of care entails. When discussing about Kohlberg's moral dilemmas in his research, Ruddick refers to abstraction as a partial source of knowledge in the forms of reasoning that parenting entails:

> To abstract is to simplify complexity, in particular to reduce the manifold issues of moral life into dichotomous choices . . . Concreteness requires inventing alternatives even when there seems to be none, . . .
> To use familiar terms, women's thinking has been called "holistic" . . . they tend to reject the demands of abstraction and instead look closely, invent options, refuse closure . . . This way of knowing requires a patient, sympathetic listening to the complexities and uncertainties of another's experience quite unlike the acceptance of the given terms required for abstraction. (1990, 95–96)

Much of the resistance to the paradigm that ultimately goes back to Kant's *Critique of Practical Reason* ([1781] 1929), has to do with the sociological cum philosophical argument that persons have an embodied and embedded existence in society and that individuality does not necessarily have preeminence in comprehensive conceptions of reality different from the liberal one. These are the critiques in which communitarianism and feminism converge, who agree with seeing a distinct moral orientation in Gilligan's ethics of care. According to Seyla Benhabib, Gilligan's work created so much recognition and controversy because it was posing Kohlberg the same kind of questions that a growing number of influential critics were making to traditional neo-Kantian moral philosophy:

> Just as Gilligan reported her female subjects' sense of bewilderment in view of a language of morals which would pose even the most personal of all dilemmas like abortion in terms of formal rights, so too Michael Sandel maintained that a polity based on the procedural and juridical model of human relationships alone would lack a certain solidarity and depth of identity. And just as Gilligan doubted that the Kohlbergian model of the development of moral judgment could claim the universality it did in view of the difficulties this model encountered in accounting for women's judgment and sense of self, others like Taylor and Walzer questioned whether the form of moral judgments of justice could be so neatly isolated from the content of cultural conceptions of the good life. (Benhabib 1992, 180)

John Rawls, the most recent representative of the contractual Kantian school of political thought, responded to these criticisms aimed at his "original position" in his *A Theory of Justice* (1971) with a political deontology in *Political Liberalism* (1996) that cannot be sustained by the metaphysics from which it arises, as his debate with Jürgen Habermas illustrates. I will engage with this debate in the last section of chapter 4, but here I only want to advance that Rawls's reply to his communitarian critics and the way he accommodates to their objections, illustrate that liberalism itself cannot escape being seen as a comprehensive conception of the good, once we produce adequate qualifications.

In this work, I consider Kantian practical rationality as a learnt ability, a product of culture in Weberian terms. I regard it as a comprehensive conception of the good, based on individual liberty, but I sustain that the moral individual is one of the finest cultural products of Modernity. Individual self-consciousness is then a disciplined practice, not an abstract "natural" trait of human beings. Modern interaction is based on the constant and systematic practice of this discipline. In the following chapter, I discuss how Modernity produced the individual idea of self as the basis of humanity and how this is related to the development of a distinct sense of morality, one that can universalize principles. I do not believe that the development of the ability to universalize abstract principles that guide our actions is the only kind of morality that human beings are able to display, but it is an important one in global, modern, impersonal interaction.[21] Moral judgment as impartiality has universal consequences, and yet, so does any other transcendentalist comprehensive conception of the good; the difference is that moral judgment is based on the individual as a value in itself, and the comprehensive conceptions on what the particular human group considers as sacred. Having considered this important difference, both moral judgment and comprehensive conceptions entail particular and distinct representations of either sacred or transcendental metaphysics. The realm of domestic life gives children their initial emotional abilities to engage in such pressing manner to their comprehensive conception(s) of good and self. Both moral reason and comprehensive conceptions are taught to children through conventional ethics, local and particular, which are always a bridge between experience and ideal ethical authority in society.

An ethics of care then is an essential ethical orientation in the life of human beings; we encounter it in the first environment in which we learn to become distinct persons within a complex of human relationships. Nevertheless, I have placed this element of our development as people in the primitive view of reality because it is conceptually displaced from being universalizable. As Benhabib contends,

> Gilligan has not explained what an "ethic of care" as opposed to an ethical orientation to "care reasoning" would consist of, nor has she provided the philosophical argumentation necessary to formulate a different conception of the moral point of view or of impartiality than the Kohlbergian one. (1992, 180)

In fact, Gilligan does not provide the principles that will clarify just how an ethics of care can have the same moral standing as the moral orientation to impartiality and justice. We are at a loss of directions as to what could replace the role of Kantian practical rationality in a moral orientation of care. This ethics of care must lose its local status and be formulated beyond the confines of domestic and primitive human life in order to get the categorical force of moral judgment. How could this moral orientation obtain universal status? This will be dealt with in the following chapters, where I intend to construct the two ideal–typical views of reality that are intimately related to transcendence. For now suffice it to say that the temporal order of events in synchronicity opens up the possibility for a postconventional moral orientation to care. But before tackling the central argument of this book, I now turn to the view of reality where human beings are historical beings as well as transcendental subjects.

4

THE HISTORICAL IDEAL TYPE
OF REALITY

The historical ideal type of reality conceives of the *beyond* as transcendence, in constant *tension* with the world within which a universal humanity progressively moves in time. This tension between world and transcendence organizes the structure of the temporal order of events as an indefinite progression. I argue that the shape of this time structure is determined by the discovery (or invention) of transcendence within the Judaic and Greek cosmology, the ulterior Christian conception of unified human kind under one God, and its related consequences for the conception of a universal human history. Historical cosmology, according to Eric Voegelin (1974), emerges through an imperial thrust that encompasses several cultures and is forced to discover or create its own sacred roots to existence. Here, I want to argue that historical reality is also conditioned by myth and it shares this characteristic with primitive and mystic types of reality. From a diachronic perspective, historical reality and mythical reality do not converge as their preeminent verbal structures cannot establish a dialogue: They are incommensurable with respect to each other in their sequential coherence, as is illustrated by the contrast between historical objective reality and fiction. Nevertheless, from a synchronic perspective (the *present moment of meaningful experience*), history and fiction can be observed to overlap and complement each other in the course of interaction at a local level as well as a global one, even as from a diachronic perspective we must differentiate between them. Here, I want to emphasize that in secular history, myth remains the shape of sequential facticity, while transcendence is transformed into the eternal *not yet* of the project of Modernity. This idea of time as a progression of events is related to the myth of the one God that would bring His chosen people to historical success, and so, myth is an essential component of the transcendental Judeo-Christian cosmos of reality.

As I have said, what differentiates the historical and the primitive types of reality is not myth—historical reality is also told and enacted by means of myth, plot, or narrative. The difference is that there is no explicit symbol or structural role for *transcendence* in the primitive type of time and reality.

As has already been discussed in this work, transcendence is regarded as a spiritual discovery (or invention) that takes place when a human being merges in consciousness with her divine root to existence; an experience that Voegelin calls *hierophany*[1]. It is only from the perspective of transcendence that the notion of universality can be conceived at all, basically because only from this imagined position can one extricate oneself completely from the mundane particularity that influences our very own embodied and contextualized experience. I argue that the concept of universality is genetically related to the symbol of transcendence. Any claim of universal validity is linked to the ability to represent a transcendental realm that gives categorical relevance to human rules. This is the basis to say with Charles Taylor, that liberalism is itself a comprehensive conception of the good life. I would add that a refusal to see this veils a form of liberal fundamentalism—a danger that all religions and views of reality with origins in the house of Abraham should learn to avoid. The liberal secular self-identity—and an analytically useful differentiation between private and public realms of interaction—displaces them from being aware that this doctrine rests on fundamental certainties (i.e., the *fact* of individuality), and this kind of truth could not but be providential in origin.

Liberalism is linked to the scientific view of reality as objectivity, conceives of the self as a historical and accountable entity, and contemplates this self as *essentially* based on individual freedom. As Alisdair MacIntyre puts it,

> The problems of modern moral theory emerge clearly as the product of the failure of the Enlightenment project. On the one hand, the individual moral agent, freed from hierarchy and teleology, conceives of himself and is conceived of by moral philosophers as sovereign in his moral authority. On the other hand, the inherited, if partially transformed rules of morality have to be found some new status, deprived as they have been of their older teleological character and their even more ancient categorical character as expressions of an ultimately *divine law*. (1984, 62; emphasis added)

As will become clear in the discussion below, I do not follow MacIntyre in what he conceives as the "failure" of the Enlightenment project. I disagree in that he considers modern moral judgments as merely emotivist and invalid; he argues that they are "linguistic survivals from the practices of classical theism which have lost the context provided by these practices" (MacIntyre 1984, 60). They may be linguistic survivals and their shape may very much be determined by their sacred origins that have been forgotten, yet they could not have possibly survived if they were not based in present practice. One may argue—as I will—that modern individual morality is imaginary and ideal, but this does not mean that it lacks a basis in the embodied life of modern people for not having objective and spelt out rules of practice.

It is important to realize that the practice of individuality as a modern identity has an astounding organizational power, with no precedent in the known history of humankind, as Max Weber pointed out in his *Protestant Ethic* ([1905] 1958). It is based on the individual responsible agent and legal–rational domination. The organizational power of individuality, specialization, and legal–rational legitimacy was viewed by Weber with a mixture of awe and fear before the totalizing force of a fully administrated society. This fear, I believe, is related to a Faustic aspect of our moral modern identity.[2] Nevertheless, this individually based power of organization sustains the global arena of interaction and is not without its noble and awe-inspiring moral roots. A legal–rational type of order may disclose a systematic nature that threatens to swallow the *life-world* of human interaction; Weber saw this and Jürgen Habermas followed him from a critical Frankfurt School perspective. Nevertheless, a type of legal–rational legitimacy requires the constant practice of moral reasoning, even if the debate involves incommensurable claims, which is MacIntyre's point of departure to diagnose modern morality as decadent. It is precisely because ongoing moral public debate involves incommensurable claims that there ought to be an ideal point of convergence between views of reality, as Rawls's *Political Liberalism* (1996) illustrates.

Modern interaction requires that actual people practice the discipline of individuality; that they consider themselves accountable individuals with rights and equality before the law—not only in principle, but also in actual and lived experience and practice. The imperative that people practice individuality is so close to our conscious selves that it is hard to see. MacIntyre wants to establish objective principles for such practice, yet fails to consider that this is already a global practice and is reinvented on a daily basis around the world. His position is liable to be criticized much in the same way as Habermas criticized Rawls's political liberalism: They prescribe the rules of validity for *justice* or *morality* for individuals instead of allowing for freedom of choice in the formation of modern preferences. In this chapter, I argue that the validity of the concept of moral reasoning resides in contemporary practice of individuality and the present allegiance that it awakens as a comprehensive conception of the good life and as an ongoing practice. In her *Narrating the Organization* (1997), Barbara Czarniawska uses drama as a useful metaphor to represent and understand modern complex interaction and also, to understand "how preferences are created, and such understanding can replace indignation, that most common of modern emotions" (Czarniawska 1997, 34; see MacIntyre 1981). The lived practice and experience of considering oneself an individual may not be the natural essence of human beings, but it is desirable that in modern and global interaction, people behave like competent individuals.

In this chapter, I argue that, although, in Modernity, human beings and institutions must contribute to the production of such individual dignity and importance by constant practice, liberalism requires that the individual human being be the principle of universality. That is, in Modernity, the individual human being is "sacred," but in a human-made moral fashion and not in a providential one. Yet, this secular "sacredness" is inherited from the particular way in which Christianity and the European culture evolved toward Modernity. This "evolution" includes the emergence of individuality as a principle of order and I argue with Paul Ricoeur (1967a) that this is related to the notion of human fault. One can say that not all cultures around the world give such importance to individuality. However, as the modern kind of order is now global, moral theory cannot but be based on the embodied (and so, particular) individual human self. And so, in spite of being aware of the particularity that embodied and contextualized human beings convey, and of stressing that reflexivity about this condition should be constant in moral philosophy—as illustrated by my primitive type—I also argue that it is essential to engage in a philosophical debate about universality and universal humanity.

To be sure, any representation of universal humanity has its origins in a particular cultural context, and the liberal tradition is no exception. As has been mentioned above, the emergence of representations of universal humanity take place in devotional and sacred contexts, and this is also true of liberalism at root. Yet, liberal universality managed to extricate itself from particular representations of sacred belief—even as it preserves their structure. I argue that, in principle, only the liberal tradition's type of universality can claim to have broken through the particular bounds of mundane representations of sacred-ness.[3] The ideal of individuality is a secular and universalistic principle that effectively organizes interaction between various conceptions of the good life within as well as beyond political associations (states). The ideal of individuality places value on diversity, pluralism, and toleration as major sources of the human drive to sustain social modern global interaction. In contrast to this, particular human groups and their comprehensive conceptions have symbological boundaries that are not necessarily closed and keep reinventing themselves culturally (imaginatively and emotionally), but this kind of particularity is displaced from being able to organize the multicultural world. That is, no conception of the good life other that liberalism could manage to function effectively as a common substantive basis for interaction without canceling diversity and plurality. Liberalism as a common substantive basis requires to be complemented, as I will discuss in chapter 5, but it cannot be dispensed with in contemporary globalized interaction.

In the first section of this chapter, I review the mythical basis of the historical ideal type of view of reality. This is a discussion of how the Christian inheritance of a sacred history structures the secular historical view of reality. I resort to Eric Voegelin on this, whose work is congenial with the communitarian position according to which an idea of self emerges from the relevant nexus of language, context, and the way the past determines human references that shape this conception of self. In the second section, I will be ready to develop further the conceptual elements of the historical ideal type of reality. In this section, I explain how it is that both the historical and the mystic views converge in conceiving a transhistorical realm to which the self relates emotionally and imaginatively. I explain how, in the historical ideal type, this relationship legitimizes the diachronic conception of time and produces a judgmental type of ethical approach to human experience. I contrast this with the relationship that mystic traditions of knowledge establish with their specific type of transhistorical reality that considers only the eternal present moment as legitimate time, where awareness of the union of all things arises. In the third section, I engage in an interpretation of Paul Ricoeur's *Symbolism of Evil* (1967a), a phenomenology of fault in the Judeo-Christian tradition, and adapt it to my theory by means of a conversation with Keiji Nishitani's idea of fault in Zen Buddhism, and other Eastern traditions of knowledge. With respect to the historical view of reality, this will establish the relationship between sacred reality and the cultural production of the individual self.

The fourth section of this chapter is a discussion of liberals (Rawls, Habermas) and communitarians (Taylor, MacIntyre), and also of constructivist organizational theory as a counterpoint (Czarniawska, Meyer). It engages with how the individual self is both the basis for the abstract liberal tradition *and*, at the same time, a product of culture that is always particular to the context that raises the individuals. From the perspective of my own theoretical definition of the historical ideal type of reality, I argue that the liberal–communitarian debate projects into the inner self the outside tension between *world* and *transcendence*. This tension is the one between the particular-embodied and contextualized self *and* the transcendental subject, an end in itself. I contemplate the individual as an institution, a very useful disciplined practice that is the product of a specific culture. In spite of this, I argue that it is a mistake to regard it as a mere Western imposition, it is de facto now a global practice—even in the postcolonial narrative of self—it is a diverse lived experience in a wide variety of human groups all over the world. In contemplating the individual as a valuable practice, and not a universal characteristic of human kind, it is possible to enact individuality in a constant interpretation of the notion itself as a cultural product. Liberal–democratic, well ordered, and just societies presuppose that individuals practice their individuality that is seen as a "universal" category. Following Kant, I propose that the metaphysics of such universality might well be all imagined and illusory[4]—we cannot *know* them—but even if we assume universal individuality as imaginary, I argue that it is necessary for us to "think" them for moral orientation. A universal principle or *ideal* is necessary as a guide to establish points of reference that are common—or that we imagine to be common—to all humanity.

HISTORICAL REALITY

Both the historical and mystic views of reality articulate and represent transcendence, while the primitive one is articulated only with respect to the world; transcendence remains unexpressed explicitly. The symbolization of transcendence conveys an organizational transformation, where human order is to be aligned with the reality of the imagined transcendental realm. In the creation of the historical type of reality, this transformation took place alongside the need to justify imperial rule that, according to Eric Voegelin (1974), was transformed from cosmological kingdoms into the Christian *ecumene*. In Christianity, the immediacy of Apocalypse was solved institutionally by the church while its symbolization of humanity as one "body" in faith produced the awareness and possible inclusion of other peoples through conversion. Both the historical and mystic views of reality contemplate a transhistorical perspective from which an awareness of the uniqueness of every instant arises. But the primitive view of reality lacks such explicit realm, which is nevertheless *lived* as an intuition in its ritual mimetic oneness with the cosmos. Historical reality is thus here portrayed as a consequence of the symbolization of an experience of transcendence, which secular reality transforms into relevant symbols of individual consciousness and value.

The modern mind regards the primitive kind of tales as unreal myths, and this is because lived experience of modern life does not confirm them as real:

> For us moderns, a myth is only a myth because we can no longer connect that time with the time of history as we write it, employing the critical method, nor can we connect mythical places with our geographical space. This is why the myth can no longer be an explanation; to exclude its etiological intention is the theme of all necessary demythologization. But in losing its explanatory pretensions the myth reveals exploratory significance and its contribution to understanding, which we shall later call its symbolic function—that is to say, its power of discovering and revealing the bond of man and what he considers sacred. Paradoxical as it may seem, the myth when it is thus demythologized through contact with scientific history and elevated to the dignity of a symbol, is a dimension of modern thought. (Ricoeur 1967a, 5)

In other words, there is a dimension of modern thought that is also mythical, on which modern life is sustained. But the sequence of its story does not converge diachronically with any other particular myth—and yet, it is an assumption of this work that various particular myths can only converge synchronically (in the present moment of awareness). Myths encompass whole universes that can only converge at present (in synchrony) because each tale follows the structural form allowed by the sequence of the tale (in diachrony) or by the particular cosmos that it shapes. Modern life, though, is sustained by taking an artificial distance from nature that can never be complete due to embodiment. As a matter of fact, most of the modern ethos is built on giving value to this distance that is also embedded in the secular scientific view of reality and its accompanying rational myths, for example, that of objectivity. We have said before that any view of reality has its own cosmological myths and, therefore, a mythical basis is not really the principle of differentiation between what I have called primitive reality and historical reality, or between the former and what I call mystic reality.

Therefore, what ideally differentiates the primitive view of reality from the historical and mystic ones is that the former lacks a clear representation of transcendence. The cultures that managed to represent transcendence also produced a new axis on which social life would be organized. The explicit symbolization of transcendence brought about organizational consequences in society. When the idea of transcendence was discovered (or created), a religious frame of order was set up, which would bring humanity closer to consciousness about this transcendental reality. In axial age civilizations, "there was a concomitant stress on the existence of a higher transcendental moral or metaphysical order which is beyond any given this- or other-worldly reality" (Eisenstadt 1982, 296). The new awareness about universality and transcendence posed the problem of bridging the gap between the two levels of existence in human life, and therefore, also in the legitimate idea of social order. In post-axial age societies, the emergence of new elites took place: The carriers of the new models of social order that institutionalized the perception of the basic tension between the transcendental and the mundane levels of existence. "Examples would include," says Eisenstadt, "the Jewish prophets and priests, the Greek philosophers and sophists, the Chinese Literati, the Hindu Brahmins, the Buddhist Sangha . . . It was the initial small nuclei of such groups of intellectuals that developed these new transcendental conceptions" (1982, 298).

Cosmological kingdoms became empires in their drive to conquer. Their cosmology and emperor lay at their center and organized them in a hierarchical imperial form, like the Chinese, Egyptian, Babylonian, and Assyrian empires. "A cosmological empire," says Voegelin, "is more than one type of political organization among others. In its self-interpretation, imperial rule is the mediation of divine-cosmic order to the existence of man in society and history" (1974, 93). This awareness of imperial order brought about the need to stabilize and legitimate its creation in "historiogenesis," or historical speculation based on current pragmatic knowledge as well as in myths, symbols, beliefs, and values that contemplate an "extrapolation of pragmatic history toward its cosmic-divine point of origin" (Voegelin 1974, 101). However, Voegelin also speaks about the role of imperial catastrophe, which produced the need to create order out of political chaos. According to him, the newer empires like the Persian, Macedonian, and Roman "originated, not in a ferocious will to conquer, but in the fatality of a power vacuum that attracted, and even sucked into itself, unused organizational force from the outside; it originated in circumstances beyond control rather than deliberate planning" (1974, 117–18). The resulting society under empire held a mixture of values and beliefs that "historiogenetic" speculation had to take into account in order to base "ecumenic" history on a cosmic-divine origin.[5] This brought about what Voegelin calls "historiomachy" (see 1974, 109–13), the phenomenon of cultural competition for the historical tale that was most relevant for the human extended group now forming the ecumene:

> When the older cosmological empires were conquered by the ascending ecumenic empires, a new constellation of problems formed, for the older symbolisms, though they continued to be cultivated, were now forced into competition with one another for ecumenically representative rank. (Voegelin 1974, 109)

These movements in social organization transform the general understanding of human nature: The qualitative jumps from tribal society, to city-state, to empire produced a differentiated consciousness of the human self and the symbols of the sacred origin of a kind of order that is shared by all human beings. "Through the hard reality of empire, there begins to shine forth, as the subject of history, a universal mankind under God" (Voegelin 1974, 95). The Greek philosophers had developed a new style of universal truth, on the one hand, through their differentiation of noetic symbols that made intellectual speculation and knowledge possible beyond the compact symbols of mythical tradition, and on the other, through a unique Hellenic interest in making the whole of humankind the subject of history. Israel's own history is based on the exodus of Yahweh's chosen people from a historical setting that enslaved them, into freedom reified in a sacred covenant with God. This produced the possibility of seeing cosmic-divine order as a direct relationship between God and the believer, not mediated by a cosmological emperor, but by universal law. Christianity, in its institutional drive to world conversion, appropriated both the Jewish and the Greek sources into its dogma and gave shape to an extended concept of ecumene that encompassed all peoples and all epochs in progress to an eternal Heaven through history and Apocalypse:

> Setting aside the fact that Christian faith is by far not the only root of Western philosophy of history—Israel and Hellas also have something to do with it—there still remains the hard fact that philosophy of history has indeed arisen in the West and nowhere *but* in the West. There is no such thing as a non-western philosophy of history. For a philosophy of history can arise only where mankind has become historical through existence in the present under God. Leaps in being, to be sure, have occurred elsewhere; but a Chinese personal existence under the cosmic *tao*, or an Indian personal existence in acosmistic illumination, is not an Israelite or Christian existence under God. While the Chinese

and Indian societies have certainly gained the consciousness of universal humanity, only the Judeo-Christian response to revelation has achieved historical consciousness. (Voegelin 1954, 23)

What Voegelin calls a "leap in being" is what I have referred to as the discovery and symbolization of transcendental reality. While in mysticism this discovery is the sole basis of reality, and thus, mysticism regards the world as an illusory effect of consciousness, a dream from which one awakens in spiritual Enlightenment, the philosophy of history took both the world and transcendence to be real, and arranged them in a progressive order with a beginning and an end for the whole of humanity in Genesis and Apocalypse. Beyond Christianity though, the secular view of history has generally been the recipient of a mixture of symbolisms that have mixed synchretically and have expanded the conception of time within frontiers of a beginning and a beyond incommensurably by an embodied mind. The embodied secular mind that thinks objectively, the one that lives the relevance of the subject–object divide, conceives of its vastness abstractly and imagines it through infinite space. But this is the kind of infinite finiteness that Nishitani calls "bad infinity"; an artifice achieved by separating space and time in abstraction to produce awareness about the factual level of reality in a mechanistic cosmos that does not end and that displaces awareness of transcendental infinity to oblivion.

The effect of the discovery of transcendence within the historical type of reality—and its relationship with the world—produced a symbolism of time that made possible a projection of human existential concerns into the future. "The typological structure and shape of the Bible," says Frye, "make its mythology diachronic in contrast to the synchronic mythology characteristic of most of the religions outside it" (1982, 83). Following Frye, the idea of causality was transformed from having effects horizontally, on the same temporal level of duration with respect to the past and renovation in the synchronic moment of the cyclical ritual; to a movement that was both horizontal and vertical in a diachronic "leap" that brought about the perspective of progress in the development of collective embodied humanity as a universal humanity. But this *mechanism* could only come about in a cosmology that considered both the world and transcendence to be real in the present before God, while assuming that there was an imminent end of the world. This imminence in primitive Christianity produced an everyday life expectation of death as an event that would be organized within a wider frame of the personal place in the sacred history of human progress toward spiritual perfection.

The idea of imminent collective death through the horrors of Apocalypse was eventually "solved" or postponed by the Augustinian institutionalization of the sacraments and their absorption and administration by the church as the "body" of Christ. Modernity transformed this Christian belief into progress toward ideal rational understanding and peaceful interaction between all human beings, and it framed this progress in universal human history with civilized rational interaction at the apex of the historical tale that it was creating. But the modern version of progress is in line with the Augustinian tale of collective spiritual progress:

> In Augustine, intellectual child of the Greeks as well as of the Jews, to this day preeminent theologian in Christian history, there are all the essential ingredients of the modern idea of progress: The vision of an unfolding cumulative advancement of the human race in time—a unified, single human race, be it emphasized—a single time frame for all the peoples and epochs of the past and present, the conception of time as linear, single flow, the use of evolving stages and epochs in the history of humanity, belief in the necessary, as well as sacred character of mankind's history as set forth in the Old Testament, and, finally the envisagement of a future, distinctly utopian end of history when the saved would go to eternal heaven. (Nisbet 1994, xiii)

However, the secularized version of this tale got rid of the spiritual element and found its own sense of reality in factual historicity. History situates its past and future in a purely mundane setting, ignoring that the qualitative jump into a conception of universal human history was brought about by contrast to the discovery (or invention) of transcendence. In Modernity, the Christian idea of the progress of humanity, as one body toward spiritual perfection in history with Apocalypse at its end, was transformed into an experienced unfolding of time as natural evolution and indefinite linear factual history, as well as *deformed* into material capitalist and political progress of the nations with respect to the enlightened ideals of Modernity.

> The Gnosis of progress toward the reason of the eighteenth-century bourgeoisie, which Voltaire tried to substitute for the Augustinian *historia sacra*, could be applied to the interpretation of phenomena only under the condition that nobody would raise the fundamental question where and how the symbolism of an historical mankind had originated. (Voegelin 1954, 16)

Modern universal human history kept the basic Christian cosmological divide between world and transcendence that fetters the latter in superior imminence and relegates the world to an inferior kind of reality, as chaos that must be controlled. And so, in historical reality, both world and transcendence are real, and this arranges all human time—universal history—as a constant enfolding, diachronic "movement" that nevertheless requires a universal *point d'appui*. I now turn to this *linchpin* that is essentially related to the achievement of symbolizing transcendence as a conception that lies beyond time as it is experienced in the world. This idea can be best symbolized by metonymic language, which is a verbal structure that is put for what is meant: transcendence can only be expressed indirectly by worldly references.

THE TRANSHISTORICAL REALM OF HISTORICITY

As has been discussed, the Christian tale of universal history is the root of the modern prehension of history, but its secular essence requires that a new modern tale of human-made linear progress be produced: the possibility to dominate the material world technically, scientifically, and morally. In its rejection of Christian dogma, the modern enlightened rational discipline downplays the fact that its intellectual notion of infinity is rooted in the Christian notion of an omnipotent and transhistorical God. "Although the views of history found in Christianity and in the Enlightenment represent diametrically opposed points of view," says Nishitani, "they both concur in recognizing a meaning in history" (1982, 211). A universal historical consciousness cannot escape the element of infinity opened up at the very root of being in the world. As has been mentioned, this is illustrated by how the predicament of nihilism haunts the modern contemporary mind.

Nishitani calls the infinity of historical consciousness the "transhistorical view" needed for a history that can be truly universal, and he says that it is unavoidably linked to a "religious prehension of history" (1982, 213). In this prehension, the transcendental realm of existence (eternity, infinity) comes about as a certainty and may be said to be analogous with hierophany, or interaction with the divine root of existence. Religious faith can be conceived as a kind of certainty, and it comes about in the life of human as what Nishitani calls the Great Reality:

> To be sure, this reality is not something merely objective and separate from ourselves; if it were, we should still be on the field of consciousness.[6]

When we ourselves are thrown into the reality of evil or faith in such a way as to become ourselves the realization of their realness, a conversion takes place within reality itself with us at the hinge: we have a *real* change of heart. (Nishitani 1982, 30)

The transhistorical view is analogous to the synchronic sacred moment of renovation of the natural cycle celebrated in archaic ritual, but here it is of a higher order that moves symbologically (and not only intuitively and experientially) in the direction of transcendence; it is the awareness and explicit representation of the new and the irreversible that contemplates infinity and therefore the uniqueness of the present moment:

The idea of a stratified formation of simultaneous time systems necessitates the idea of an infinite openness at the bottom of time, like a great expanse of vast, sky like emptiness that cannot be confined to any systematic enclosure. Having such an openness at its bottom, each and every now, even as it belongs to each of the various layers accumulated through the total system, is itself something new and admits of no repetition in any sense. The sequence of "nows" is really irreversible. Accordingly, in the true sense, each now passes away and comes into being at each fleeting instant. (Nishitani 1982, 219)

Nishitani observes that this transhistorical realm lies at the center of the mystic Zen notion of time and, while it produces an immediate kind of historical consciousness—the present view that history has no beginning and no end—it does not unfold into the mature science of factual and descriptive history. Nishitani's discussion shows that the transhistorical is itself radicalized in Zen mystic practice as Absolute emptiness as the root to reality that discloses the factual realm as ultimately illusory. In Christianity, it is radicalized as the human transcendental identity in a personal relationship with God conceived as a willful *being* in a transhistorical dimension. In Modernity, this is transformed into a secular relationship between the universal human self and human personality, her freedom, and her will. When scientific objectivity becomes the prominent way of conceiving reality in Modernity, history finds its legitimacy in describing stories based on facts, expressed preeminently in demotic verbal structures.

Nevertheless, before Modernity, it is important to pay attention to the culturally ascendant verbal structures that refer to time and transcendence: While the mystic realm of transhistorical time defines a domain of synchrony that legitimizes the notion of a collective non-anthropocentric mind, the historical realm defines a domain of diachrony that legitimizes the notion of universal humanity as a collectivity advancing in progress and constant betterment. In Modernity, this was transformed into the uniqueness of the individual mind that is seen as a feature of infinity, an end in itself. In both cases, and in awareness of a religious prehension of history, the dominant verbal structures are metonymic as either synchronic or diachronic legitimate symbols of time that are put for a transcendence that is both immanent and imminent. In the historical view of reality though, after the Modern mind and the humanities were well established in Europe, and time had become an indefinite progression, its expression of reality changed to become descriptive, demotic verbal structures, in line with the legitimate type of objective reality.

Nishitani argues that in the Western philosophical tradition, the legitimate realm of transhistorical reality is placed at the "far side" of ordinary consciousness:

> [W]hen Plato conceives of a world of Ideas as the far side of this sensible world, the beyond he has in mind is only such to the extent that it is something like a celestial world. It is a far side viewed perpendicularly from the earth upward. . . . Similarly a personal God who is thought to reveal himself vertically from heaven down to earth, as commonly represented in Christianity, is considered to be seated beyond, on the far side. Since in this case we speak of a revelation from beyond, the far side is more to the far side than it was with Plato. (Nishitani 1982, 104)

The distance placed between God and human is meaningfully represented in diachrony and, as we will see, also in the notion of sin as an anthropological root to individual human existence. But this absolute breach between God and human can be represented as a metonymic "unrelatedness" in a rational philosophical plane of dialectical thought: "[A]n unrelatedness can be represented as a sort of relationship of 'unrelatedness,' that is, as a 'dialectical' relationship" (Nishitani 1982, 105). In secular facticity, this unrelatedness is translated into a cognizing subject and its object of analysis, but here, the prevalent verbal structures are descriptive. In the historical view of reality, the object/subject relationship enfolds both the occularcentric tradition of science and the moral mission of knowing the self who does the cognizing, always keeping the diachronic division that allows for cause and effect to be clearly seen and for sequential explanation to be performed by the discipline. It could be said that secular history attempts to shift the "far side" of the transhistorical realm to the "near side" of the cognizing subject—and as Nishitani argues, this was best achieved by the nihilists in Modernity—but we will see that it fails to accomplish the absolute near side because it is still couched in, and determined by, the duality of a divided reality. In contrast to this, in the mystic view, the legitimate realm of transhistorical reality is placed at an absolute "near side," one of Absolute emptiness from which being emerges, where "both the abyss of nihility and the personal relationship of God and man can come about . . . and be represented" (Nishitani 1982, 105).

To be sure, the absolute near side of mystic traditions is also metonymic and is put for immanent transcendence, but one that enfolds salvation and nihility, heaven and hell, and that is displaced from judgmental reason and distinction between absolute good and absolute evil. What Nishitani calls religious love (*agape*) or compassion (*karuna*) illustrates this notion of the near side where love is absolute and impersonal as in the Buddhist "Great Compassionate Heart [*maha-karuna*], the essential equivalent of the biblical analogy that tells us there is no such thing as a selfish or selective sunshine" (Nishitani 1982, 60). Similarly with Jesus' injunction to love one's enemies as one's friends, and the Buddhist virtue of "non-differentiating love beyond enmity and friendship" (Nishitani 1982, 58), this is the prevalent absolute near side of transhistorical reality in the mystic view of reality. Discursively, its compact metonymic symbolism of experience allows for factual ambiguity, and fails to organize a descriptive sense for universal history; but in disciplined practice, a factual historical awareness is organizationally necessary in an immediate sense with respect to one's own present life and situation, one's own particular emotional attachments and lived predicaments. This is a near side that becomes personally pressing and, according to Nishitani, must break through the field of nihility that lies beyond the horizon of the field of consciousness; or that of self as cognizing subject, ego, or personality.

Nishitani's considerations on a philosophy of being "take their stand at the point that traditional philosophies of religion have been broken down or been broken through. In that sense they may be said to go along with contemporary existential philosophies, all of which include a standpoint of 'transcendence' in one sort or another" (1982, xlix). Nishitani considers the nihilistic philosophies of Sartre, Heiddeger, and Nietzsche, as well as the religious existentialism of Kierkegaard, in order to find a Western common ground with Eastern concerns about nothingness. But he also considers how, even these Western existentialist dilemmas are still very much couched within the assumptions of the traditional philosophy of Christianity. A radical change of heart in these cultural conditions, in the sense of conversion to a "Great Reality" (discussed above), has produced either the negation of the existence of God as a willful personality (an atheistic humanism), or in the case of Kierkegaard, a philosophical–spiritual vocation. After all, the kind of certainty on a Presence in the believer has much in common with the certainty of such absence in an atheist.

Modern philosophical thought is based on the reality of the personal self, and therefore, on the reality of its division from the world *outside* itself. The Cartesian "*cogito, ergo sum* expressed the mode of being of that ego as a self-centered assertion of its own realness" (Nishitani 1982, 11). But according to Nishitani, it is an ego that seeks its own realness and mirrors itself in what it finds at every turn. This kind of self-centeredness is displaced from looking at itself beyond the actual fact that it considers itself as real. As I have argued in chapter 3, this has to do with the multiple emotional interactions in which the ego is engaged, which give shape and consubstantiality, objective reality, to the "integument of culture" where it lives. But according to Nishitani, this field of consciousness must go through an existential doubt in order to contemplate its own nonreality as impermanence, and experience the grounds on which it stands as emptiness:

> Only when the self breaks through the field of consciousness, the field of *beings*, and stands on the ground of nihility is it able to achieve a subjectivity that can in no way be objectivized. (Nishitani 1982, 16)

This "standing" though is existential as well as intellectual knowing. According to Nishitani, this is the only comprehensive standpoint for modern human because, in every other standpoint, contemporary human is shattered into little abstract pieces that separate consciousness from mortality, the unavoidable return to nihility (death).

According to Nishitani, the problem for this existential modern position is that it does not radicalize the experience of emptiness, but remains couched in its intellectually cognizing discipline that depends on the reality of the subject itself. This is why the Great Reality of the existential nihilism that Nishitani criticizes does not perform a complete conversion into a religious quest, even if it seems closely related to it in its certainty about the absence of a Presence—atheism. Nishitani argues that in nihilism, nothingness may be posed as the ground of existence; the problem is it still sees the self as poised on some kind of objective grounds:

> [T]he nothingness that means "there is no ground" positions itself like a wall to block one's path and turns itself into a kind of ground so we can still say that "there is a ground." Only absolute emptiness is the true no-ground (*Ungrund*). Here all things—from a flower to a stone to stellar nebulae and galactic systems, and even life and death

themselves—become present as bottomless realities. They disclose their bottomless suchness. True freedom lies in this no-ground. Sartre's freedom is still a bondage, a kind of hole that has the ego projected into it like a stake driven into the ground for the self to be tied to. (Nishitani 1982, 34)

In atheistic nihilism, individual human selfhood is defended with religious zeal as the source of freedom and autonomous will. In the Western forms of existential nihilism, the "far side" transhistorical realm is attempted to be brought to the "near side" by the transcendental identity of human, but it fails to do so because this identity is couched in the personality of the cognizing self who is displaced from prehending infinity existentially.

To say it with Nishitani, an excessive identification of the self (collective or individual) with the particular personal selfhood or ego is precisely the predicament in which modern culture finds itself: "If we grant that Cartesian philosophy is the prime illustration of the mode of being of modern man, we may also say that it represents the fundamental problem lurking within that mode" (Nishitani 1982, 19). The abyss of nihility that opens up at the bottom of self brings out infinite nothingness that human personality on its own is unable to deal with because of its own inherent finiteness. A tension between a transcendental identity (infinity) and the individual personality (finiteness) of human arises in the symbolism of the historical view of reality, and this tension organizes the legitimate factuality of universal history. In contrast to this, in the mystic traditions, infinity itself produces awareness of universality, not only with respect to other human beings, but also with respect to any type of consciousness. This fails to produce universal symbolism of factual human historicity because the infinite vastness of time for all forms of consciousness (animals, plants, even objects!) cannot possibly be represented factually, but it can be understood (and represented in metonymy) in the search for the present mystical moment of Absolute emptiness, where it is apprehended. Nihilistic nothingness still shows the bias of objectification in which the self, cognized as an ego, regards nothingness as a kind of objective *thing*.

In contrast to this, the mystic standpoint of Absolute emptiness is the immanent "near side" of the transhistorical realm needed for consciousness of infinity with no beginning and no end. But this is not simply a cyclical predicament because in cyclical time, recurrence signals finiteness, and the beginning and end can be organizationally arranged according to that finiteness. Nevertheless, the "once and for all" essence of factual reality, that which cannot be repeated and is therefore unique, can only be expressed in realization that the beginning and end are contained in the present moment of existence:

> Kierkegaard speaks of a "transcendence" in the "moment" and along with that of a "simultaneity" coming to be in the "moment." In fact, past and present can be simultaneous without "destroying" the temporal sequence of before and after. Without such a field of simultaneity not even culture, let alone religion, could come into being. We can encounter Sakyamuni and Jesus, Basho and Beethoven in the present. That religion and culture can arise within and be handed down historically through time points to the very essence of time. (Nishitani 1982, 161)

We will say for now that the Eastern "near side" transhistorical realm of Absolute emptiness, conceives of an immediate kind of factual historicity based on the simultaneity of newness and impermanence experienced in time. From that point of experience, self is simultaneously nonself; it is one with emptiness and therefore free of all horizons of objective cognition, where emptiness is identical with being. I will attempt a clarification of these notions further below when I define the ideal-type mystic view of reality.

We are now in a position to say that the development of a historical consciousness depends on the symbolization of the notion of universality. Historicity, therefore, depends on a symbological dimension that is transcendental or transhistorical either on a "far side" or on a "near side" with respect to the human self. But while the legitimacy of the mystic "near side" as Absolute emptiness remains synchronic and a present spiritual dimension, as it seeks personal morality to point metonymically toward the experiential reality of what Nishitani calls "religious love" (*agape*) or "great compassion" (*Maha-karuna*), the legitimacy of the historical "far side" embodies the metonymic dialectical symbol of a divided reality between world and transcendence arranged diachronically with respect to each other. This was originally expressed in our Western tradition as the tale of Genesis and Apocalypse, and later in secular historicity, as the division between subject and object where the former is an end in itself and seeks factual knowledge and causal explanation about the latter. As we have said, the transhistorical or transcendental realm in the historical type of reality is positioned in the "far side" or the *not yet*, and through this, diachronic factual historicity acquires its institutional importance. To be sure, this experience of movement in time is also represented organizationally in an ideal mystic view of reality, but it does not acquire institutional legitimacy as reality. In the mystic disciplines of the East, immediate facticity (*samsara*) is contemplated as an illusion and as a burden that is given up in spiritual Enlightenment (*Nirvana*).

As we shall see, in Christianity, legitimacy of diachronic time comes from the institutionalization of both a group relationship and a personal relationship with God, which in secular reality becomes a universal kind of morality that should be internalized through history by all rationally enlightened individual selves. The ancestry of this kind of legitimacy goes from religious exegesis, to a personal conscience, to academic factual analysis. In mysticism, the organizational role of diachrony is to regard the phenomenal world as mere illusion of forms and is therefore not engaged with its factual analysis as if it were legitimate reality. But it does produce interrogative thought about the factual relationship between past intentions, the present personal situation, and future expectations. Therefore, historicity as a relevant category for the realm of human order is better disclosed for our purposes in the notion of human fault. In their diachronic and synchronic considerations of a transhistorical (transcendental) realm, the historical and mystic symbolizations of fault can illustrate the tension between, on the one hand, sinful humanity and a personal relationship with God, and on the other, worldly suffering and the transcendental realm of *Nirvana*.

Human Fault and the Responsible Agent

It is in the formation of distinctive types of *ethos* that the notion of fault becomes a relevant object of analysis. Following Paul Ricoeur's study of the Judeo-Christian symbolism of evil and Nishitani's considerations of the Eastern-mystic notion of fault, I have distinguished three types of fault to which the human self can relate according to each view of reality: the primitive view conceives of fault as defilement; the historical view as sin and guilt; and the mystic view as "worldly suffering" or *karma* in Eastern disciplines. Nevertheless, in the Judeo-Christian tradition, worldly suffering is seen as a condition of sinful humanity. The notion of fault is constant in any cosmology and it clarifies how each view of reality tends toward an ideal individual self or to a collective self. I argue that defilement and worldly suffering or *karma* highlight the importance of a collective self, either embodied in community or conceived as a sacred collective mind, while the historical, legal–rational notion of fault (especially in guilt) tends toward individuality as the locus of self conceived as the responsible agent either in the religious imputation of fault or in the secular one. Symbols of fault can only be overlapped and compared from a phenomenological perspective, in present awareness, because their prevalent verbal structures produce imaginary paths that do not converge symbolically through time conceived as past and future; they unfold into the shape of the relevant mythical tale: The transmigration of souls beyond the individual lifetime (the wheel of birth and rebirth), eternal damnation and salvation, or universal history. From this perspective, guilt and sin are observed to open up an unavoidable abyss between the self and the "far side" realm of transhistorical reality, while the mystic notion of emptiness reconciles the self with the transhistorical realm in an absolute "near side" of spiritual love.

In his *Symbolism of Evil* (1967a), Paul Ricoeur carries out a phenomenological analysis of the experience of fault. His three stages— defilement, sin, guilt—represent the symbolic evolution of the Judeo-Christian tradition toward deeper awareness about the responsible individual self in Modernity. I will take his first stage, that of defile-ment, to be an ideal type of symbolism of fault for my primitive ideal-type view of reality, one that is lived and cognized right now as a mixture of emotion and imagination and expressed in metaphoric-poetic language. From defilement, the phenomenological path toward sin and guilt defines the symbological development of the historical view of reality, while the notion of fault as *karma* defines that of the mystic apprehension of a "leap in being" toward transcendence. Ricoeur identifies the symbolic evolution of the experience of defilement, to sin, to guilt:

> "Guilt," in the precise sense of a feeling of the unworthiness at the core of one's personal being, is only the advanced point of a radically individ-ualized and interiorized experience. This feeling of guilt points to a more fundamental experience, the experience of "sin," which includes *all* men and indicates the *real* situation of man before God, whether man knows it or not. It is this sin of which the myth of the fall recounts the entry into the world and which speculation on original sin attempts to erect into a doctrine. But sin, in its turn, is a correction and even a revolution with respect to a more archaic concept of fault—the notion of "defilement" conceived in the guise of a stain or a blemish that infects from without. Guilt, sin, and defilement thus constitute a primitive diversity in experience. Hence the feeling involved is not only blind in virtue of being emotional; it is also equivocal, laden with a multiplicity of meanings. This is why language is needed a second time to elucidate the subterranean crises of the consciousness of fault. (Ricoeur 1967a, 7–8)

In this symbolism of fault, Ricoeur also identifies a movement in language, from an elementary language of confession (metaphorical) to the elaborated language of gnosis and counter-gnosis (metonymic). He also says that there is a heavy emotional involvement every time there is explicit description of the personal or collective experience of fault. This is congenial with the idea that fault, and ultimately the idea of self, is emotionally cognized. Ricoeur's three categories are thus a typology that is determined by emotional response to the relationship with God's interdictions, and to his divine Will.

The most archaic or basic type of fault, that of defilement, is generally expressed in metaphorical verbal structures of disease and pestilence in order to point toward exclusion from the human group, originally constituting the human self. In synchronic legitimation of time and reality, the locus of the self is the known human group and its verbal structures are arranged as artistic representations of reality cognized physically and emotionally. Defilement is seen as offense against the human group, the collective self, human personality repre-sented as gods and goddesses who engage in cosmic dance and play and produce the experienced reality of newness and impermanence, and is expressed in compact symbolism of mixed emotion and imagination. This dance and play is the most archaic form of divine human identity as lying beyond the world in the shape of absolute joy, but in a similar manner, this other-worldliness is also lived emotionally in an absolute manner in the despair and experienced physical pain reified in the symbols of defilement. Our embodied experience constantly conveys the nuances between extreme joy and extreme pain, going through boredom and indifference, which are emotional and thus physical and which most strongly express the relationship between what is allowed and what is forbidden, what is expected and what is a necessity for individual embodiment to be and to produce. Human emotional development through ontogeny carries the most basic and archaic relationship to self as goddesses and gods, even if these symbols become emotionally and intellectually differentiated and trans-formed into legitimate self as personality couched in a transcendental identity or into self as Absolute emptiness.[7]

Defilement is related to the boundaries of permissiveness; "we have to transport ourselves," says Ricoeur, "into a consciousness for which impurity is measured not by imputation to a responsible agent but by the objective violation of an interdict" (1967a, 27). Under this regime, the list of faults is vast while it is poor when it comes to considering the intentions of the agent. Here, evil and misfortune are still associated; "the ethical order of doing ill has not been distinguished from the cos-mobiological order of faring ill" (Ricoeur 1967a, 27). To us, this lack of differentiation on the side of intentionality is irrational because it connects physical contingency with fault. Defilement is typically symbolized as a form of impurity by contagion that infects from without, "but this infectious contact is experienced subjectively in a specific feeling which is of the order of Dread" (Ricoeur 1967a, 28). Taboos, which define primitive boundaries of permissiveness, are basically punishments emotionally anticipated in transgress of cosmological interdicts. There is an archaic relationship between defilement and vengeance that, according to Ricoeur, is the oldest and most primitive form of representation of fault. From a primitive need for vengeance emerged the first human modes of expression of order in the language of retribution.

When this expression discovers the symbolic direction of transcendence, verbal structures become preeminently metonymic to point toward transcendental infinite joy and freedom, but at the same time, to the infinite abyss of despair and nihility, also generally used to point to divine punishment or cosmic debt that is also eternal, and so, absolutely terrifying. This is the reason why the symbolism of defilement is actually never left behind because it is the most explicit one in physical analogies and metaphors, and it is resorted to in every type of symbolism of fault.

> It is because the symbolism of defilement still clings by its manifold root hairs to the cosmic sacralizations, because defilement adheres to everything unusual, everything terrifying in the world, attractive and repellent at the same time, that this symbolism is ultimately inexhaustible and inerradicable. As we shall see, the more historical and less cosmic symbolism of sin and guilt makes up for the poverty and abstractness of its imagery only by a series of revivals and transpositions of the more archaic, but more highly surcharged symbolism of defilement. The richness of the symbolism of defilement even when this symbolism is fully interiorized, is the corollary of its cosmic roots. (Ricoeur 1967a, 12)

The kind of language used to represent fault appears in mixed symbolism, so the difference between the categories of fault is phenomenological rather than linguistic or historical, and it is progressive only in the sense that it points to the discovery and representation of transcendence in human social order.

The notion of *karma* in Eastern spiritual discipline keeps the connection to the primitive language of vengeance and retribution, but transforms it into a cosmic burden of infinite embodied debt in pain and attachment that can only be absolutely paid through spiritual Enlightenment. It keeps the archaic relationship between doing ill and faring ill, but gives it an ethical arrangement that trusts in fate as a learning device that arises as the product of our own actions:

> This force of destiny is not a destiny in the ordinary sense of something that simply rules over us and controls us from without. Nor is it merely

something like blind will. It is a destiny that appears only in the shape of the acts we ourselves perform, only as one with our own actions. (Nishitani 1982, 104)

This is why the realm of historicity that this notion of fault discloses is immediately related to factual consciousness of individual self ontogenetically, and not to any legitimate realm of universal human history. The notion of *karma* transforms the archaic trust in cosmology toward the direction of transcendence as a trust in contingency as fate. This Eastern trust in contingency as fate is displaced from the critical discipline of factual historical analysis; it defines an intuitive attitude of submission to experience and contemplation of the cosmobiological links between all things in the particularity of the present situation.

The notion of *karma* is emotionally grounded in a view of reality that situates itself wholly in transcendence, which does not lie in a "far side" but which becomes radicalized, especially in Buddhism, as an absolute "near side" of emptiness. *Karma* is existentially cognized as the worldly field of causality that ties human action to human fate indissolubly and that is identified as taking place in an "endless sea of suffering," *samsara*, which is ultimately illusory, but which is "grasped in a keenly existential fashion" (Nishitani 1982, 169). This experienced suffering is described as ontologically illusory for the practitioner who seeks absolute redemption or liberation exemplified by the enlightened masters; diachrony is *aspirationally* illusory for the seeker.

> [W]hen we speak of illusory appearance, we do not mean that there are real beings in addition that merely happen to adopt illusory guises to appear in. Precisely because it is *appearance* and not *something* that appears, this appearance is illusory at an elemental level in its very reality, and real in its very illusoriness. (Nishitani 1982, 129)

Here, the realm of history is unimportant as an institutional (legitimate as real) program that would embrace the whole of humanity in a universal tale of a beginning and an end.

Nevertheless, the notion of factual historicity is an important organizational principle in Eastern mystic discipline; each particular embodied individual contemplates it as a personal story of causality. As has been said before, mystic apprehension of the universal realm of being concentrates on the universe within, and therefore, every practitioner who strives for redemption from the sea of suffering does so, not only for her own benefit, but also primarily for every other "sentient being." To seek redemption for one-private-self is still regarded as a form of slavery to the illusory nature of embodiment in *samsara*, when the universe within in identity with every conscious being, has not yet been apprehended. In order to grasp the ontological priority of universal wholeness, an apprehension of Absolute emptiness is required through experience, where any notion of individual human identity of self is dissolved into the infinite ocean of nonbeing (more on this in chapter 5). This transhistorical realm of being–nonbeing is the absolute "near side" that discloses a universality that goes beyond the boundaries of Self as human self, it apprehends existence as nonexistence and merges in consciousness with the universe itself. It is the Absolute emptiness that in Mahayana Buddhism, Nagarjuna calls *sunyata* that must be experienced to be known.

In contrast to this, the Judeo-Christian opposition to trust in fate may be said to lie in personal responsibility about acts and the cosmo-logical impossibility of the notion of *samsaric* "transmigration" (eternal birth and death), which is secularized as a "once and for all" unique individual life. However, it can be argued that the root of this attitude originally lies in the personal relationship with a God who dwells in a transhistorical "far side" and that relates to His chosen people through prophetic indignation and historical exegesis as the expression of His Will. This is illustrated in the anthropological myth of the fall and the figure of the serpent, which is told as an event that took place "springing up from an unknown source, it furnishes anthropology with a key concept: The *contingency* of that radical evil which the penitent is always on the point of calling his evil nature. Thereby the myth pro-claims the purely 'historical' character of that radical evil" (Ricoeur 1967a, 252). In the Christian view, radical evil is contingent in history, in the world, even in the flesh but it is not the sole nature of human, and humanity's only mission is to overcome evil through its transcendental identity. Under this circumstances of reality, it would be irrational to trust in contingency, as radical evil may at any time spring out of nowhere in the course of historical time. This defines an attitude that must be intentionally active, dominating evil, controlling circumstances, and finding proof of success in the world.

The Hebrew representation of an avenging God is rooted in an archaic representation of order. The emergence of Yahweh as the only God of the universe with a chosen people was originally symbolized as a collective relationship with a local sacred entity who would lead them to historical success. "What there is in the first place," says Ricoeur, "is not essence but presence; and the commandment is a modality of the presence, namely, the expression of a holy will. Thus sin is a religious dimension before being ethical; it is not the transgression of an abstract rule—of a value—but the violation of a personal bond" (1967a, 53). Revelation transformed this local relationship into the figure of the Covenant, and gave it its transcendental possibilities. It is with respect to the Covenant that the notion of sin is defined: Sin is an unavoidable human characteristic according to the myth of the fall, the awareness of which unites the chosen people before God's judgment. But this judgment is expressed as an infinite distance between God and man, between His transcendental power and the deeply rooted human evil. This distance is expressed in the form of prophetic accusation, indignation, and the wrath of God:

> The initial situation of man as God's prey can enter into the universe of discourse because it is itself analyzable into an utterance of God and an utterance of man, into the reciprocity of a vocation and an invocation. Thus this initial situation, which plunges into the darkness of the power and violence of the Spirit, also emerges into the light of the Word. It is in this exchange between vocation and invocation that the whole experience of sin is found. (Ricoeur 1967a, 51–52)

The figure of the Covenant, of unlimited demand and finite commandment, defines a dialogue between God and each individual from which an unavoidable collective experience of sin emerges. The law teaches people how they are already sinners and this accusation deepens the experience of being oneself, but alienated from oneself: "Sin, as alienation from oneself, is an experience even more astonishing, disconcerting, scandalous, perhaps, than the spectacle of nature, and for this reason it is the richest source of interrogative thought" (Ricoeur 1967a, 8). While alienation from oneself in defilement—the primary experience of the cosmos—is alienation from the community, in sin, this kind of alienation is related to exile from the transcendental realm symbolized in Paradise: It defines the worldly human condition that must struggle to defeat evil till the end of time. Sin is thus universalized as a condition that, as it were, unifies humankind. This condition is symbolized in the terror that the prophets experience when they must face God:

> [T]he religion of Israel is imbued with this conviction that man cannot see God without dying. Moses at Horeb, Isaiah in the temple, Ezekiel face to face with the glory of God, are terror-stricken; they experience in the name of the whole people the incompatibility of God and man. This terror expresses the situation of sinful man. (Ricoeur 1967a, 63)

The infinite demand of God and the finite command of the ritual codes create a tension with which the sinner is never finished. When there is pardon as deliverance, it is symbolized in a theology of history for the whole of the people of Israel; otherwise, pardon is never reached in actual personal deliverance. It is, however, lived in the punishment that the ritual codes prescribe because, in it, sin loses its aspect of irrevocable condemnation: "[P]ardon does not abolish suffering but grants a respite which is interpreted as a horizon determined by divine patience" (Ricoeur 1967a, 79). In the language of the confession of sins, this symbolism of fault provides the grounds for interrogative thought in the personal relationship with God, which is symbolized as a whole in the Covenant:

> [I]n addition to mitigation of the punishment, pardon appears as the transformation of an obstacle into a test; punishment becomes the instrument of awareness, the path of confession. Pardon is already fully evident in this restore capacity of knowing oneself in one's true situation in the bosom of the Covenant. (Ricoeur 1967a, 79)

Sin is therefore individual and communal at the same time, and it is entwined with the "Day of Yahweh," the historical events, and their penal interpretation by the prophets. Prophecy joins the promise of salvation to the threat of calamity; there is a double imminence of catastrophe and deliverance. "This double oracle," says Ricoeur, "keeps up the temporal tension characteristic of the Covenant" (1967a, 68).

Ricoeur speaks of a crisis that came about due to the deepening of the feeling of sin. The experience of evil in the self as a deeply rooted human characteristic, symbolized in the fall, produced constant contemplation of the individual self in obeisance to the Law of God. But this relationship to ritual finite law is always experienced as emotionally attached to the infinite demand of God himself. This is the symbolism of historical time of man *before* God, or the root to the experience of being seen by God:

> [T]he primordial significance of this seeing [being-seen-by-God] is to constitute the *truth* of my situation, the justness and the justice of the ethical judgment that can be passed on my existence. That is why this seeing, far from preventing the birth of the Self, gives rise to self-awareness; it enters into the field of subjectivity as the *task* of knowing oneself better; this seeing, which *is*, lays the foundation for the ought-to-be of self-awareness. (Ricoeur 1967a, 85)

The emergence of personal guilt occurs when sinful man internalizes and personalizes the experience of fault, not only as responsibility in being the cause of a violation of interdiction, but also now as being the author of ethically wrong deeds in the eyes of the divine gaze. "That is why," says Ricoeur, "the consciousness of guilt constitutes a veritable revolution in the experience of evil: That which is primary is no longer the reality of defilement, the objective violation of the Interdict, or the Vengeance let loose by that violation, but the evil use of liberty, felt as an internal diminution of the value of the self" (1967a, 102).

When interdiction is not only ritual but also becomes ethical, human beings are radically called to a perfection that goes beyond their *objective* obligations; it becomes a *subjective* assumption of responsibility. It is in this internalization of fault and in this awareness of being seen by God that individuals face the alternative "God or Nothing" (Ricoeur 1967a, 103). When all possibilities are reduced to this simple alternative, human beings must look at themselves as the authors of their acts together with the motives of their acts; this "raises up, over against itself, a subjective pole, a respondent, no longer in the sense of a bearer of punishment, but in the sense of an existent capable of embracing his whole life and consider it as one undivided destiny, hanging upon a simple alternative" (Ricoeur 1967a, 103).

According to Ricoeur, at the time of the Jewish prophets of the Exile, when Jerusalem had fallen to Babylon, a historical situation took place that corresponds to the change from communal sin to individual guilt:

> The preaching of sin had represented a mode of prophetic summons in which the whole people was exhorted to remember a collective deliverance, that of the Exodus, and to fear a collective threat, that of the Day of Yahweh. But now that the evil hour has arrived, now that the national state is destroyed and the people deported, the same preaching which had been able to appeal for a collective reform has become a cause for despair; it has lost all the force of a summons and become nihilistic in its import. (Ricoeur 1967a, 105)

Ezekiel, who had been brought captive into Babylon before Jerusalem was taken, preached for the individual responsibility of fault. No communal choice was open, collective sin had become a symbol of failure according to which the wrath of God had already condemned a whole people. Hope could, therefore, only be found on the individual side of sin; this took place in the same kind of preaching as accusation, which produced a solitary experience in the form of individual guilt. Nevertheless, if sin was now individual, so would salvation be: "Even if the Exodus from Egypt could not be repeated in an exodus from Babylon, even if the Return was to be indefinitely postponed, there would still be hope for each man" (Ricoeur 1967a, 105).

It is in the subjective emergence of the experience and symbolization of fault that the notion of *conscience* as individual and solitary conscience emerges. As a religious experience, and in an intimate relationship to sin, it is lived in the presence of a higher spiritual order on the "far side" of transhistorical reality from which the human being is displaced, and which observes her. However, it is in the assumption of a transcendental identity that human makes the ethical choice to take the side of this divine presence and judge her own deeds. The experience of a complete cleavage between sin and guilt can be, then, formulated in the emergence of an individual conscience that judges the doings of the mundane self from a transcendental standpoint of either the Law or the personal "law" or moral principles, one's own judgment and critical mind, which in secular reality may no longer be transcendental *qua* God, but is still transcendental *qua* part of the human identity.

> Let the "I" be emphasized more than the "before thee," let the "before thee" be even *forgotten*, and the consciousness of fault becomes guilt and no longer sin at all; it is "conscience" that now becomes the *measure* of evil in a completely solitary experience. It is not by accident that in many languages the same word designates moral consciousness (*conscience morale*), and psychological and reflective consciousness; guilt expresses above all the promotion of "conscience" as supreme. (Ricoeur 1967a, 104)

In the historical type of reality, the basis for this "conscience" is individual due to the fragmentation of symbolism of the human self. Self is conceived as preeminently collective in primitive fault as defilement; in the Judeo-Christian tradition, it is alternatively collective and individual in consciousness of fault through original sin and the personal relationship with God, and ends up being constructed as preeminently individual in the hope for salvation and the reality of mundane evil as guilt. In secular modern reality and moral behavior, it is conscience as guilt—either projected or assumed—that shapes morality, which becomes a supreme entity liable to be worshipped in the temple of personal individuality and the private realm: The transcendental identity of a subject who is cosmologically divided from its object of cognition and holds an emotional relationship and attachment to that division.

In the divided universe of historical reality—between world and transcendence—boundaries are defined with respect to typical Judeo-Christian categorizations of good and evil. This structure of belief is based on the Christian collective spiritual practice as one body in the church (*ekklesia*).[8] The political organization of the church was very powerful in a universal world order because, as opposed to all other empires based on cosmological kingdoms, it empowered an impersonal organization to act for God through the people in its ranks.

> The central royal metaphor—that we are all members of one body—was expressed in terms of unity and integration, as the unity of a social body into which the individual is absorbed. The Church claimed to be the continuing Body of Christ in history, and as early as the letters of Ignatius we are completely in the atmosphere of the Church Militant, with its emphasis on military analogies and its disciplined organization, where no authority is to be followed except what comes through the bishop. (Frye 1982, 99)

When this organizational principle became secularized and put into the hands of liberal democracy, an aura of distance, congenial with the idea of a gaze from the "far side," was given to the institution of the state or the law, in the Anglo-Saxon one. The way in which the globalized order of today conceives of institutions is tied up with the Augustinian institutional arrangement. The Augustinian tale, however, in its transcendentalist implications foresaw a city of God of perfect justice; this tale was transformed into a secular one in which the spiritual quest is out of sight. In its place, there remains the discipline of a modern ethos that poses the individual human self as an end in itself and organizes morality as a private quest for the prehension of the self.

I have argued that conscience is an essential aspect for the construction of the moral individual self in Modernity, and that conscience emerges from the Judeo-Christian sacred cosmology, which in Modernity becomes the *responsible agent*. This section explored phenomenologically the sacred source of our moral identity in order to find where ideal individuality comes from. My argument is that Ricoeur's portrayal allows for such exploration of our modern conscious selves in a phenomenological depiction of the transformations of conscience, individually borne in practice. In what follows, I argue that ideal individuality is a socially constructed identity required to sustain modern organizations—however imperfectly it is reproduced in daily interaction. Individual human identity is the practical as well as the ideal basis for legitimating the primacy of individuality in liberalism.

THE COMMUNITARIAN–LIBERAL DEBATE: THE INDIVIDUAL AS AN INSTITUTION AND UNIVERSAL HUMANITY

Individual liberty is the substantive basis of the liberal tradition. However, in contemporary political philosophy, there is a fundamental rift around the conception of the human self *qua* individual. Liberals promote an idea of the human self as unrestrained and not determined by anyone or anything but herself, free to make her own choices and live her life according to her own conception of the good, as long as this chosen lifestyle will not interfere with other people's rights. Along the history of political theory, this principle of individual liberty as a universal conception of self has unleashed objections grounded on historical–sociological arguments. In the eighteenth century, Edmund Burke's ([1790] 1999) dismissal of an excessive use of abstraction in order to define an individuality that had not been earned historically, illustrates a well-known reaction of the type I am now referring to. In the twentieth century, though, one cannot as easily and aristocratically invoke the providential role of history and whatever human groups can learn from it. Communitarians conceive of the individual self— as well as a sense for individual morality—as a product of history and culture, and criticize liberals for regarding individuality as an abstract–universal characteristic of human beings, disregarding its social constitutive characteristics. I discuss what in contemporary polit-ical theory debate has been regarded as "communitarian positions" that stress and aspire to the constructive creation of the self by means of disciplined practice, tradition, and the sociological datum of an ethical life that produces meaning. With this I want to argue that indi-vidualism may well be a product of European religion, values, and culture; a disciplined practice that is sustained by human enaction, but is now the basis for modern global interaction. Even as we can see its ideal roots as imaginary, the universalizing principles that emanate from individual experience of morality are essential to interaction in globalized Modernity *qua* ideals. This is no longer an imposition of the colonial West, but a lived experience at various levels of interaction around the world.

I argue, within my own theoretical framework, that both sides of the liberal–communitarian debate arise from the tension between world and transcendence in the historical ideal type of reality and that this opposition has no logical solution. Here I want to situate the tension between liberals and communitarians structurally within my ideal type historical view of reality and propose that, if we adopt the present moment of meaningful experience as a phenomenological perspective, this historical time framework and view of reality deems it unsolvable.[9] In the previous sections of this chapter, I have referred to how the reality of world and transcendence produces a mature philosophy of history. Their tension is "outside" the individual consciousness of self; it organizes historical reality and is the virtue by which the order of events in diachrony is seen as taking place irrevocably. I have postulated the diachronic representation of time as characterizing the historical ideal type, which is framed in the tension between world and transcendence, both conceived of as real at the same time and with a moral calling for the world to chase after transcendence. In Modernity, this structural arrangement of time produces historical reality as a sequential story of facts interpreted in the light of relevant historic-political-economic values, according to the ideographic methodology. However, within the individual subject, the inner reality of world and transcendence as a product of such history, displays the "inside" perspective of another tension: An internalized *world* as the worldly identity of the embodied individual entity, attached to a particular embodied personality and a specific cultural context, versus an internalized *transcendence* that places intrinsic value on human life and its uniqueness in every individuality, a reflection on the self as a transcendental subject. The individual self is seen as either determined by the particularity of her context, or as the individual bearer of the right to freedom (even *from* her context)—the individual condition being a general characteristic of embodied humanity, and so a very practical principle for organization. On the one hand, when seen as determined by context, the historical aspect of Modernity and the formation of the individual self as a product of culture is stressed. On the other, when seen as a universal feature of selfhood, the stress lies on the transcendental subject, or in humanism; it is expressed in universal and abstract all-encompassing terms (even by Rawls), and as I have argued above, it is ultimately based on a sacred prehension of the self.

The value of this "inside" perspective has to do with how Modernity interprets the uniqueness of its own cultural tradition in terms of, on the one hand, the historical particular self who is part of the social whole, and on the other hand, the moral self who considers herself as ideally pertaining to a well-ordered and just society. The tension between human embodied and context-specific ethos and the metaphysical basis for universalizability of maxims—the modern transcendental identity—characterizes the liberal–communitarian debate. The latter has produced a very rich enquiry into how it is that the human individual self is conceived of and interacts in the modern world, yet it has arrived to a stalemate. Either individualism or communitarianism on its own is conceptually displaced from being able to represent a convincing characterization of the human ability to be ethical and/or moral. Individualism dispenses with particular context and social conditioning as an essential part of what it is to be an individual;

communitarianism is structurally displaced from providing a valid basis for ethical/moral interaction beyond local cultural references.

I find that both abstract-individual liberalism and communitarianism have limitations of their own and, in a way, complement each other. However, I find that when we speak of global interaction, that is, interaction across the very diverse views of reality in the world, it is essential to find a secular common ethical basis. Only the liberal tradition managed to culturally produce such basis for a universal humanity. I have revised how the abstract–universal language of liberalism is ultimately rooted in a religious prehension of the self. Yet, this idea of self is the structural basis for modern organization, which is now a public and global good. We find ourselves with it and, eventhough our own tradition of knowledge has produced the theoretical basis to be critical of the systemic order it produces, the practice of being and behaving like an individual shapes the way we moderns conceive of ourselves. The construction of human *ethos* is essentially a human endeavor. When it is regarded as a private endeavor, this reflects an essential liberal value with universal moral pretensions. I am comfortable with holding this essential value to be true, much like a Christian, a Muslim, or a Jew would hold and even defend with their lives the essential conviction of the One God of the universe to be true, much like a Buddhist or a Hindu would hold the existence of *Nirvana* to be true.

As much as these systems of beliefs might at times find themselves in stark contradiction with each other, modern people hold a handful of them at various stages of their ontogeny at the same time. Disciplined practices overlap, confront, and assimilate each other in whatever creative ways the conscious embodied individual manages to bring forth as the mental and emotional space she was born to and lives in. This is the reason why practices have a cross-cultural essence and are never closed systems of rules—not even the most rigid ones. They might produce an illusion of constancy, as Luhmann has pointed out in his *Social Systems* (1995), but they are also constantly interpreted and reinterpreted, built and rebuilt. I believe that MacIntyre's hope for objectivity by means of such rules discloses his own modern sense of self and feelings of moral indignation before what he contemplates as the contemporary absence of a sense for virtue. This modern feeling, I believe, is very much related to an old style of calling upon people (preaching) and scolding them for not having it clear that they should aspire toward a higher order of life, excellence, whose root is transcendental, sacred, providential. Different cultures have different worldly manifestations of various orientations to the good, but I argue that these ideals do not really have closed borders—especially not in modern individual awareness. This is an illusion of analytical thought that allows for an identification of diverse phenomenal domains. The common basis for all these orientations to the good to converge, as I will argue in chapter 5 of this book, lies beyond language and symbols. And so I regard liberalism as a comprehensive conception of the good with universal pretensions that are analogous to other religious-philosophical-spiritual comprehensive conceptions of the good that people practice on earth right now.

In spite of holding the above liberal conviction as essentially true, my hermeneutical–critical mind entices me to consider that other views of reality might hold essential values other than individual autonomy to be right and true—at times, I myself might, depending on the ethical decision to be made. This does not lessen the fact that in a global arena of interaction, individuality is an ideal value that ought to be enacted. In practice, in the embodied human world, this will result in diverse forms of individuality enacted through a variety of cultural environments around the world. Individuality can be seen as an institution or a set of habits that are learnt and sustained by meaningful and constant enactment of interaction according to social–cultural rules. This is congenial with Meyer's definition of an institution as "cultural rules giving collective meaning and value to particular entities and activities" (Meyer et al. 1987, 13). Following March and Olsen (1989), Czarniawska interprets the concept of "cultural rules" as "the 'rules of narration' that are typical for a given time and place" (1997, 42). The individual self can be regarded as a legitimate institution that acquires an aura of "sacredness" in Modernity; the individual is a product of culture that is only sustained in meaningful and ongoing disciplined practice:

> Society is rationalized as rooted in the behavior and choices of individuals and as functioning for their benefit; it is, as it were, not quite sacred itself but rather the product of its sacred individual members. It is justified, not by its history, but by the extent to which it benefits the individuals who are both its ultimate producers and its ultimate consumers. (Meyer 1986, 209)

Meyer tells us that modern organizations need properly trained individuals to function in a systematic and efficient manner as such, and so individuality is not merely the product of people who are understanding and organizing in this way their own experience for themselves. Rather, it is a large-scale endeavor, that is the product of "various bodies of professional officials—religious ideologues, their secular counterparts (e.g., psychologists, teachers, lawyers, administrators)—and by other institutions of the modern state" (1986, 208). While the critical discipline entices us to be alert about such influences, we can be so only from an individual rational perspective, which such "bodies of professional officials" help construct. It is a principle of the critical mind to doubt that these formal influences are solely devoted to my own good. In liberal democracies, ideally, the relationship of people with the figure of authority ought to be a critical one, constantly demanding accountability. In practice, while the person builds her individuality, either in a critical manner or not, the product of her construction builds her own sense of self back. The individual ideal may be enticing, but the complex self does not behave in a critical manner with respect to all aspects of her life—nor is it desirable that she does.

Modern society is individualistic in the broad sense that it allocates the value of human life in the coordinated social action of individual persons with a private life. Meyer tells us that individualism has expanded historically as the market and state have expanded, as both institutions require individually based interaction: The market requires that everyone pursues their own benefit and the state is rooted in the doctrine of individual citizenship. Modern National States make it part of their job to legitimize the constant production of competent individuals and so education is regarded as a right in many national-state constitutions of the world: "[education] is seen as directly linked to progress and justice" (Meyer 1986, 216). Further, individuality is expanding even more as global interaction expands; it has become a constitutive doctrine of modern society. The structural environment of modern and complex organizations, such as the government, and institutions, such as the state and the market, need such ideal to be held to carry out their reification and enactment. And so, there is a continual reinforcement of its importance and a constant production and re-production of an idea of autonomous individual selves around the world.

Meyer locates the actual enactment of the most extreme form of individualism geographically in southern California, but his portrayal is more accurately posed as an ideal type of individuality. The definition that I borrow from Meyer to designate this ideal–typical individuality portrays it as facing the natural world and the moral world directly, without any mediation, nor social or cultural (1986, 210). This is, of course, an ideal type, if we consider that people are biologically born to a nexus of references and language, and can never live completely disembedded from a human conversation, view of reality, or cosmos, as my primitive ideal type of reality illustrates. This is also Charles Taylor's position in his *Sources of the Self* (1989), where he refuses validity to naturalist conceptions of the self (abstract–individual–liberalism and utilitarianism), and insists that this conception is unacceptable in moral philosophy. To him, it is unacceptable because a naturalist conception of the self contemplates individuality as unmediated by social conditioning and essentially as independent and self-sufficient.

To Alisdair MacIntyre, the portrayal of the modern identity as essentially autonomous leads to disastrous consequences in the ethical life of actual people. MacIntyre argues that this is because everything is understood in abstract and universal terms and this does not link the moral self to any valid practice or tradition that would give rationality and consubstantiality to ethical action. And so, to MacIntyre, in Modernity, we are ruled by emotivism, according to which our moral decisions are no more than arbitrary personal preferences and are impossible to justify objectively:

> The specifically modern self, the self that I have called emotivist, finds no limits set to that on which it may pass judgment for such limits could only derive from rational criteria for evaluation and, as we have seen, the emotivist self lacks any such criteria. (MacIntyre 1984, 31)

Modern culture assumes that anyone is already a moral and rational agent, but this ignores the importance of the social roles or practices for the self to learn how to behave as such. This is the reason why MacIntyre sees failure in the Enlightenment project: It uses universal language to speak about personal and particular preferences that are chosen arbitrarily in the absence of dense social references and objective rules. The individual self is such only within the framework of social references that defines this self.

Taylor attempts a portrayal of the modern identity as a starting point of the self-understanding of Modernity proper. He speaks of "our" identity and explains that the "self" in the title of his book designates an "ensemble of (largely unarticulated) understandings of what is to be a human agent: The sense of inwardness, freedom, individuality, and being embedded in nature which are at home in modern West" (1989, ix). Taylor's work describes the genesis of the modern identity, and this history is justified by an ethical theory of "frameworks," constructivist shared references, and language. To Taylor, frameworks or "socially mediated interaction" between the self, her moral existence, and the world, necessarily have an orientation to some idea or conception of the good. He interprets such mediation as an essential aspect of what

I have portrayed as the imaginative and emotional construction of the self. My understanding of Taylor's views on language and shared references (frameworks) is that they are the *materials* in which the self identity is *carved*. Taylor's theoretical position is that the modern identity or self—who understands herself as an individual—is inextricably entwined with ideas of the good or ethical orientations. Frameworks are important because they let us differentiate experiences and see how these are entwined with our existence as agents, as individual selves. This is why, according to Taylor, the self and an orientation to the good have qualitative differences between themselves, but they are not isolated phenomena. Rather, they are like two different perspectives of the same phenomenon: "Selfhood and good . . . turn out to be inextricably intertwined themes" (Taylor 1989, 3). In order to know who one is, one has to resort to shared references according to the "map" of our "moral space." For this orientation to occur, Taylor uses spatial metaphors to stress that without the map and without knowing where one stands on such map—which is socially provided—the individual self would be lost. Such orientation is necessarily related to how we conceive of the good or goods that we pursue within our frameworks. Taylor tells us that people can be ethically oriented by various goods and this is why they find themselves in the need to rank them. There will be a good of highest importance that will determine my identity, for it is an orientation to this good that comes closest to defining it:

> [W]e acknowledge second-order qualitative distinctions which define higher goods, on the basis of which we discriminate among other goods, attribute differential worth or importance to them, or determine when and if to follow them. Let me call higher-order goods of this kind "hypergoods," i.e., goods which not only are incomparably more important than others but provide the stand point from which these must be weighed, judged, decided about. (1989, 63)

According to Taylor, then the modern moral self stands before alternative goods that are ordered according to qualitatively higher goods in this manner.

Taylor argues that liberalism is a comprehensive conception of the good and that our modern–liberal framework of references makes our individuality a supreme value. Autonomy and independence constitute frameworks of shared references about the self in Modernity. I believe with Taylor that this produces social enaction of such individual selves. That is, this understanding conveys the competent enactment of individuality in the modern arena of interaction. Individuality may be a utopia and an ideal, but it is also already the basis for disciplined practice of such individuality all over the world. Alisdair MacIntyre resorts to the concept of "practice," and the bigger one of "tradition," to explain that frameworks, common standards, or evaluative allegiances are of the essence for the imaginative production of sense and meaning in human lives.[10] As I have explained above, I consider individuality a disciplined practice in MacIntyre's sense. Individuality is already a legitimate way of experiencing reality for modern selves, perceived as the value of the inner individual self, a product of culture as well as a way of bringing forth the world in an embodied and a substantive manner.

The concept of "practices," in the plural, illustrates that one person's allegiance and devotion to various practices may well survive even as they contradict each other. A typically hybrid person will find herself taking into account her own autonomy and individuality as well as communal and particular rules of interaction in her specific culture (or mixture of them) and particular set of relationships and emotional attachments in order to make a moral decision. Historical reality was born in a teleological movement of the kind "from the city of man to the city God." But both Taylor and MacIntyre project this movement into individual consciousness and how one lives one's life in unitary coherence in time, in order to organize intelligibly the story of one's personal ontogeny. I find this quite illustrative of how the historical type of view of reality privileges the idea of self as an individual morally moving through historical, factual, and diachronic time. To MacIntyre, the unity lies within the coherence of the narrative of every personality, internally seeking her *telos* and enacting virtues that give substance to practices and traditions. This is such a dense and complex nexus of elements that he cannot give credence to analytical philosophy, which breaks down human actions to analyze them separately, nor to existentialism, which separates artificially the self from her roles.

MacIntyre's portrayal of the virtuous self, I argue, is actually the portrayal of how one practices at being and becoming an individual accountable self, within the modern–liberal tradition. This self strives for constant betterment in the realm of historicity, the constant search for an Aristotelian *telos*. MacIntyre regards this *telos* as the basis for the unity of human life, one that strives to fulfill the criteria of excellence within given practices. This is the root of the romantic notion of individuality, one that exists within the freedom of an imaginative creation of the self, an aristocratic sign of humanity, which Ortega y Gasset also speaks about in his *Rebellion of the Masses* (1937). But this search is supported by an awareness of historical context and the particularity of each "tradition" in MacIntyre's language. I agree with a central thesis of MacIntyre's work: "[M]an is in his actions and practice, as well as in his fictions, essentially a story-telling animal" (1984, 216). People tell stories with their actions, but such actions are enacted and disappear, and soon they are not embodied in anything but the story itself. Narratives are all there is left to approach selectively the volatility of human action. I believe that in such circumstances, the line between fact and fiction is not absolutely clear. Yet stories, plots, or narratives, as I have argued above, are of the essence in portraying and perpetuating what is important to human groups.

The "tale" of the individual self is told over and over again all over the world, its criteria of excellence are enacted in the products of human creativity and originality . . . and this tale is constantly enacted and re-enacted—however imperfectly. I do not agree with MacIntyre's portrayal of decadence for the whole liberal–moral tradition; his three archetypes of modern selves may illustrate the kind of vices that modern life also entails, but I believe he sees decadence where there is only human fallibility. In his *After Virtue* (1981), MacIntyre wants to describe how the Enlightenment project failed and how Modernity may be prevented from falling further into a fateful moral decadence. But I believe that what he succeeds in doing—and therein lies the power of his theory—is in describing the practice of imaginatively building one's individuality through a quest for excellence within the narrative unity of one's life. This practice allows us to be responsible individuals, and so "what is crucial to human beings as characters in enacted narratives is that, possessing only the resources of psychological continuity, we have to be able to respond to the imputation of a strict identity" (MacIntyre 1984, 217). Such identity is imaginatively constructed with the cultural materials that shape the individual sense of self as a moral and rational agent.

Meyer poses four principles of modern identity as individuality, and locates the first two as far as St. Augustine, and the last two already developed in Modernity: self-respect, competence, autonomy, and flexibility, or the ability to detach oneself from a specific perspective, the basis of a continual reconstruction of individuality according to the changing cultural structures of Modernity. Following Meyer, self-respect may be seen as descending from the City of God and medieval ideas of the virtuous self. However, I also propose to contemplate the phenomenological experience of the value of the self in modern moral-individual life as conscience. According to Wolfe, it is not that we are social entities because we are moral entities; rather, we are moral entities because we live with other people and should be accountable for what we do

(1989). The second principle that Meyer postulates is competence, which he regards as also coming from the Augustinian value of the self in a celebration of orderly nature and the efficient involvement of the self in such order. However, I relate both the origin of self-respect and competence to the Judeo-Christian internalization of fault that allows for a phenomenological experience of the value of the self with respect to a personal appreciation of one's own behavior morally, historically, and functionally.

Individual morality and competence are so dependent on the sanction of institutional public arenas, that there is the constant Frankfurt School-type of critical fear about manipulation of the life-world by means of such institutions, with a corresponding loss of autonomy. About this Meyer says,

> So reconstructing individualism—finding and legitimating the true, hidden individual behind the masks of social rationalization—has been a continuing and active process. . . . This process goes on, as always, under the guidance of the professional elites of individualism—intellectuals, theologians, psychologists—but the lawyers are also at work constantly giving the individual new rights, such as privacy, personal space, environmental purity, and welfare. (1986, 219)

Individualism is itself the aspiration that allows us to contemplate ourselves as moral selves—deciding by ourselves the maxims that will rule our moral life. I will contemplate individuality as an institution that sustains modern organization. This ideal relies in much abstraction to produce an individual personality who is always embedded in a particular culture and lived as an actual experience of human consciousness. The ideal of the individual self is also the structural basis for interaction in modern societies and can be regarded as a meaningful practice that sustains organization in a world scale. Individuality is an ideal that we even project unto functional groups of people—organizations—because it gives such enterprises shape and the possibility to portray respectability:

> Seeing individuality as an institution and identity as a narrative provides us with a possible answer to why the image of organization as a super-person persists. In the first place, it is because the notion of the individual is an institutional myth developed within rational theories of choice, and thus close to the core of organizational analysis. Second, and as a result, organizations are anthropomorphized to reproduce the notion of accountability, which is central to modern culture. (Czarniawska 1997, 46)

The third principle postulated by Meyer, autonomy, has historical legitimacy in the religious transformation and political development of England and the rest of Europe. It stemmed from autonomy to choose one's religious belief and expanded to the intimate realm of conscience, thought, and of course, a personal and private life. This is the principle that lies at the foundation of any liberal theory—even the communitarian reaction. The fourth and last principle is that the practice of individuality is continually under re-construction and this is related to the recent twentieth century "definitions of the legitimate self as beyond sex and gender" (Meyer 1986, 220) and, we could also add, beyond culture. Czarniawska interprets this last principle as the modern ability to detach the self from a specific point of view, as flexibility in the creative construction of the modern self who is aware of global organization, complexity, and plurality of identities (1997, 47–48). What Czarniawska calls flexibility is what I consider the basis for the modern self to not only practice and experience tolerance, but also to reinvent itself, in principle. That is, the individual is *ideally* competent to take a cool distance from context and contemplate it from an outside perspective.

In order to clarify the notion of individuality as an institution, Czarniawska quotes Vytautas Kavolis (1993) to say that there are three elements required for perception of identity, that have been identified as such by anthropological research: (1) *coherence* in perception and expression about the perceived world, (2) *continuity* of such perceptions in human ontogeny and within the human group, (3) a conscious *commitment* to the way one understands, perceives, and deals with one's self—even as we may not always be faithful to such commitment. To Czarniawska, the modern self identity is essentially understood and practiced as the individual self that is continuously acted out. What is being represented is the individual ideal, and she finds in autobiography the literary genre that may be used metaphorically to understand how it is that the modern individual identity is built. To her, modern individual identity is reified in interactions, but it creates the impression that the self can remain independent of people's reactions and involvement with the imaginary and emotionally cognized world that backs up such interactions. That is, the modern self identity tries to reify itself as autonomous from people's emotional involvement with each other. Also, when compared to heroic societies, as described by MacIntyre (1984), modern identity's character is individual and oriented toward a future that is yet to be experienced, rather than the past. Czarniawska believes that autobiography is the best genre analogy to modern individual identity:

> The analogy obviously lies in the fact that autobiography is a self-narrative of identity but also, less obviously but just as important, in

autobiography's claim to factuality. Autobiography belongs to literature, but not to fiction. (1997, 49)

MacIntyre's narrative unity of a human life is analogous to
Czarniawska's use of autobiography as a metaphor that illustrates the
imaginative construction of individuality in modern interaction. But
here one has to differentiate their attitudes toward modern identity
that can be found in the way they express themselves about individuality:
Czarniawska speaks of autobiography as an illustrative metaphor of
this modern institution and practice, while MacIntyre has not abandoned demotic language; human tales expressed in actions should
coincide with the narrative unity of a human life.

I find his portrayal of a coherent narrative unity for each person
somewhat forced, because, on the one hand, such linear thinking
ignores the complex nature of human relationships within the intricate narratives and conversations that we build, and on the other, we
cannot know whether the public tale that is lived in such unity has
actually been acted out as it is told a posteriori or if it is comprised of
imaginary actions that have been inserted into the tale. Thus, narrative unity is not only an ideal but also an aspiration of a disciplined
practice at the same time. My contention is that individual autonomy
might not always be the supreme good that validates all our ethical
decisions, as in deciding whether to donate one's kidney to a sibling.
However, individuality as the hypergood of the liberal tradition is
always there as a point of reference that gives order and precision to
specific modern interactions when we might find it essential to validate ourselves as such, for example, in our life as citizens or in legal
imputations of fault. In a similar manner, MacIntyre's idea of the
"narrative unity of a human life" portrays individuality as the coherent
story of embodiment and its actions, whose life story is told in such
unity. Again, the ethical decisions might well be shaped by the cultural
context of such embodied entity, but the final decision to behave ethically comes from individual consciousness. MacIntyre does not refer
to a convincing source for such decision, besides speaking of a quest
for the fulfillment of a (personal? individual?) *telos*. Here I resort to
my own theoretical framework to situate his account: MacIntyre's
idea of a narrative unity in the life of people is determined by the historical idea of reality projected into the ontogeny of each person in
order to be able to regard them as moral entities within such narrative.

Nevertheless, MacIntyre, and also Taylor, succeed in pointing at
the most important source of criteria for the practice of modern
individuality: the nexus of social and cultural references that give

consubstantiality to this identity at all. They regard individuality as a product of culture and history. I agree with their views, congenial with Meyer's and Czarniawska's, about individuality as a social construction, or institution. Nevertheless, I drop their apocalyptic views on the moral "decadence" of modern humanity—quite congenial with the style of preaching of Israelite prophets. I have discussed that the formation of the modern self is an ongoing practice that is based on concrete and particular expressions of culture and conceptions of reality that change according to the constant changes of cultural imaginary and universal ideals of individuality. As I have mentioned, I regard these communitarian critiques as representing one side of the historical ideal-type tension between world and transcendence. Communitarians tie their conviction about the modern self firmly in worldly and culturally embedded historical existence, and in that way, deny that their own representation of self benefits from the use of very powerful symbols, such as the inherent transhistorical realm of historicity. This position allows them to slip into the perspective of the hermeneutic observer, and contemplate the relative validity of cultures and conceptions of the good life, which feed a creatively alive plural society. The problem with communitarian relativism is that it leaves us with no convincing common standards for morality beyond the social structures of meaning where the self is formed and lives, as if the individual self did not have any basis (however imaginary) to transcend them—or reinvent them.

An essential source of reflection in political theory is the need for common substantive principles on the basis of which a human group may flourish. A contemporary ingredient to this is that one should assume that there is no homogeneity within such groups, and so, a plural array of views of reality must coexist in the same political association. Further, I want to concentrate on how global interaction produces the need to expand the substantive basis for agreement beyond national borders. The liberal answer to this is that human consciousness itself—individual conscience, with its moral undertones—ought to be the source of such basis. Contemporary human interaction around the world benefits from the expansion of the ideal of individuality, which influences the experience of belonging to comprehensive doctrines, or of using their symbols. The modern self (ideally) has no use for providential or sacred sources of common substantive principles, and yet, embodied and practicing individuals do. The modern type of reflection on the self, as somebody who conceives of herself as part of a specific national political association, is also rooted in her strong sense of self *qua* embodied individual. But this does not preclude this self from having a spiritual identity at the same time as she sees herself as an individual as well as experiences the primitivity of her embodiment. The theory of human agents as rational beings leaves to one side that they are also primitive beings and may conceive of themselves as spiritual beings. The need for common substantive principles for interaction in a globalized world ought to take into account all aspects of our human existence, yet it also requires the notion of ideal individuality at its center. The theoretical construction of a "moral space" that is appropriate for global interaction cannot make do without ideal individuality, but it should allow for our sense of morality to transcend this ideal individuality as well as the hypergoods of nonliberal comprehensive doctrines that might inform human interaction. Chapter 6 of this book will concentrate on the inner process by which overcoming comprehensive doctrines may be achieved.

Here though, I argue that by conceiving both world and transcendence as real at the same time, the historical view of reality determines a structural differentiation between comprehensive doctrines in a way in which they seem to be absolutely closed off from each other. Monotheistic religions from the house of Abraham have absolute requirements for the believer that pose the alternative "God or nothing" (see Ricoeur 1967a). The enlightened reaction against theistic reality in Europe in the eighteenth century produced practical rationality that would extricate itself completely from such type of alternatives in the ethical life of man. From this enlightened attitude and a close relationship to such type of doctrines, there remains the idea that all religions hold an absolute command for believers. This produces a "theoretical hygiene" in which it is assumed that comprehensive doctrines are lived in essential closure from each other, with no possibility for them to be lived as imaginative mixtures of their symbols and cross-cultural values that are cognized emotionally. Human creativity has it that such diversity of traditions as there are in the world will have different rules of practice to achieve what is considered to be good in a human life. Likewise, their cosmological tales present themselves in such a rich variety of forms that it might seem natural that they remain closed up within themselves.

However, I believe that the borders of comprehensive doctrines are generally more porous than many political philosophers concede. Granted, some traditions (mostly those that come from the house of Abraham) require for their borders to be firmly established and membership sanctioned by specific requirements (sometimes by birth within the group). Nevertheless, this conception does not necessarily hold in many comprehensive spiritual and philosophical traditions in the world, specifically the ones that are legitimized in transcendental mysticism. In the case of historical or Judeo-Christian–Islamic traditions, when the modern individual sense of self has acquired a degree of validity for the human group—and global interaction makes this happen—people can see worth and validity in comprehensive doctrines other than their own. As has been said, the liberal-individual sense of self finds itself entangled with conceptions of the good that may come from different symbological sources and traditions. What gives them their unity—not necessarily their coherence in practice—is the individual consciousness that tells her own tale and adapts and adjusts the values she takes from different traditions. Ideal individuality is a product of culture that is the substantive basis for well-ordered modern political associations, but people within such associations will use in practice the symbols that bring substance to their lives in spite of their own cultural inheritance—especially in modern environments where the individual sense of self thrives.

As has been argued above, the way we interact in global Modernity and in modern institutions (the state, the market) requires that we see ourselves as rational individuals within such interactions and institutions. We should bear in mind though that in spite of this seeming natural to us, as Charles Taylor objects, modern individuality is a product of a particular cultural context and history. It is so close to ourselves that it is very hard to see. Nevertheless, this cultural product holds the substantive principles that managed to overcome religious or sacred representations of substantive reality and rooted such representations in the transcendental, albeit embodied, individual self. The Kantian representation of the rational and moral subject is rooted in a sacred prehension of the self that cannot be genetically extricated from its transcendental roots. The historical type of reality contemplates its own universal identity as an extension of the eternal diachronic, linear progression of time in universal history—there are moral undertones in the name of this curricular subject taught in universities to young minds. *Telos*, the concept that MacIntyre borrows from Aristotle, is experienced or reified as a life-quest that does not end. In Kant's *noumena*, "immortality," one of the concepts that cannot be known but must be thought, signals the moral aspirations of the individual self that must act in history. Such aspirations to universality show us that liberalism is a comprehensive conception of the good life in which the construction and experience of human individuality ought to be enacted as a constant moral and even spiritual disciplined practice. The scrupulous maxim of knowing oneself is related to the reflexive consciousness and conscience of the moral individual. This scrupulousness may result in Kafkian pathological guilt, or even violent exclusion of the nonmodern other, but no discipline or source of order is situated beyond the constant danger of exerting too strong a force on people that it may actually crush them or urge them to crush each other. However, escaping the dangers in comprehensive doctrines of the good life (including liberalism) is the constant moral–ethical predicament of human beings.

A common substantive basis for contemporary humanity is essential for interaction in global environments, yet we should bear in mind that world diversity demands that people build and sustain borders between themselves, and between them and the world to be able to approach reality in any way. Humans use symbols and conceptual tools to interact with each other and with the world. I believe that the most essential moral predicament of humanity lies on the appropriateness of the relevant borders that we build between each other, and between us and the world in order to interact. We need those borders, for they also give us the ability to grasp the difference between things and mental substances, and their similarity, in order for languages and systems of symbols to produce sense and meaning. Borders between people, and between people and the world may be very useful, they help us grasp aspects of the world that would otherwise remain undifferentiated and blended into the whole; they put us close to factual knowledge and help us categorize and understand it in ways that can be very helpful practically and technologically. This is the reason why, in this book, I have postulated language as one of the essential materials of which views of reality are made. And yet, borders may become terrible and insensitive things that may help us evade ourselves, not see, be careless, be blind to aspects of reality that lay beyond the secure borders that contain objective sets of rules. This is the reason why the human systematic need to build borders carries in itself a constant moral predicament, one that is present at every instant of embodied interaction and cannot be solved in *a once and for all* manner. And so, a common substantive basis for interaction in global times is rooted in individual awareness of this constant predicament and also on the fragile essence of the ideal of individuality. Human consciousness of a scope wider than our embodied individuality could also be seen as a source of universal validity, but this type of validity lies beyond language, which my mystic ideal type of reality will clarify in chapter 5. Here, I want to concentrate on how the concept of individual worth, which has a providential ancestry, occupies a central place in the liberal tradition of thought, and why this ought not to be ignored, or elegantly sidelined, in order to be able to produce substantive basis that will be appealing to all individuals and comprehensive doctrines alike.

In his book, *Political Liberalism* (1996), John Rawls wants to outline substantive principles of justice that legitimate the idea of public reason as the common basis for the liberal type of public order. According to Rawls, his political principles of justice are based on the conception of persons as free and equal and so "with a duty of civility to appeal to public reason" (Rawls 1996, 226). In other words, in human interaction, resorting to public reason is legitimate because it guarantees that people recognize that all are free and are of equal worth *qua* individuals. He argues that this is the common assumption for all types of political liberalism, which he insists in conceiving as merely political, not metaphysical (see Rawls 1985). Rawls gives his version of political liberalism a type of neutrality—justice as fairness— that he postulates as appropriate for ruling substantively the public sphere of interaction—and leaving the private realm to be ruled by whatever comprehensive doctrine individuals may find appealing or real. This, to Rawls, constitutes the common substantive basis for liberal political associations that dispense with metaphysics, and yet, it is not merely a pragmatic arrangement. I will discuss, following Habermas, the problem of this merely political conception. Rawls conceives of political liberalism as a moral position that can organize the public life of individuals whose comprehensive conceptions of the good life are diverse (and reasonable). He insists that this view "offers no specific metaphysical or epistemological doctrine" (1996, 10), and in doing so, he seems to be answering to communitarian objections about the essence of self in his "original position" and "veil of igno- rance" in his *A Theory of Justice* (1971) (asocial, unencumbered, artificially disembedded). These objections lead toward the theoretical problem of justifying a common substantive basis for interaction in modern societies. Rawls summarizes the two elemental question of his enquiry in this book as "how is it possible for there to exist over time a just and stable society of free [and equal] citizens, who remain profoundly divided by reasonable religious, philosophical and moral doctrines?" (1996, 3–4). He regards such pluralism as the unavoid- able consequence of interacting in a society based on the principles of freedom and equality. I would add that it is an unavoidable conse- quence of the way people are constituted as imaginative and emotional beings.

Jürgen Habermas criticizes Rawls's need to extricate his theory from metaphysical considerations on the basis of philosophical arguments. I criticize Rawls for the same reasons, although I admire his attempt at looking for common substantive grounds for human–political interac- tion without enshrining one comprehensive doctrine (liberalism) over the rest of them. His theory illustrates a serious attempt at approaching the fact of pluralism as a problem that cannot be solved by merely speaking of "philosophical neutrality" that postulates universal maxims, without caring to look at the arguments of philosophical traditions other than the one with its roots in Europe. Nevertheless, Rawls fails in his attempt because he tries to justify his liberal merely political position, by stripping the liberal tradition of its metaphysical, universal roots, thus, bringing it to a political neutrality that does not hold because it still relies on individual autonomy and worth—the original source of liberal values. According to Rawls, the terms for the possibility of a well-ordered society where individuals see themselves as free and equal exist within the qualifications that he uses for the society as well as for the elements that interact within it. Society, citizens or individuals, and doctrines or comprehensive conceptions of the good might seem like pretty neutral sociological categories. However, if we have a look at the adjectives he uses for them—"just and stable society," "free and equal citizens," and "reasonable doctrines"—we are left with most of the major ingredients for Rawls's idea of what he conceives as an essentially neutral political establishment. My contention is that the above qualifications cannot be neutral, and indeed ought not to be seen as such, in order to prevent the modern view of reality from colliding rather than having a conversation with other comprehensive conceptions of the good life.

A "just" and impartial society, as modeled by Rawls's "original position" and "veil of ignorance," obviates the worth of individuality in such circumstances. Communitarian objections to such portrayal of people are based on sociological arguments that question whether people's sense of individuality can be represented at all in such terms in order to make moral decisions. Rawls's answer to this has generally been to remind them that he is solely presenting a hypothetical mind experiment, and not a realistic portrayal of the experience of self as an individual. Nevertheless, individuality's axiomatic worth remains intact within this experiment. As communitarians have argued, there is much historical and traditional baggage in the assumption that individuals should be seen as free and equal. This assumption has led to the liberal idea that the public arena of interaction should function with principles that differ from those of the private realm. Public principles of justice should be based on the worth of the individual citizen and her rights, and they ought to have a primacy over diverse and often clashing ideas of the good, based on comprehensive religious and philosophical doctrines. Private and diverse manifestations of values, the ethical value of human life, and substantive principles that define ideas of the good should remain in the intimate realm of human inter-action. In other words, we should separate the right from the good and allow for the former to rule the political association where we live. However, there is not much clarity in the mechanisms to separate arti-ficially the private and the public realm in the ethical life of people, and neither are those for the separation of the individual self from its constitutive elements that come from the human group. Rawls pro-poses such separation by means of what he calls the "public use of reason," which leads to the reasonable elements in every comprehen-sive doctrine in order for them to legitimize the substantive basis he proposes for political liberalism.

The impossibility of separating the good from the right in actual human interaction contrasts with the way it is done analytically and theoretically. Of course, to a liberal mind, it is obvious that this is the way one ought to think about human liberty and individual self-determination in principle. Yet, these two realms constantly touch each other in the practice of being an ethical entity. Rawls's limits between the private and the public realms are thus artificial and arranged conveniently when dealing with comprehensive doctrines. When Rawls says that the doctrines or comprehensive views of the good are reasonable when they limit the exercise of their beliefs to the private realm of interaction, he is basically saying that they must value the worth of individuality as much as the democratic–liberal tradition does when it comes to interacting in the public sphere . . . otherwise, they are not reasonable. He resorts again to a cultural imposition of values when he explains his idea of the "burdens of judgment" and how a reasonable conception is able to see those within its own tradition and those within other traditions in order to refrain from imposing its own. He ascribes far too much reflexivity to such doctrines, which is a characteristic of our individual sense of self and our modern intellectual tradition. Further, it relies on the modern individual identity of the people who choose to have faith in the prin-ciples of such doctrines. I have referred above to this characteristic as the individual's ability to be *flexible*, to take distance and contemplate her own beliefs with a critical mind. However, Rawls assumes that this can be done from within any "reasonable" comprehensive doctrine. Sociologically it can, but this will come from the modern identity of those who belong to comprehensive doctrines, for individuality and comprehensive conceptions of the good life are not mutually exclu-sive. But he is thus relying on the modern identity of those who belong to comprehensive conceptions and not in those conceptions themselves.

What Rawls does in his *Political Liberalism* (1996) is to illustrate that political associations need a common substantive basis and principles in order to be able to organize public life at all. This has to do with the American experience of having to deal with various self-contained comprehensive conceptions of the good life within the same political association. His solution to the problem of common principles was to imagine that his "freestanding" political basis ought to be legitimized from within the comprehensive doctrines themselves. This effectively trusts that political liberalism can be appealing to every single comprehensive doctrine for he assumes that—if they are reasonable—there will be what he calls an "overlapping consensus" among comprehensive doctrines that will legitimate the principles of justice chosen by a society modeled as a cooperative scheme of free and equal citizens:

> In such a consensus, the reasonable doctrines endorse the political conception, each from its own point of view. Social unity is based on a consensus on the political conception; and stability is possible when the doctrines making up the consensus are affirmed by society's politically active citizens and the requirements of justice are not too much in conflict with citizens' essential interests as formed and encouraged by their social arrangements. (Rawls 1996, 134)

I regard Rawls's idea of how the public sphere ought to be legitimized by values that come from within "reasonable" comprehensive conceptions of the good as a failed attempt to rid the liberal–political tradition of its universalistic pretensions. To say it with Mulhall and Swift:

> Rawls's latest defence of the limits of the political itself fails to respect those limits; the purely political Rawlsian state must inevitably base itself upon elements of a comprehensive doctrine, and so fails to live up to its own claims to neutrality. (Mulhall and Swift 1996, 245)

The elements that Rawls relies on, and does not make explicit, are the ideal qualities of the individual self that the European Enlightenment produced in the eighteenth century.

Habermas criticizes Rawls for exchanging the Kantian categorical imperative for a new intersubjective category—the overlapping consensus—whose strength emanates from the comprehensive doctrines themselves (1995, 1996, 1998). He contemplates this as a suspicious move, for he regards it as a tuned down portrayal of the political need for legitimation within what Rawls characterizes as "reasonable" doctrines or worldviews. To Rawls, individual people are rational and they are made reasonable by virtue of their belonging to a wider political association that might comprise a variety of closed off doctrines or comprehensive views of reality. The latter are reasonable because they know this plurality and do not impose their own values, as they would not want for other doctrines to impose of their own. This is fair enough, and he attempts to solve the problem of needing a common substantive basis by proposing what he calls political liberalism as such basis, and then strip it from its comprehensive essence, thus escaping the problem of he himself imposing this worldview on the others. That is, he solves the predicament by leaving on the side liberalism's own roots of its claims to universality. Habermas explains that when Rawls speaks of the "reasonable" character of comprehensive conceptions, he is really referring to the *true* character of liberal values for them to have preeminence in public life (1996). To Habermas, this discloses a paternalistic attitude of the philosopher, for Rawls provides the basis for people to agree upon from the outset (his original position) without allowing citizens to enlarge their interpretive perspective by themselves by means of public argumentation:

> If we wish to preserve the principle underlying the Kantian universalization principle, we can respond to this fact of pluralism in different ways. Rawls imposes a common perspective on the parties in the original position through informational constraints and thereby neutralizes the multiplicity of particular interpretive perspectives from the outset. (Habermas 1995, 117)

Habermas has a much wide-ranging proposal that he develops fully in his *Between Facts and Norms* (1998), an explanation of which lies beyond the scope of the present work. Suffice it to say that he believes that he can reconcile the liberties of the ancient world with the modern liberties by proposing a discursive ethics based on practical reason according to Kant. And yet, the problem of the Habermasian project is that he regards as nonproblematic the fact that such enterprise situates the particular European philosophical tradition over and above any other worldview or comprehensive conception of the good. This is inevitable when trying to overcome the problem of a common substantive basis for interaction that is valid for all people and all times solely from within the historical view of reality, as Rawls's failed attempt illustrates.

The problem of a common substantive basis that will be valid in the global realm of interaction remains in contemporary political philosophy. I do not believe that it can be posed as a universal and abstract system of rules, but it cannot dispense with conceptions of universality. We should bear in mind that the contemporary way of interacting in the global arena is a product of much history and culture, and so, the solution can be found as an imaginative construction that allows for various views of reality to overlap. This, in fact, was Rawls's strategy. Nevertheless, his strategy was also to dispense with metaphysics and universal conceptions for the political arena. I, on the contrary, think that liberalism ought to go back, not only to its post-metaphysical grounds for universalism, but also to the sacred roots of individual autonomy as its hypergood. The experience of the inner self in Modernity is a function of the moral self, the one that grounds the categorical strengths of liberalism. This existential value of the self, the transcendental subject, an end in itself, is the only liberal principle similar in stature to Absolute emptiness in the mystic ideal type, and the only grounds for convergence of the two transcendentalist types. I argue that liberalism ought not to make do without these references, even in a secular representation of such principles or in what Jürgen Habermas calls "post-metaphysical thought." I believe the world and global politics is in major need of symbols that will convey a *together-ness* and *one-in-anotherness* that the liberal–political debate is not conceptually equipped to refer to, as it is carried out right now. People ought to imagine at least one universal, common human principle for universalization that lies beyond rationality, and get emotionally attached to it in their own cultural way. Yet, the ongoing human predicament is to keep constructing and revising the narratives that arise from such an ideal: the moment one thinks that a particular narrative may be seen as valid for all peoples at all times, fundamentalism arises. As MacIntyre says,

> When men and women identify what are in fact their partial and partic-ular causes too easily and too completely with the cause of some universal principle, they usually behave worse than they would other-wise do. (1984, 221)

The danger with an abstract liberalism that considers itself to have been completely extricated from its sacred roots is that it is unable to see just how universally imposed principles of rational interaction are a type of veiled fundamentalism. Only the structure of the historical ideal type of reality is in danger of falling into this kind of extreme moral situation. In the next chapter, I discuss why it is that only with a universal principle of love can it break through such rigidities. I pro-pose a form of liberalism that can embrace a hermeneutics of cultures and can see value in every single one of them. This entails a critical hermeneutics of the type proposed by Ricoeur (1981), the critical perspective though should be founded in a refusal to endow practices that hurt other humans (physically, psychologically, and emotionally), based on the one universal emotion that the individual self is able to identify by means of the principle of compassion or universal love. With this principle, I am referring to the mystic idea of universality, based on Absolute emptiness of the self. Only on these grounds (or absence of them) can the individual self attain selflessness, a morally inspired alienating distance from comprehensive conceptions (including liberalism) that can be conceived of as an ideal aspiration toward spiritual Enlightenment. Compassion is the source of the moral principle that we can for now refer to as universal love, which emanates from Absolute emptiness. And this in turn must be put conceptually beyond language, in order for it to be truly universal. This is the only way to emphasize that morality and ethical conduct is a constant human dilemma within a vivid awareness of the synchronic order of events and how they inhere in our own very intimate subjective perspective about reality. In chapter 5, I show why, and the best way to characterize it and identify oneself with it is the present moment of meaningful interaction.

5

The Mystic Ideal Type
of Reality

The mystic ideal type of reality is rooted in transcendence as the legitimate essence of what is considered to be real. This type of reality is expressed in metonymic verbal structures and symbols, as worldly references that are *put for* a reality that lies beyond the world. However, metonymy always remains short of conveying the experience of what Voegelin calls "hierophany," or universal openness of the self, conceived of as interaction with the divine root to human existence. Mystic reality is experienced in spiritual Enlightenment that can only be reified synchronically in an ongoing eternal present moment, which views past and future as determining worldly life. From the mystic perspective, the latter is seen as an illusion of our attachment to our external mundane needs, which are temporary, and so they ultimately lack the permanent and real essence of transcendence. In the second section of chapter 4, I have discussed the transhistorical conception of the synchronic aspect of time, or the simultaneous order of events in time, in contrast to the sequential order of events in legitimate time as diachrony in history. In this chapter, I want to explain, on the one hand, how it is that the mystic view of reality situates itself beyond diachronic time, and on the other, how it is that this position allows for a philosophical conception of universal compassion that is conceived of as absolute synchrony, as simultaneous mutual recognition of universe and self. In chapter 6 of this book, I argue that universal compassion discloses the synchronic realm of time in human experience and that *trust* lies within this order of events in simultaneity. And so, it is useful to define the philosophical conditions for awareness of the synchronic order of events in time, where trust resides. The mystic ideal type of reality discloses the temporal basis for the construction of a *common human moral space*. This common moral space will be based on the simultaneous presence of universal compassion and moral reason, toward a liberal–cosmopolitan moral philosophy of the human self under contemporary conditions of globalization.

Universal compassion, conceived in the way I propose and not merely as a particularistic emotion, gains the stature of a philosophical universal category. And yet, moral reason cannot be dispensed with. I believe that moral reasoning and universal compassion can be seen as complementary in the ethical life of people. This is the reason why I explain how this can come about with the construction of a common human moral space in the concluding chapter of this book based on a hermeneutical–critical methodology. Universal compassion is the ideal source of benevolence, which in political theory has generally been regarded as a problematic category as it is displaced from the realm of rational analysis. However, the synchronic essence of universal compassion and benevolence discloses a realm of time where events are ordered in simultaneity with respect to each other. This synchronic realm of time organizes trust and trusting behavior that is even more crucial than benevolence to sustain modern–liberal interaction (economic, civic, political, democratic). In this chapter, I attempt to point at the experiential and imaginative sources of universal compassion. I refer to *experience* and *imagination* because the philosophical portrayal of universal compassion is aware that this type of emotion cannot be apprehended through the powers of abstraction. Universal compassion remains beyond language and representation, ultimately standing on the experience of Absolute emptiness or what Keiji Nishitani calls *sunyata*.

I have stated that universal compassion lies beyond particularity, but fraternal compassion, together with its related emotions—sympathy, empathy, pity, mercy—are seen as conceptually inferior or "underdeveloped" with respect to the idea of moral reason, in spite of the constant acknowledgement of the importance of these emotions to our ethical life. This is illustrated by the debate in moral psychology between Lawrence Kohlberg and Carol Gilligan, who in her *In a Different Voice* (1982) postulated what she considered a novel orientation in ethical decisions, an "ethics of care," that is of a different quality yet complimentary with what she calls an "ethics of justice," or morality based on universalizable principles of action. The "ethics of care" highlights our embodied humanity as needy and vulnerable, instead of idealizing it as ultimately individual and autonomous from constitutive elements of self, and so, it is congenial with communitarian objections to abstract individualism. Yet, the problem of an "ethics of care" is that it remains parochial and confined to personal ties:

> An ethics of care, it may be argued, is ultimately inadequate from a moral point of view for the objects of our care and compassion can

never encompass all of mankind but must always remain particularistic and personal. An ethics of care can thus revert to a conventional group ethics, for which the well being of the reference group is the essence of morality . . . An ethics of care yields a non-universalizable group morality. (Benhabib 1992, 181)

As I have said, it is generally obviated that our finite and embodied condition is displaced in its particularity from constantly experiencing and practicing the soul-enlarging emotion of universal compassion. Nevertheless, I argue that it is enough to be able to imagine that someone on earth can be (or could have been) the embodiment of such awareness to motivate people emotionally toward conversion, universalistic spirituality, religious faith.[1] The role of the spiritual leaders and masters who originate universalistic religions is to be the embodiment of such absolute emotion. Universal compassion (*karuna, agape*, religious love) may remain unattainable on a regular basis by common people, but it does not fail to inspire and move vast masses of believers, even if from a secular perspective it is only regarded as an imaginary possibility.

Nevertheless, universal compassion need not be conceived as a mere religious category, and thus dismissed as useless for political theory. I believe that this type of emotion can be isolated from its religious undertones philosophically in order to postulate it as a useful *ideal*. This ideal is congenial with the ideal of individuality that I have proposed to regard as such in chapter 4. I argue that it is desirable that the modern individuals be moved by universal compassion in their moral reflection in an analogous way as actual embodied people are moved by compassionate historical figures, such as Mother Theresa. I argue that moral reason is incomplete without the notion of universal compassion and I postulate universal compassion as the one ideal emotion that can be the philosophical basis to ground the conception of a universalizable "ethics of care." I argue that this concept may become the grounds for the legitimacy of compassion in ethical reflection, with a stature commensurable with the notion of the autonomous morally reflecting individual. The fact of plurality, the diversity of worldviews, cosmologies, and/or comprehensive conceptions of the good life in the world requires imagination and emotional investment in the construction of a possible common ethical basis for global interaction. This global realm already inherits modern institutions, such as the state, the market, and the law, and modern technological capabilities to put in touch people around the world. These communication technologies are constantly changing, being updated, and the interaction that they aid is ultimately based on actions of embodied individuals who may have an emotional attachment to ideal individuality.

As I have argued in chapter 4, individuality is a *practice* and an ideal that is constantly reinvented in a variety of cultural environments, and it is desirable that people aspire to an emotional cultivation of historical individuality, in MacIntyre's way, in a quest for excellence. Here I want to propose that although the practice and quest for an ideal individuality is desirable, it is certainly not enough to sustain moral reflection when facing the fact of the diversity of worldviews in the global realm of interaction. I argue that historical individuality ought to situate itself philosophically within present awareness of universal synchronicity to allow for an ethical reflective exercise of the expansion of the self beyond the individual self. This present awareness may be regarded as ideal, yet only here will it lie beyond its universalistic diachronic temporal horizons that confine it within a Judeo-Christian type of judgmental morality. In the first section of this chapter, I discuss Nishitani's concept of Absolute emptiness, experienced as the dissolution of the personal ego-self that identifies itself with the universe. I explain how this experience is rooted beyond the diachronic order of events in time, which nonetheless discloses awareness about the immediate embodied realm in an essential connection with everything and everybody else. In the second part, I discuss how Absolute emptiness is related to the ideal of universal compassion and I contrast this notion with how compassion is conceived of in the historical tradition, following Martha Nussbaum's admirable *Upheavals of Thought* (2001). From the perspective of the mystic ideal type of reality, this chapter defines what I consider to be the conceptual elements lacking in the historical ideal type of reality in order to be able to define a common substantive basis for global interaction.

BEYOND HISTORY: ABSOLUTE EMPTINESS AS A PHENOMENOLOGICAL CENTER FOR UNIVERSAL MORALITY

Even if Absolute emptiness cannot be described, as its experience lies beyond language and symbols, here I refer to it as a useful "signpost" to organize a universally relevant realm of morality as compassion. I have said that Absolute emptiness lies beyond diachronic historical time and I show this by a discussion of its conceptual constitution as compared to what I call the historical view of reality. This view of reality hosts the philosophical tradition that has its roots in Israel and Greece, is then assimilated into Christianity, and finally becomes secular in academic European circles that have now been exported all over the world.[2] Absolute emptiness or *sunyata* is a spiritual existential experience that takes place through the field of nihility, or the vivid awareness of nothingness as the root to existence. A radicalized emptiness is the root source of newness and impermanence, and thus it discloses its temporal quality within the eternal present moment, where both the positive and negative aspects of life are encompassed. While in institutionalized Christianity evil is willfully expelled through repression into a mythical realm of eternal damnation, in mysticism, it is apprehended and dissolved in the midst of the transcendental source of experience. The mystic self is not related to the embodied personality, but to the collective sacred mind—the essence of mystic notions of selflessness or non-ego. Here I resort to the language of Eastern spiritual traditions, such as Taoism, Buddhism, and Hinduism, where the mystic type of moral reality, an orientation to the "near side," has an ascendance over an orientation to the "far side" in what I have defined as the historical type of reality.[3] While in the Western philosophical tradition, oneness is the negation of multiplicity and differentiation is a dialectical opposition of concepts, in mystic Eastern traditions, oneness and multiplicity are enfolded in an absolutely empty unity that must be cognized existentially through the field of nihility. In Absolute emptiness, infinity is conceived as the spiritual entwinement of all things, where things are contemplated in their *suchness*.

The Indian philosophical duality that precedes the notion of Absolute emptiness is couched in the oneness of *Brahman* and *atman*, which could be considered as analogous to Judeo-Christian notions of Divine Being and the self. However, the unity of *Brahman* and *atman* is expressed only in negative terms "as the seer who cannot be seen and the knower who cannot be known" (Abe 1985, 125). Christianity saw the oneness of this duality in the idea of Godly Being from which everything emerges in all its multiplicity. The Greek duality is symbolized by Plato in the "mystery of *being* as existence between the poles of the One (*hen*) and the Unlimited (*Apeiron*)" (Voegelin 1974, 184). But in Greek philosophy, nonbeing is merely a privation of being (Abe 1985, 122). This illustrates that, in the historical type of reality, the positive side of being is stressed and the negative is expelled to oblivion or to a realm of "nothingness," which effectively constitutes a domain of darkness that human is engaged in dissolving through intellectual knowledge and substantial rationality:

> To sum up, in the West such positive principles as being, life, and the good have ontological priority over negative principles such as nonbeing, death, and evil. In this sense, negative principles are always apprehended as something secondary. By contrast, in the East, especially

in Taoism and Buddhism, negative principles are not secondary but co-equal to the positive principles and even may be said to be primary and central. This is so in the sense that the realization of negativity is crucial to reveal ultimate Reality, and in the sense that the nameless Tao or Emptiness is realized as the root-source of both positive and negative principles in their relative sense. (Abe 1985, 133)

Emptiness at the root of both positive and negative principles discloses a realm of historicity that does not constitute itself as a factual universal program for the union of humanity (historical reality), but which produces a fertile ground for personal contemplation of fault in present suffering and about redemption in the experience of present compassion.

The field of *sunyata* is displaced from description, but a field of immediate ontogenetic historicity—regarded as *illusory*—is disclosed around this transhistorical realm of legitimate reality, situated in the absolute "near side" of self (or no-self). It therefore reveals a realm of morality that the secular universal program of human historicity expels to oblivion in its institutional and factual diachronic structures, but which is present in the religious Judeo-Christian tradition as *agape* or divine love. In *karma*, the immediateness of personal involvement with everything else that exists, not only with one's own factual fate, but also with that of all other beings—which involves one's own constant actions, emotions, and thoughts—puts emphasis in a factual universal historicity that, nevertheless, is not legitimate reality. This realm of immediate factual historicity, however, acquires consubstantiality with respect to Absolute emptiness that constitutes ultimate legitimate reality, the source of all that we experience for it carries the universe within. Here, ego or personality is experienced as unreal: "In the Existenz of non-ego, non-ego does not mean simply that self is not ego. It has also to mean at the same time that non-ego is the self" (Nishitani 1982, 251), or that "I am the universe" where "I am" is not me *qua* ego. According to the enlightened masters of this tradition, this experience is therefore absolutely humbling and absolutely empowering. The experience of Absolute emptiness is therefore real in its existential *realness*, but its source is the universe itself, not mediated by a sacred personality or a monotheistic God, and even less by subjective or objective cognition of the individual self. Experience as universe is also particular experience at the same time and this simultaneity can only be lived in the *hierophanic* discovery (or invention) of transcendence, the mystic moment of union to the divine root of existence, or Absolute emptiness (*sunyata*). According to Nishitani, this is illustrated in the mysticism of Meister Eckhart: "Absolute nothingness signals, for Eckhart, the point at which all modes of being are transcended, at which not only the various modes of created being but even the modes of divine being—such as Creator or Divine Love—are transcended" (1982, 61).

The mystic "near side" of a transhistorical realm as Absolute emptiness and legitimate reality is nonobjectifiable, as it transcends the "subjectivistic nihility" of existential nihilism (Nishitani 1982, 98) and acquires the dimensions of what can only be considered as an ideal type. This ideal may be compared metonymically to *pure subjectivity* from an objectivist discipline like ours, but Absolute emptiness is not identical with it for subjectivity presupposes the ontology of an individual self. Absolute emptiness cannot be found in empirical reality, not because it may not actually be experienced or lived by humans, but because it is displaced ontologically from being observed scientifically, just like love. Absolute emptiness as *sunyata* or as the point where all modes of being are transcended is an absolute abyss, "an abyss for the abyss of nihility" (Nishitani 1982, 98). In that field, the self as ego is unreal, as it has identified itself experientially with the universe. We could use a metonymic verbal structure to say that self in *sunyata* is analogous, but not identical, to being a collective self in the experienced actuality and connection of all things. But *sunyata* is a spiritual realm immanent to the world, where difference is unreal, yet experienced in its substantial manifestation—diversity is real, but irrelevant in this essential union. This is how self is collective: in connection with all other things. This is not only an anthropomorphic self as personality, but also one for whom experience and universe are the same thing and so are multiplicity and oneness. To illustrate this position in the Christian tradition, Nishitani resorts to the figure of St. Francis of Assisi:

> The case of St. Francis may be rather exceptional in Christianity, but it serves us with at least one example of religious Love overstepping the boundaries of the human to reach out to all things. (Nishitani 1982, 281)

For the anthropomorphic self, the end in itself is the human self, the transcendental subject, the one that lives in historical universal human time. This standpoint defines the limits of the integument of culture with respect to nature (and inadvertently also with respect to other less "civilized" cultures), with the intention of excluding nature from the human world. It corresponds to the archaic metonymic definition of borders between the sacred and the profane, only in the shape of the human and the natural—or culture and nature—in secular reality. This movement defines for Nishitani an essentially dogmatic point of view that shelters a self-contradiction in the relationship between the "thing in it self" and objective "reality":

> [T]he Kantian critique with its split between two completely irreconcilable modes of being, phenomenon and noumenon, came to be advocated. On the standpoint of *sunyata*, where these two irreconcilable modes of being are pushed to their limits, they are both seen to come about as one and the same mode of being of the thing. (Nishitani 1982, 138–39)

As discussed earlier, oneness in the Western philosophical tradition is defined as the negation of multiplicity and differentiation, in a dialectical opposition. In contrast to this, mysticism enfolds both oneness and multiplicity in an absolutely empty unity. What this means is that before uniting them in an intellectual relationship, oneness and multiplicity must be cognized existentially through the field of nihility. This involves the knower into questioning her own existence, and moves from the realm of intellectual knowledge or historicity to that of spiritual knowledge:

> The questions brought up by nihilism, at first heeded by only a few gifted thinkers have since come to haunt us in modern life. In Nietzsche, and in more contemporary figures like Heidegger, for instance, nihilism is dealt with on the horizon of the so-called "history of being." This sort of situation does not exist in the East. Still, the East has achieved a conversion from the standpoint of nihility to the standpoint of sunyata. (Nishitani 1982, 168)

This is a spiritual realm because it is directly related to the prehension of one's own death or of one's own self as standing on nihility, leading to what Nishitani calls a conversion to "Great Reality." It depends on a "religious quest" that awakens in human beings when tragedy, disillusion, or even closeness to one's own death *quicken* one's awareness and preoccupation with things religious; "when death, nihility or sin . . . become pressing personal problems for us" (Nishitani 1982, 3).

Only from the field of nihility can the ego be posed as non-ego, and then be reassumed as the spiritual knowing of non-knowing, where there is absolute autonomy (freedom) as the absence of autonomous identity. In the mystic Christian tradition, this nihility is spoken of as the "dark night of the soul," the existential detachment from ego experienced as "the whole being's surrender to the All" (Underhill 1995, 400). Nihility is an essential step to Absolute emptiness of the self because, even if we may posit objective things as independent of our own immediate consciousness, they cannot be seen as independent of nihility:

> No thing, whatever it be, can be divested of nihility. Sooner or later all things return to nihility. Things cannot be actual without being deactualized; things cannot really exist except as unreal. Indeed it is in their very unreality that things are originally real. Moreover, in nihility the existence of existing things is able to be revealed, questioned, perceived. (Nishitani 1982, 109)

Only from the perspective of nihility, which is known existentially, is the self able to move on to an Absolute emptiness that is also known existentially, where self can contemplate itself at one with the universe. It is in this contemplation that infinity can be apprehended. "True infinity as reality," says Nishitani, "refuses to be encountered anywhere but along the path of Existenz" (1982, 177).

Sunyata, then, is described as a "field" of Absolute emptiness only metonymically and for heuristic purposes, because it is experienced as having its center everywhere and its circumference nowhere:

> For multiplicity and differentiation to become truly meaningful, then, the system of being is seen as something that opens up *nihility* as its ground, and not merely as a system of *being*. The circle must not be looked at from within the circle itself, but as something that includes tangents at all points on the circumference. In so doing, it becomes apparent that all those points imply an absolute negation of the orientation to return to oneness at the center (the orientation given to them as properties of a circle), such that each point implies an orientation toward infinite dispersion. They then cease to be merely the defined loci of points situated equidistant from a common center. Of themselves, these points are not merely uniform and undifferentiated. They do not sink into a One that has had all multiplicity and differentiation extracted from it. Instead, each of them displays an orientation toward pluriformity that absolutely denies such a reduction to oneness, an orientation toward infinite tangential dispersion. And these orientations, showing up as they do in a unique manner at each particular point, as belonging only to that point, bring about an infinite differentiation. (Nishitani 1982, 144)

This kind of infinity refers to the entwinement of all things *qua objects* in time both simultaneously and sequentially, and to their spiritual entwinement with each other. This does not only include embodied humans, but also all the orders of things great and seemingly insignificant.

Even if the field of *sunyata* describes its discoveries with respect to the substantial things that we posit as such from the field of consciousness, things are not experienced as having the same kind of substantiality as they do in objective reality because here the self is still a subject. According to Nishitani, the field of objective reality, "on the one hand, it is the field on which things come to display what they are in themselves; and on the other, the field on which we grasp what things are in themselves. Such are the distinguishing features of the field of logos or reason" (1982, 113). From the field of Absolute emptiness, though, knowledge and praxis are indistinguishable; this is where things are known in their absolute suchness. Here, the existence of things is not cognized as how they appear to us; rather, it is experienced as the mode of being of things as they are in themselves, which means to say, how they are in their own "home-ground."

To give us an idea about the notion of the home-ground of things, their suchness, from the standpoint of *sunyata*, Nishitani resorts to metonymic language used in Buddhism to point toward emptiness that entails the knowledge of non-knowing. He refers to old sayings according to which "fire does not burn fire," "water does not wet water," and "the eye does not see the eye," and goes on to argue that these things sustain their own being in their intrinsic suchness by not being able to overstep themselves: Being is sustained by nonbeing.

> Just as the essential function of the eye, to see things, is possible by virtue of the selfness of the eye, whereby the eye does not see the eye itself; and just as the fact that fire burns things is possible by virtue of the selfness of fire, whereby the fire does not burn itself; so, too, the knowing of the subject is rendered possible by the not-knowing of the self in itself. Thus we can say in general that the self in itself makes the existence of the self as a subject possible, and that this not-knowing constitutes the essential possibility of knowing. (Nishitani 1982, 156)

It is only in this field that the self can be experienced as absolutely subjective and free from objectifying reality. But this does not mean that the substantial manifestation of things disappears, only that our existence in time becomes radicalized as a synchronic awareness of things in themselves because we identify with them at their home-ground, in a negation of being that is no mere nihility, but an Absolute emptiness that is an absolute fullness at the same time. Such is spiritual knowledge, which is essentially nondiscursive, since verbal structures can only point at such knowledge but may never aspire to convey it on their own.

However, for Absolute emptiness to be useful in political theory as a concept, it is necessary to be able to use it in the mundane time of daily interaction, and not merely in the mystic exercises of the ones who aspire to spiritual Enlightenment. If we move from Absolute emptiness to the Cartesian "field of consciousness" where things are cognized *qua* objects, we realize that *sunyata* can still be considered from the *present moment of meaningful experience* as an ideal signpost.[4] Absolute emptiness can be seen as lying in the "near side" transhistorical realm to organize moral experience, as explained in the second section of chapter 4. Two concepts—*ontogeny* and *phylogeny*—emerge from evolutionary biology and are useful to illustrate the kind of historicity that emerges from the historical and mystic types of transhistorical realms.[5] Ontogeny denotes the individual lifetime of living beings, and phylogeny, the evolution of a species through time. If we translate these biological concepts into historical ones, giving them the relationship between personal history and universal human history, respectively, we could relate ontogeny to our embodied present as living beings and phylogeny to the known history of humanity. We could also say that the historical facticity of the mystic type tends toward ontogeny, while that of the historical type tends toward phylogeny. Nevertheless, this arrangement can only be done phenomenologically and synchronically, that is, from the present moment of meaningful experience. The whole organizational symbology of both types of tradition cannot be overlapped diachronically onto each other because they follow divergent symbological paths in human imagination. In this manner, the mystic diachronic consciousness can be seen to organize an "ontogenetic" type of historical facticity—related to a particular life path, which is nonetheless illusory—while the historical consciousness can be seen to organize a "phylogenetic" type of historical facticity legitimated as real—or the life path of historical humanity.

When we pose *sunyata* while standing in the present moment of meaningful experience, it can be done as an aspiration or an ideal, much in the same way as I have already discussed autonomous judgmental individuality also as an ideal. Absolute emptiness lies beyond history and yet can disclose this aspect of our factual existence from the transhistorical "near side" ideal mystic realm. Nevertheless, the identification of self and universe aspires to an ideal union of the self with all that exists. In contrast to this, in the historical "far side" transhistorical realm, the self aspires to an ideal separation of the self from its human and natural background, which is never complete, but which aspires to produce autonomous moral judgment. This autonomy is the one basic principle or "hypergood" of liberalism, essential to produce moral reflection and universalizable principles of action. However, this is done in the recognition that this disciplinary principle must be based on some form of *mythos*, just like that of any other discipline. What we are left with is two disciplinary realms that are helpful to establish the relationship between two types of ethical reflection from the present moment of meaningful experience: ideal Absolute emptiness that tends to the transhistorical "near side" a transcendental union with the universe, and moral autonomous individuality that tends to the transhistorical "far side" to take a transcendental distance from the world and judge it accordingly. I have explained how the ideal of Absolute emptiness discloses awareness of an immediate personal historicity, a realm of present synchronic existence and involvement with all other things and living beings, which the temporal horizon of the historical type of reality is displaced from contemplating. I now turn to discuss how universal compassion arises from Absolute emptiness in this temporal realm of synchronicity.

COMPASSIONATE MORALITY: TOWARD A LIBERAL–COSMOPOLITAN POLITICAL PHILOSOPHY

In her *Upheavals of Thought* (2001), Martha Nussbaum poses the question of whether emotions are suitable to guide our ethical reflections as adults and if there are any reasons to rely on people's emotions: "Why should a social order cultivate or appeal to emotions, rather than simply creating a system of just rules, and a set of institutions to support it?" (2001, 298). In order to answer this question, she investigates the emotion of compassion and how it has been regarded in moral and political philosophy as having good consequences when displayed in human interaction. She considers the "resources for good" in compassion, as well as its limitations as a source of ethical reflection. The result is an investigation of the "cognitive structure of compassion" as an emotion that is "most frequently viewed with approval in the tradition, and most frequently taken to provide a good foundation for rational deliberation and appropriate action, in public as well as private life" (Nussbaum 2001, 299). I argue that Nussbaum explores the subject of compassion as a particularistic emotion (and its related ones—empathy, sympathy, pity, mercy) due to the fact that she does this solely from the perspective of what

I call the historical ideal type of reality. Compassion in this tradition or view of reality, as I have mentioned before, is seen as limited because of its particularistic *essence*. In contrast to this, I argue that when taken away from the historical diachronic temporal horizon and seen as emanating from Absolute emptiness, compassion can be conceived as a universal moral principle and not as a mere mundane emotion. Universal compassion, as I have defined it here, lies beyond the historical time horizon as it is located in an eternal present where past and future are ultimately illusory. In what follows, I discuss Nussbaum's position on compassion who argues convincingly that it is essential to moral reasoning. Nevertheless, her reflections being located within the historical type of diachronic timeframe, regard compassion as a particularistic and mundane emotion, and thus displaced from producing universalizable moral principles. I discuss why compassion is conceived as essentially particularistic when considering it from within the structure of historical reality, and I explain how compassion can be regarded as a universal principle of morality when seen as emanating from Absolute emptiness. Universal compassion is then an ideal that organizes an orientation to moral conduct that is lacking in the ideal of human individual autonomous will that is able to accept, internalize, and obey rational rules.

Nussbaum defines compassion as "a painful emotion occasioned by the awareness of another person's undeserved misfortune" (2001, 301). She follows Aristotle to postulates three cognitive elements of compassion: First, the belief that the suffering one witnesses is serious rather than trivial; second, the belief that the sufferer does not deserve her plight; and the third is the "eudaimonistic judgment," which comes in two steps. Initially, there is a belief that great undeserved suffering may happen to anyone, including me, which is the judgment of similar possibilities. This last element may not be essential for compassion, but it is initially postulated as an epistemological principle that bridges the gap between one's own goals, the judgment according to which "others (even distant others) are important part of one's own scheme of goals and projects, important as ends in their own right" (2001, 320). This is the second step that constitutes the "eudaimonistic judgment" as an essential cognitive element for the feeling of compassion. Based on this cognitive element, it is remarkable that Nussbaum finds a relationship between compassion manifested in altruism and the moral point of view that John Rawls built in his *A Theory of Justice* (1971): "Rawls himself invites the comparison, stating that he has attempted to model benevolence in an artificial way, by combining prudential rationality with constraints on information" (Nussbaum 2001, 340).

In other words, self-interest is the root-source of compassionate eudaimonistic judgment, much in the same way as it is the basis to want a just society in Rawls's terms. But Nussbaum poses no hypothetical reflective exercise; she considers self-interest as a developmental point of departure in the ethical life of a human being: Children will learn to be compassionate by recognizing that they have similar possibilities of suffering, identifying themselves with the sufferer, deploring the fact that anybody should suffer greatly and undeservedly, and thus elevating the other (even distant others) in their appreciation. I cannot but agree with Nussbaum that this is a desirable process of cognitive development to further people's ability to feel compassion for distant others in their ethical reflection about public life, which ought to be aided by public institutions and more support for education in the arts and the humanities.

The reason why I find these *cognitive elements* of compassion problematic is that when regarded from a historical perspective, they are always determined by cultural particularity. This is where traditionally the major objections to compassion arise: It may be a valuable emotion in certain cases of moral reflection, but it cannot be ensured that when this particular emotion arises, it will lead to proper moral behavior. Fraternal compassion is partial by definition. Nussbaum solves this problem by stating that in spite of partiality, each of the cognitive elements of compassion should be equipped with a correct ethical theory:

> The judgment of seriousness needs a correct account of the value of external goods; the judgment of non-desert needs a correct theory of social responsibility; the eudaimonistic judgment needs a correct theory of proper concern. (2001, 386)

And yet, eventhough I find it admirable that Nussbaum attempts to ground the three judgments on a correct ethical theory for each of them, I observe that she forgets the fact of plurality, of a diversity of worldviews, cosmologies, and conceptions of the good. I do not believe that there could be *correct* ethical theories of the value of external goods, responsibility, and proper concern that would not impose cultural values to the plurality of worldviews by means of so-called philosophical neutrality. This would be the case especially with respect to the first cognitive element: seriousness. Nussbaum accepts that societies and individuals vary in what they take as a serious source of suffering, but she argues that the central disasters to which a human life is exposed are fairly constant. They are constant inasmuch as all people will deal with their own death and that of a loved one, but even death is experienced around the world within a wide variety of symbological universes. In the case of loss or damage to external goods, the spectrum seriousness attached to the same kind of loss across the world will face an even wider variety of perception. The second cognitive element would also be exposed to the same kind of objection, yet I believe that an even stronger one can be elaborated on the basis of its cultural partiality. Nussbaum says that compassion will be felt as long as suffering is not deserved: "Insofar as we believe that a person has come to grief through his or her own fault, we will blame and reproach, rather than having compassion" (2001, 311). I believe that this kind of judgment emanates from a historical type of judgmental morality with Judeo-Christian ancestry. Here, the idea of responsibility of the individual agent takes precedence over compassion, even when seen as a partial and mundane emotion. However, my feelings of compassion are very much in order for a loved person who has made moral mistakes and now suffers for them and even for somebody I do not know who is found guilty and sent to the death row. This latter case is illustrated by the kind of feelings that Camus makes us to feel for Mersault in his *L'Éstranger* ([1942] 1989). I do not agree with defining nondesert as a cognitive element for compassion, where it may justify the presence of this emotion rationally and make it more akin to normative rational thought, but it does not necessarily determine the presence or absence of compassionate feelings in all cultural settings and in every embodied person around the world.

The third cognitive element in compassion that Nussbaum defines is the one judgment that I believe may transcend cultural and contextual particularities. Initially, Nussbaum poses it as the judgment of equal possibilities, the one that is congenial with Rawls's "original position." As has been explained, children learn to be compassionate by means of a qualitative jump from self-centered interests, to being able to imagine themselves in the situation of somebody else who suffers. This is the reason why education in arts and humanities (Nussbaum refers to the literary use of tragic predicaments) may help the imaginative efforts of people in this direction, especially when growing up. This initial judgment is still very much couched in self-interest and, according to Nussbaum, is not yet legitimate compassion. However, it allows for people's imagination and emotional concern to be extended until people genuinely regard the absence of suffering in other people's lives (even distant others) as an important part of their own "scheme of goals and ends." This is the eudaimonistic judgment through which somebody can feel compassion when witnessing somebody else suffering: "She must take that person's ill as affecting her own flourishing.

In effect, she must make herself vulnerable in the person of another" (2001, 319). I believe that Nussbaum considers this a position of "vulnerability" because her own philosophical enterprise is situated within the historical ideal type of reality. In this type of reality, liberalism regards the autonomous individual as a value in itself, and so the individual makes her autonomous self vulnerable when she shares someone else's plight. On the other hand, and from a republican tradition (communitarian), the individual is also a historical entity, a self with constitutive attachments and external needs. According to Nussbaum, compassion is also a type of love in which the self is seen as partly constituted of attachments to other things and persons. The idea of a wider self constituted by its attachments helps us conceive of the possibility to extend such self beyond individuality: "compassion pushes the boundaries of the self further outward than many types of love" (Nussbaum 2001, 300). The problem with an extension of self into its own constitutive attachments is that compassion remains a particularistic emotion, a category that only allows for the self to be extended up to a limited amount of relationships and objects of concern. As will be shown below, the aspect of attachment related to love is problematic when seeing love and compassion as arising from Absolute emptiness.

I propose to contemplate compassion as a universal category. This arises, not from actual human interaction, but from a philosophical position that conceives it as emanating from ideal Absolute emptiness. As has been explained earlier, *sunyata* takes place in an aspiration to merge the self with the universe, which includes people and all living entities as well as everything else. This union is not anthropocentric, and yet it includes the intentional union of the "I" and the other. Here, particular experience can reflect universality in its uniqueness, but this is a spiritual union that does not take place discursively—even as it leaves its marks on ordinary human interaction, in the synchronic figures of forgiveness, compassion, and trust. I will deal with these elements and how they relate to a wider political theory in the concluding part of this book. However, here I want to stress that they are human emotions pointing to the ideal transhistorical "near side" beyond existential nihility, that of *agape* and compassion (*karuna*). This is what Nishitani calls the structure of religious love:

> Here the absolute self-negation that sees the *telos* of the self not in the self but in all things and the absolute self-affirmation that sees the original selfness of the self in all things are one. (Nishitani 1982, 277)

When Absolute emptiness is an ideal of disciplined interaction, one sees oneself in everyone else, each conscious self becomes a monad that will reflect oneself in the constant expansion of consciousness: The other is everyone that I perceive as an embodied self and interaction should lead me to the realization of the illusion of otherness.

Here, it will be helpful to contrast this type of expansion of self with how Husserl conceives of the relationship between transcendental Egos and how they relate to the world and to their own as well as other's mundane or empirical egos. In his *Cartesian Meditations* (1977), Husserl distinguishes a succession of four levels of constitution, and each of them presupposes the one before: First, the constitution of "other Ego," then Ego-community, the objective world, and the last, the constitution of "people as objects in this objective world and as giving worldly sense to transcendental Egos" (Hammond et al. 1991, 215). But this ultimately produces a community of transcendental Egos that can never overcome their individuality, for this is fettered to their worldly sense. According to transcendental phenomenology, every person that I encounter is a transcendental subject that their empirical person refers to. The problem for this type of investigation, as Sartre in his *Being and Nothingness* ([1943] 1995) and Luhmann in his *Social Systems* (1995) contend, is that in it Husserl gives no apparent basis for connecting the consciousnesses of transcendental Egos in what he calls an "intermonadological intersubjectivity." As Ricoeur puts it;

> The descriptive spirit and the requirement of constitution tend to meet but fail to blend into each other for according to the idealistic requirement of constitution, the Other must be a modification of my Ego and according to the realistic character of description, the Other never ceases to exclude himself from the sphere of "my monad." (1967b, 130)

Nevertheless, from a phenomenological perspective, awareness of embodiment allows for diversity in the modality of "appearance." I believe that Husserl's *epoché* or "bracketing" of reality as mere appearance, of suspending judgment about reality's existence, is congenial with the mystic type's contemplation of the world as an illusion of actuality. As the world becomes the "world-perceived-in-the-reflective-life," it is inappropriate to ask at what point the phenomenologist will remove the brackets and establish direct contact with reality. To be able to do that would mean that we are able to access knowledge without limitations. Husserl shares with Kant the attack on traditional theory of knowledge in the sense that his phenomenology conceives of "transcendence" as the external world that transcends my experience, my sphere of ownness:

> Husserl has a different idea of what "transcendence" is. One has experiences of something "out-there." This "out-there" is an aspect of

the experience. One experiences, for example the die, with all its horizons, as something which is an object which goes beyond one's particular perception or experience of it. One has a sense of what is beyond particular experiences; but it is a sense which is explicated by describing all the other possible experiences which are implicit in the actual one. It is seen as transcendent because one can never have all the possible experiences of it. That is the sense in which the transcendent world "goes beyond" experience. One has this *sense* of the transcendent; and for Husserl this is all we need. (Hammond et al. 1991, 85)

And so, the only reality that there is, is the one articulated by the transcendental Ego about the transcendent reality, the consciousness that grounds any phenomenological experience of reality. Again, this is congenial with the reflexive orientation to the "near side" transhistorical realm, to Absolute emptiness. In this reflexive orientation, the self is existentially vividly aware of the suchness of people in bodies, living entities, and things, whose existence is based on their nonexistence, in their constant de-actualization and renewal, and so may be considered a mere appearance. The problem of intermonadological intersubjectivity, the union of transcendental Egos, cannot be solved for the purposes of producing valid knowledge. However, it may be solved philosophically in awareness that Absolute emptiness allows for them to merge in an ideal all-encompassing emotion of universal compassion or perfect love.

Universal compassion arises in the synchronic moment of mutual recognition of self and universe, and moves ethically toward contemplation of the "near side" transhistorical realm. This is an ideal or an ethical orientation that moral reflection cannot dispense with. I argue that only from the perspective of universal compassion can we overcome non-compassionate objectification of the other, where the master objectifies the slave through exploitation and the slave objectifies the master through desire. The relationship between the self and the other is complementary from a synchronic perspective of phenomenological observation. It is in this sense that Luce Irigaray considers that only the gaze of the Buddha in "selfless, nurturant relation to the world" escapes the dialectics of domination (Jay 1993, 538). The synchronic perspective of the mystic type is based on an absolute "near side" of transhistorical reality as *agape* (religious love) and *karuna* (compassion). In contrast to this, the divided universe of the historical type of reality between world and transcendence is unable to conceive of universal union with the other because it sees the realm of wrongness as real, and its existence is regarded as a border horizon with otherness—even if there is an assumption, in the notion of progress, that this horizon will eventually disappear. It is important to bear in mind that this division came by through a *particular* cosmological *mythos* and a culturally determined vivid awareness of individual responsibility (see chapter 4, third section).

In spite of this critique on moral reflection that is solely based on historical reality, the ideal of autonomous individuality has produced and grounded institutions that sustain and coordinate global interaction. It is important to stress that the historical view of reality is an essential step in the development of human creativity toward the possibility of global interaction. The moral individual, even if produced by contrast to evil, is a gem of the Judeo-Christian tradition that eventually became secularized in its universalistic responsibility toward the rest of humanity, in its ideal clarity about intentionality, in its intellectual discipline, and in its formal organizational possibilities. The historical possibility of internalizing the concept of universe, even if only as an abstract conception, creates awareness of a shared ideal as the basis of civilized interaction. This kind of refined interaction is produced by belief and practice of autonomous individuality as a universal ideal, but I argue that the synchronic order of events in time brings to the fore awareness about important aspects of modern interaction, which is now global. The new disciplinary chore for our tradition of knowledge is to suspend judgment upon the other, which according to mystic metaphysics, is only a constant judgment upon the "I." If the "I" and the other are not embraced as one, the moral individual remains trapped in an ontological, albeit transcendental, individuality.

For the purposes of moral reflection, I propose the convergence of the ethical orientation to the "near side" and that of the "far side" transhistorical realms—even as we may contemplate them as imaginary. The "far side" orientation regards both world and transcendence as real, the lowly world aspiring to reach the exalted transcendence. I have tried to show in chapter 4 that this orientation produces responsible agents with moral scruples. My position is that this ideal individual self ought to encounter the ideal self who aspires to its own dissolution in the emptiness of non-ego. This encounter will organize what I call a *common human moral space* as the basis for a moral philosophy of the global age. Here, it is illustrative to resort to foundational symbols of the historical type as well as of the mystic type. Apocalypse can be seen as a spiritual symbol that signals the end of history in Absolute emptiness, the absolute "near side" of transhistorical reality. This transhistorical realm is seen as an ideal-type signpost around which the synchronic perspective of ethical reflection and emotional involvement can be organized. This synchronic perspective is built here as contemplating both the "near side" as well as the "far side" transhistorical realms simultaneously. These ideal realms that lie beyond history can be regarded as guiding principles for ethical reflection or as ideal–typical signposts that mark different orientations toward universe. The "far side" tendency describes complex multiplicity following the disciplinary mandates of factuality and idealizes the autonomous individual person; the "near side" tendency points toward transcending physical separation and regards human mind as an ideally collective spiritual universe.

"History symbolically ends," says Frye, "at the point at which master and servant become the same person, and represent the same thing" (1982, 91). In the Christian historical symbolism, this possibility has a "once and for all" quality in the life of Jesus Christ, the perfect Son of God, who took the form of a historical character and walked the earth, but it is based on the expectation of an end of time (and the world) in Apocalypse. From a synchronic perspective, it is possible to conceive of this kind of love without the need of a factual Second coming, yet with a symbological one in the acceptance of a transhistorical realm located on the "near side" of the self. From this standpoint, every object of historicity has its origin in Absolute emptiness and the notion of self is extended to everything and everyone. From this standpoint, no intellectual or positive criteria may be defined in order to rule interaction and equality. This is why it still needs the "far side" transhistorical realm to differentiate human rules and agreements that are constantly actualized. Nevertheless, the "near side" is an ideal realm of self from which the most authentic kind of morality emanates without falling into the problems of legalism; it is an ideal realm of universal compassion. As Nishitani puts it:

> True equality is not simply a matter of an equality of human rights and the ownership of property. Such equality concerns man as the subject of desires and rights and comes down, in the final analysis, to the self-centered mode of being of man himself. It has yet to depart fundamentally from the principles of self-love. And therein the roots of discord and strife lie ever concealed. True equality, on the contrary, comes about in what we might call the reciprocal interchange of absolute inequality, such that the self and the other stand simultaneously in the position of absolute master and absolute servant with regard to one another. It is an equality in love. (1982, 285)

6

CONCLUSION

In this concluding chapter, I discuss why it is that the source of our morality—the *present moment of meaningful interaction*—ought to be based on compassionate moral maxims that aspire to universal justice, mediated by experience, tradition, and rationality. The present moment of the conscious and embodied self may aspire either to autonomous individuality or to universal compassion, or may regard itself simply as an embodied part of a particular collectivity with its own traditions, but I argue from a phenomenological perspective that these aspirations and conceptions of self are not mutually exclusive and may be experienced at the same time. What this means is that the ethical/moral human self is a lot more complex than it has been generally conceded in political philosophy and that it may go beyond mere individuality. I argue that the only meeting point for worldviews is the synchronic moment of interaction that takes place in the present, which ought to be based on a simultaneous mutual recognition between the self and the other. I also argue that this ought to be a critical–hermeneutical, as well as a compassionate recognition. The reason why this model is able to conjugate all of these theoretical perspectives is because it is grounded on synchronicity: the present moment of simultaneous recognition. A further argument based on this model is that the temporal essence of *trust* abides in the synchronic aspect of human interaction, and it is a better perspective from which to deal with it conceptually. I argue that trust generally escapes the definition of how it is produced because, when regarded from the perspective of diachrony, we can only appreciate its beneficial effects but not its source.

In this book, I have forged the theoretical basis to construct a *common human moral space*, based on the model of human cognition that I proposed in chapter 3 and Keiji Nishitani's transhistorical "near side" and "far side" perspectives as developed in chapter 4. A common human space for the practice of morality is based on what I call the present moment of meaningful experience that is absolutely particular and determined by the cultural worldview conveyed in its referential frameworks (Taylor 1989). Nevertheless, even in the most intimately and particularly determined worldview, cosmology, or personal narrative, I argue that it is desirable that both the *ideals* of universal compassion and autonomous moral reason be the neutral arbiters that could control the arbitrariness of local particularities. Nevertheless, in spite of wrapping the conclusion in such moral universal basis, I assume that this common moral space ought to be defined at the same time as never losing sight of our embodied individuality, our concrete embodiment, which cannot escape the particularities of its local existence. Both of the transcendentalist views of reality (historical and mystic) can only produce moral ideals to be pursued ethically and particularly from each of the concrete corners of the world where people live and experience their particular type of reality. So both the transcendental subject autonomous self *and* the mystic Absolute emptiness are moral ideals that people aspire to by means of disciplined practice—but precisely because of this, they are not reified in human interaction in an absolute manner. In chapters 4 and 5, I argued that in globalized Modernity, it is desirable that the *ideal* of autonomous individuality be complemented by that of universal compassion in people's disciplined practice of being moral selves. Yet, it is important to bear in mind that these ideals are seen as guiding the interaction of an embodied and vulnerable humanity that never ceases to be primitive and embodied, enacting reality in a huge variety of particular narratives and cosmologies (what people believe to be real).

What I call the *global age* refers to the contemporary importance of the global level of interaction in which the main actors are not national states, but embodied individuals connected through organizations. They are the source of ethics in the global realm of interaction for, at that level, all forms of republicanism breakdown—even Habermas's universalistic Kantian republicanism (1998). This is because, at the global realm of interaction, there is no unitary political association backed by what Weber called the "legitimate monopoly of violence," and so, there is no enforceable legal realm of the type that traditionally sustains contractual political philosophy. Granted, there are rules in the global realm of interaction, but they more readily coordinate than govern it. Here, the main problem is not the autonomy of the individual self and how she relates to others through legal and impersonal institutions. Rather, the problem has to do with the question of whether there can be a common substantive basis for global modern interaction that is displaced from the national state type of legality.

To be sure, as has been said in chapter 4, modern institutions—the market and the state—shape the ways in which people interact in the globalized world. And yet I pose the problem this way because this allows us to see our human condition beyond the institutional achievements of Modernity, beyond the comfortable confines of people holding membership to different political associations in the world—which of course, produce different types and qualities of citizenship.

Why do I pose the problem this way, after having insisted that the global realm of interaction is ruled by modern institutions? I believe that an obliged point of departure is the disciplined practice of the modern ideal of individuality and her cognitive ability to lead her life according to autonomously achieved universalizable principles of action. However, as has been explained in chapter 5, this type of morality does not cover all aspects of what it is to be a moral person on the basis of universality. A common human moral space goes beyond modern individuality in order to be able to include the possibility of universal compassion as an ideal. Also, as the primitive type of reality illustrates, this moral space ought to take into account the embodied, vulnerable, and frail aspect of being a human animal, especially when growing up. And so, my proposal is liberal *and* cosmopolitan: It is liberal because it is based on individual and embodied consciousness that practices the *ideal* of autonomous individuality—however imperfectly. It is cosmopolitan because it acknowledges that embodied autonomous individuality is not enough to rule the ethical life of people in general in the world, especially not when interaction ceases to be mediated by modern institutions, and incompatible cosmologies become the justification for conflict. This is the reason why the cosmopolitan element of my proposal is based on a hermeneutical will to *understand* nonliberal human conceptions of the good life, worldviews, cosmologies that coexist with that of individual autonomy—sometimes in the same person. But this simple type of hermeneutics is not all that is needed, for following Paul Ricoeur in his *Hermeneutics & the Human Sciences* (1981), I argue that there is also a need to create the possibilities for a *critique* of such world cosmologies—even of the liberal one—with respect to embodied experience and particular context. And so this common human moral space is the meeting realm for a *hermeneutics of tradition* as well as a *critique of ideology* that can be practiced by an individual embodied self orientated both to moral reason and universal compassion.

My proposal is framed within Ricoeur's challenge of what he characterizes as the "fundamental gesture of philosophy" that discloses an alternative between *either* submitting to the power of history over us for the sake of understanding *or* defying the benightedness of inherited ideas, ideologies, or narratives:

> Is this gesture an avowal of the historical conditions to which all human understanding is subsumed under the reign of finitude? Or rather is it, in the last analysis, an act of defiance, a critical gesture, relentlessly repeated and indefinitely turned against "false consciousness," against the distortions of human communication which conceal the permanent exercise of domination and power? (1981, 63)

Here, Ricoeur refers to hermeneutical consciousness and critical consciousness. He questions the very fact that the fundamental gesture of philosophy be posed as an alternative between these two types of consciousness, and challenges that these gestures be necessarily "foreign and purely hostile" to each other. Rather, he proposes them as complimentary, even if he does not propose to fuse them in the same system. He is well aware that they both aspire to universality from very different perspectives: Hermeneutics is *humble* because it recognizes that people are located in history and context, and also that the basis of what people *can* know is always a particular tradition of knowledge, or "prejudice." Critical theory is *defiant* because it universalizes what Habermas calls the "interest in emancipation," or the necessarily constant and indefinite questioning of concealed forms of arbitrary domination. Nevertheless Ricoeur wants to explore the possibility of hermeneutics and critique to recognize each other as raising legitimate claims, even if they do so from very distinct points of departure. "I readily admit, along with Gadamer," says Ricoeur, "that each of the two theories speaks from a different place; but I hope to show that each can recognize the other's claim to universality in a way which marks the place of one in the structure of the other" (1981, 64). Here, Nishitani's conceptions of the "far side" and "near side" transcendental realms are helpful in explaining why Ricoeur sees in the structure of both theories a place of convergence within the other. These transcendentalist perspectives also allow us to frame the universal ideals of compassion and moral reason within what I am trying to define as a common human moral space.

In the second section in chapter 4, I referred to the "far side" transhistorical realm as the type of transcendence that ideal historical reality legitimizes as real. I have also argued that the conception of universality in any view of reality is genetically tied to that of transcendence. On these theoretical bases, I now want to propose that the transhistorical "far side" realm organizes reality for both hermeneutics and critical theory so that we can recognize one in the structure of the other.

With respect to hermeneutics, its stance values tradition and refuses to judge it from an imaginary absolute autonomous perspective: my tradition produces the disciplinary basis of my knowledge. Hermeneutics creates the possibility for *understanding* particular traditions and this attitude can be said to be critical of abstract ideas of self that do not contemplate history or context. In Gadamer, this may seem as an aspiration to emptiness of self that may be seen as congenial with the "near side" transhistorical realm. However, he never really achieves it, as hermeneutics is tied to ontological assumptions about the reality of the individual historical ego—that is, the ego *qua* embodied personality. This displaces hermeneutics from achieving the Absolute emptiness of the "near side": When the nonreality of the reflecting self is apparent, her "being" is seen as supported by her historical consciousness. With respect to the critical stance though, it is not even close to approaching the "near side": It stands on the substantive basis of emancipation and depends on the "far side" perspective to be able to extricate itself from the ruling ideology, judge, and criticize the hidden workings of power and domination in it. Gadamer's meta-critique, or his "critique of the critique," is very clear when pointing exactly at where the critical substantive basis lies; "an exhaustive critique of prejudice—and hence of ideology—is impossible since there is no zero point from which it could proceed" (Ricoeur 1981, 71). I argue that the "zero point" from which it actually proceeds is precisely the "far side" transcendental realm of historicity.

Nevertheless, I also argue that hermeneutics resorts to that "zero point" as well, as a "far side" organizing principle of time and history—even if it refuses to *stand* on it. In the historical ideal type of reality, the "far side" renders diachrony as the legitimate type of order of events in time, and it is to the legitimacy of this diachrony to which hermeneutics turns when it realizes that it cannot stand on the subjectivity of the reflective self on its own. This is why Ricoeur tells us that a historical consciousness' "prejudice" precedes "judgment": "History precedes me and my reflection; I belong to history before I belong to myself" (1981, 68). This is illustrated by how in his *Truth and Method* (1989), Gadamer rejects the Diltheyan reliance on the conscious self, where subjectivity remains the ultimate source of reflection. The notion of the subjectivity of a conscious self gives credence to the divide between subjective reflection and an objective world, which is characteristic of the Enlightenment. The latter legitimized objectivity as truth while the Romantic tradition saw in subjectivist representations of reality an escape to the totalizing thrust of reason. But, as has been said, this produced a mere opposition that is anyway determined by the Enlightenment's conception of self and reality. In contrast to this, Gadamer rehabilitates phenomenologically the Romantic concepts of prejudice, authority, and tradition in order to find their essence that the Enlightenment devalued, and thus ground consciousness beyond subjectivity. Prejudice to Gadamer is essential for understanding, the point of departure for anyone to know anything further than what they already know. This is grounded in an opposition to the conception of traditional authority that in the Enlightenment is essentially related to blind obedience, but Gadamer highlights that authority is also sustained by recognition. Such recognition makes it possible for traditions to be practiced and handed down in history: "A tradition must be seized, taken up and maintained; hence it demands an act of reason" (Ricoeur 1981, 73). This leads Gadamer to the importance of historical consciousness in such endeavor, which the reflecting subject on her own could not possibly sustain. This marks "the resurgence of the historical dimension over the moment of reflection" (Ricoeur 1981, 68). However, as I have argued in the second section in chapter 4, this historical dimension is organized with respect to the "far side" transhistorical realm. With Gadamer, hermeneutics abandons observation of the ideal autonomous individual self in order to highlight the historical essence of embodied selves who can only reflect within the cultural consequences of such historicity. But the possibility of this type of reflection is ultimately grounded in the "far side" transhistorical realm of historicity; the zero-point that produces indefinite time progression, the organizing axis of such infinity. In contrast to this, in Absolute emptiness, hermeneutic historicity still needs to apprehend the un-reality of the embodied individual in the "near side" transhistorical realm. Thus, both the hermeneutic and the critical consciousnesses are structured with respect to the "far side" transhistorical realm of absolute judgment *and* history.

As I have mentioned, I propose the construction of a common human moral space that takes into account both the "far side" and the "near side" transhistorical realms, as well as the embodied and mundane primitive aspect of being human. In order to do this, I resort to the model of cognition proposed in chapter 3 (see figure 3.1), where the present moment of meaningful interaction lies at the center and is regarded as the source of human experience and morality. This present moment is necessarily determined by its particularity and so I do not intend to define a human space that imposes itself universally and thus cancels particular views of what it is to lead a moral/ethical life. This common space of morality is proposed from a hermeneutic reflexive awareness of the culture-specific analytical tools that it uses. That is, its reflexive basis is modern–liberal thought, even as it includes structurally an interpretation of the "near side" transcendental realm of mysticism. This can only be an interpretation because, according to the mystic *ethos* and practice, this realm must be experienced in silence; it cannot be merely spoken of, for in that way it loses its empty essence. Absolute emptiness as an experience is necessarily silent and so is the "near side" transcendental realm. Nevertheless, as I have argued, the "near side" and "far side" transhistorical realms may be posed as ideals and aspirations. The "near side" realm remains silent and the realm from which we can speak in analytical and abstract language is the "far side" transcendental perspective. From this ideal perspective, both the hermeneutic and the critical modern attitudes toward knowledge are very useful in order to define the cognitive possibilities of the common human moral space that I propose.

This common space has its center in the present moment of meaningful interaction and its moving horizons expand phenomenologically either toward the ideal "far side" or the "near side" transhistorical realms. The latter is characterized by its Absolute emptiness, and so in our mundane musings about an ethical life, it may be seen as an ideal center within the intimate sphere of the present moment, a signpost for our moral orientation to universal compassion. In mystic practice though, Absolute emptiness is conceived to be experienced as a spiritual Enlightenment that necessarily takes place synchronically within the present moment of meaningful interaction—interaction with transcendence, as it were. But this interaction is displaced from the realm of critical or hermeneutic analysis—as I have said, it remains silent because it is absolutely compassionate and absolutely forgiving, and so nonjudgmental in essence. In contrast to this, the "far side" transcendental realm organizes a type of morality that demands constant attention to worldly reality, either in a substantive search for freedom or in an awareness of the universal effects of history on human understanding and knowledge. The morality that arises from the "far side" can be enunciated as universalizable maxims of action, the liberal and critical thrust toward human worldly emancipation, but also the hermeneutic awareness that it is impossible to seek absolute and universal validity for any form of human knowledge.

And so, the ideal movement of critique toward the "far side" defines the critical attitude to *stand* beyond ideology or prejudice in order to judge it, and the ideal movement of hermeneutics away from it defines the attitude to understand the relative validity of all forms of human particularity. From the "far side" transcendental realm emerges critique, the transcendental subject that dares to use judgment instead of appealing to tradition, and so is able to display *moral reason* and arrive at universalizable principles of action. This poses the possibility of considering, both the critical–Marxist tradition and that of the Enlightenment as having a common thrust toward human emancipation—this is illustrated by the intellectual development of a thinker like Habermas, in whom both traditions meet. Critical theory and liberalism share the substantive orientation toward a celebration of human freedom while in the world—freedom from arbitrary power, particular bondage, ideology, tradition. Nevertheless, Ricoeur reminds us that even if we could be too ready to see the critique of ideology as opposed to hermeneutics of tradition, critical theory itself has traditional roots that frame the power of its emancipating mission:

> Critique is also a tradition. I would even say that it plunges into the most impressive tradition that of liberating acts, of the Exodus and the Resurrection. Perhaps there would be no more interest in emancipation, no more anticipation of freedom, if the Exodus and the Resurrection were effaced from the memory of mankind . . . (1981, 99–100)

Ricoeur basically tells us that the liberating mission emanates from a "tradition" sustained by means of its own "prejudices" and principles of authority. Only, it is a tradition of "emancipation" rather than one of "recollection." This is the hermeneutical point in which tradition and critique meet. And so, a common human moral space is both hermeneutical and critical at the same time. It is hermeneutical because it is aware that both embodied individuality and group-ethics cannot be transcended in an absolute manner—not even by means of philosophical neutrality. And it is critical because although it recognizes that it speaks from a transcendental imaginary place, this ideal perspective enshrines the normative principle of emancipation. And so, eventhough both hermeneutics and critique are theoretically organized from the "far side" transcendental realm, they can be placed in an expansive tension with respect to each other: Critique ideally moves toward the "far side" transhistorical realm and hermeneutics structurally moves away from it toward the particularity of contextualized consciousness, which in my model is represented by the present moment of meaningful interaction.

I have defined ideal orientations toward moral reason and critique ("far side") and universal compassion ("near side"), and I have also pointed at how the historical reality that the "far side" transcendental perspective discloses, structures the hermeneutic attitude of understanding particular tradition also sustained by a universal assumption about a *common humanity*. It is to this attitude that I now turn in order to show that the common human moral space that I propose may be *guided* by distinct moral orientations, and yet it will always be framed by particular worldviews and personal narratives—sometimes by a few of them that coexist simultaneously in the present moment of meaningful interaction. The *space* that I refer to is formed during childhood, in the midst of "love and play": Caring relationships and a constant mimicking of the adult particular world where the child grows up. This is congenial with Charles Taylor's representation of the "self in the moral space" in his *Sources of the Self* (1989). Taylor uses spatial metaphors to argue against naturalist reductions of the human self, and to remind us that what he calls frameworks or shared references, especially ethical ones, are culture and context specific:

> To articulate a framework is to explicate what makes sense of our moral responses. That is, when we try to spell out what it is that we presuppose when we judge that a certain form of life is truly worth while or place out dignity in a certain achievement or status, or define our moral obligations in a certain manner, we find ourselves articulating inter alia what I have been calling here "frameworks." (Taylor 1989, 26)

He uses the metaphor of a map to represent the orientation to the good within those frameworks. For the map to be useful in this orientation, the important places need to be marked and people also need to know where they stand with respect to those important places. This representation of a moral space includes three elements: First, "our understanding of what makes a full life" usually related to a comprehensive conception of the good; second, "our sense of respect for and obligations to others" or the fact that human interaction is mediated by socially upheld principles, and last "our sense of ourselves as commanding (attitudinal) respect" (1989, 15), or a sense for personal dignity. An idea of a good life, respect for others, and self-respect—including a display of such attitude in the public sphere—constitute the three moral dimensions that provide the basis for the qualitative discriminations that we make in moral decisions. Taylor is aware that this representation is not without its Western cultural bias, yet it includes some of the elements that we can imagine to be important in the vicinity of the present moment of meaningful interaction. The actual way in which these dimensions, or any others that may arise from culture specific references, can only be approached hermeneutically is by means of an act of understanding through empathy.

The embodied individual, her integrity, and her dignity are also related to how she manages to sustain as valid her worldview or conception of the good. A hermeneutical attitude of understanding ought to be applied in the first instance, to concentrate on the historical and narrative particularity of those whom we interact with. This is the reason why I include the need of a hermeneutic of traditions in this model for human morality. The common human moral space that I propose seeks understanding of the diverse human practices in the world before any critical or liberal judgment is passed on them. Autonomous individuality and a normative direction toward political and/or financial worldly emancipation are not necessarily every single culture's absolute objectives, even if the world order makes them every national state's objectives. One could argue that such hermeneutic attitude before critique may sanction collective practices that may diminish the value of the individual self. Nevertheless, in this moral space, the autonomous individual as an abstract principle does not necessarily have an ascendance over other ethical principles that may arise in a situation where a moral decision has to be made. This space contemplates embodied individuals as prior to abstract individuality and this is the basis for it to conceive of itself as a liberal position. Yet, this is also the basis for seeing how universal compassion, as the alternative moral universal principle, may temper the absolute presuppositions of individual autonomy as the moral basis of modern society under the conditions of globalization. It is remarkable to realize that both universal compassion and the hermeneutics of tradition may be seen to converge in this aspiration, even if they arise from different transhistorical perspectives. In the model I propose, the "near side" is an ideal center that overlaps with the embodied, contextualized, and particular present moment of meaningful experience, while hermeneutics *moves* toward the particularity of this present moment from the "far side" perspective.

Throughout this book I have tried to ground the validity of ideal–typical worldviews alternative to the modern one, in order to highlight the importance of the ideas of *time* and *language* in their construction. As has been discussed, the hermeneutical–critical stance is engaged in an attempt to understand historically and empathically not only the particular ways in which people interact through language, but also judge them from the perspective of worldly emancipation. I now turn to the two perspectives on time that I have referred to in this book: synchrony and diachrony. The historical type of reality, Modernity, contemplates diachrony as the legitimate order of events in time, while primitivity and spirituality converge in legitimizing their cosmological order through synchrony. As has been explained in chapters 3 and 5, there are qualitative differences in this convergence, yet, the disclosure of this realm of time allows for the human self to expand beyond the confines of the embodied individual toward the human group, and farther still, toward the universe itself in Absolute emptiness and universal compassion. The synchronic order of events in time, in simultaneity, is an important source for moral reflection: It helps us see each other standing on the same planet right now and it helps us see that it is not only idealistic to propose a common human morality that contemplates universal compassion, but also an urgent necessity. As has been mentioned before, it is a modern emotion to hold a Faustic fear when facing the power of the modern self and the modern way of knowing and controlling the world; but this is only a cultural habit: The power of Modernity breaks down in the face of our animality in death and also when human faith displaces moral reason as a valid universal basis against fundamental imperatives. When modern institutions lose their power to coordinate human interaction, it can only be reinstalled through the common human language of universal compassion.

The ideals of Absolute emptiness and universal compassion emerge from the "near side" transhistorical perspective and they disclose synchrony as an absolute timeframe for reality. That is, it conceives of no reality apart from the eternal present moment, here and now, a perspective from which all historical time and the stories it tells are considered as ontologically illusory. From the perspective of diachronic historical time, the eternal present of the "near side" has no ontological reality; the movement from past to future in consciousness does. However, one ought to bear in mind that both of these orientations are ideal types. In the daily reality of our embodiment and the concrete world that we experience, both time perspectives can be seen to organize human order. I argue that the historical view of reality of the modern world is still to discover the practical aspect of the synchronic order of time, and this aspect has become more notorious in contemporary awareness about global interaction. In the modern world, we are very familiar with how the diachronic order of events in time organizes interaction, and this is a very concrete aspect of the modern conception of time as a type of commodity. However, the order of events in simultaneity presupposes mutual recognition between the ones who converge in their productive–creative endeavors. Awareness about simultaneity has gained importance in globalization, which in contemporary Modernity has multiplied interaction throughout the world in a much more intense, diversified, and extended manner than ever before in history. Through the global network of communications, we can make part of our daily life relevant facts, and political, economical, social, and even cultural concerns of far away lands almost at the moment when they happen, as well as interact with people in those lands systematically, based on such knowledge. We see in diachronic time the beneficial effects of such interaction, but I have tried to develop in this book the conceptual tools to see that their source is cooperation based on trust, which abides in the synchronic order of events in time.

As has been argued, the mundane experience of trust is an essential element in the preservation of liberal institutions, but trust is one of the most problematic concepts in sociological theories of human interaction (Luhmann 1979; Misztal 1996). I argue that this is the case because trust has a synchronic essence that has not been defined conceptually to approach this "slippery" concept. It is hard to define trust systematically, because it involves emotion, risk, and uncertainty. In her book *Trust in Modern Societies* (1996), Misztal tells us that the concept of trust has many connotations and that the oldest one refers to faith, or trust in a supernatural power that the human being feels dependent upon. Whoever trusts takes a risk under conditions of uncertainty, and in spite of them, and this type of risk is essential in modern interaction. For example, technological innovation—the source of wealth in contemporary Modernity—is a type of trusting behavior that is systematized in big companies, and that can be considered as *heroic* and isolated in small entrepreneurs. In the former, this has become an imperative to remain competitive; in entrepreneurs, one can explain it as a "calling" to an emotional involvement of their personalities with risk. This idea will be expounded upon in a different work, for it lies beyond the scope of the present one. However, trust is not risk, nor is it uncertainty—even if it involves these concepts.

I propose to define trust within the temporal realm of events that happen in simultaneity. The person who trusts, even as she considers past and possible future experience before this decision, at the moment of displaying the trusting behavior, she must suspend judgment: Trust takes place at the realm of synchronicity. Before and after a trusting behavior, many reasons may arise to reflect about the appropriateness of such decision. Yet, the essential instant of trust is absolutely framed in the present and absolutely necessary for cooperation. In interaction, synchrony discloses a realm of events where we are aware of each other's existence in simultaneity, and trust is a synchronic recognition between embodied individuals, without which there is no productive and creative cooperation. And so trust takes place in an embodied recognition of the other in an instant that is empty of past and future. It is essential to realize that human interaction and cooperation in general are made of such moments, but global interaction multiplies them. This brings to the fore the synchronic order of events in time as a useful conceptual aid for understanding contemporary human behavior.

Nevertheless, a synchronic realm of interaction also reveals the phenomenological position that I have held throughout this book, according to which what we know ought to be "bracketed," seen as mere appearance, not taken to be absolute truth. It also leads us to a moral emptiness of self, where all concrete reality is an illusion of our attachment to our ego. This stance is aware that any conception of human order—such as the theory proposed in this book—is also always essentially a metaphorical tale, as it is based in useful myths or ideals that are imaginatively and emotionally cognized. I have proposed that contemporary global interaction of all types (political, economic, social, commercial) ought to be based on a common human moral space organized as the tension between moral reason and universal compassion. However, the reflective moral self standing at the present moment of meaningful experience ought to be simultaneously aware that she is a primitive entity, the human animal, telling tales to shelter her embodiment and consciousness of self while experiencing the world.

NOTES

1 LEGITIMATE REALITY AND ETHICAL AUTHORITY

1. "Well known scholars of a radical turn of mind, Valla in Italy, Reuchlin in Germany, Colet in England, were, like Erasmus, attracted to the humanist theology made possible by Renaissance scholarship which the rediscovery of the original Hebrew and Greek texts of scripture, hitherto available only in the Latin Vulgate of St. Jerome, brought into existence. Concerned to take the dust-covers off the Latin Vulgate Erasmus published in 1516 a fresh edition of the Greek New Testament which if not free from error at least showed up the mistakes and even doctrinal tendentiousness in Jerome's version. . . . Humanism fertilized the ground for the Protestant reformers, making possible a more sympathetic response to Protestant criticism of the contemporary Church and to its stress to scriptural theology. . . . Yet though it was to be popularized, humanist theology was pabulum for only a small scholarly elite, some of whom, like Sir Thomas More and even Erasmus himself, remained loyal to the Catholic faith" (Green 1996, 125–26).

2. There exists a "mountainous literature on the so-called 'reception' of Weber" (Hennis 1988, 107) that Hennis compares in content to the "game of Chinese whispers." I will avoid elaborate interpretations of what Weber really meant and will concentrate on literature about Weber's background and methodological sources and elaborations that, according to Roth and Schluchter, "on the level of historical inquiry the articulation of Weber's substantive theories and practiced methodology" have not been paid much attention (1979, 1).

3. This idea follows Bruno Latour's perspective on science studies.

4. Thomas Burger argues that Weber's involvement with methodological issues is related to the dispute (*Methodenstreit*) that took place between the economists in the German Historical School (mainly Gustav Schmoller, Wilhelm Roscher, Bruno Hildebrand, and Karl Knies) and the Austrian Classical School of Economics (founded by Carl Menger). For both sides of this dispute, "scientific knowledge constituted a mental picture of the empirical phenomena in question; it was conceived as a replica of the object in the mind. Consequently, the question which was fundamental to the whole controversy was: What counts as a satisfactory replica?" (Burger 1976, 141).

5. With this position, Weber opposed the initial rise of Marxism in academic circles.

2 Ethical Authority According to Three Ideal Types of Reality

1. This is the new institutionalism that concentrates on organizational analysis. See Powell and DiMaggio (1991), and Hall and Taylor (1996).
2. In this sense, I disagree with the institutionalist tradition, which may have its origins with Thornsten Veblem that considers institutions as mere habits. Eventhough I agree that these habits leave past dependencies and determine the shape of an organization, the habits are materializations of institutional arrangements; they are not the institution itself.
3. Human consciousness is a most complex object of analysis; any conceptual description should be regarded as just a model that must be assumed to remain short of encompassing its vastness. This is not only the acknowledgment of a negligible margin of error between the model and the object of intellectual knowledge, but it is also the realization that this margin of error represents infinity itself.
4. Quoted by Laurence Coupe from Frye's *Anatomy of Criticism* (1971) where he sees "the 'apocalyptic' vision as the permanent possibility which inspires the secular imagination. Thus by 'apocalyptic' he means, not the literal expectation of catastrophe, not even a religious doctrine, but the imaginative anticipation of the not yet" (Coupe 1997, 166).
5. This is only a metonymic resource because to assume that the eternal present moment of time is the same as simultaneity in space is what Nishitani calls "bad infinity," or when the finite goes on infinitely (1982, 170).
6. Synchrony has generally been considered as a kind of "stasis" artificially subtracted from the flow of time, like a photography, a view that was a source for the demise of structuralism (Merquior 1986). Here, synchrony is unavoidably linked to diachrony where both notions are seen as perspectives on time and both move and rest, in their own ways, at the same time. Yet, the observer can only consider one of them at a time in a way that is analogous to the uncertainty principle of measuring the position and the momentum of microparticles in physics (see chapter 1, second section).
7. See chapter 5.
8. As Frye puts it, "The universe may have started off with a big bang billions of years ago, but the question of what happened before that goes on nagging" (Frye 1982, 71).
9. I. M. Lewis follows R. A. Knox (1950) to say that in contemporary studies of Shamanic and primitive religions, it has been observed that "religious leaders turn to ecstasy when they seek to strengthen and legitimize their authority" (Lewis 1989, 29).
10. I will discuss this Eastern notion of *karma* in chapter 4, third section. About it Nishitani says: "Being obligated to the infinite drive from the home-ground of the self itself to be constantly engaged in doing something

and consequently being obligated also to keep entering into relation with others and co-determining the self with others endlessly, but yet remaining forever incapable of taking leave of the self that presses onerously down upon us—this, it seems to me, is by and large the state of affairs that has arisen to awareness through the concept of karma. It can be termed a self-awareness of the essence of existence in time, conceived as a dynamic nexus of being, doing, and becoming" (Nishitani 1982, 242).

11. This was in spite of the simultaneous rise of a vernacular *ricorso* of metaphoric verbal structures in popular rhyme and alliteration.

3   THE PRIMITIVE IDEAL TYPE OF REALITY

1. This is true even for modern consciousness: An emotional involvement with particular myth or (personal) narrative rules our domestic lives. One of the most important objections to liberal political theory is that it over-looks the "narrative unity of a human life" (MacIntyre 1984). I argue that emotional involvement with particular (personal or group) narratives, in a mixture of spiritual and ethical topics, rule human preoccupations and imperatives (even if they are seen as private).

2. I first came across the concept of autopoiesis in Niklas Luhmann's theory of social systems (1995). Nevertheless, I learnt from him that he took this term from two Chilean biologists: Humberto Maturana and Francisco Varela. I resort to the latter all through this book, as Luhmann's theory dispenses with the human embodiment or consciousness of self and discards the notion of individuality as a modern invention. While the latter might be true, one cannot deny the presence and importance of individual human bodies and awareness to create and sustain any social system, complex or not in Luhmann's terms.

3. These archetypes have been related to fertility rituals of Neolithic origin. See Levy (1948). But the primitive roots of symbology in the shape of the cycle of life and death remain present in transcendental notions: A Beginning and a Beyond in Christianity or the endless circle of birth and rebirth in Eastern religions (Hinduism, Buddhism). The transcendental "leap in being" is organized either around the notion of a collective humanity or with respect to that of the individual life span of a human being that seeks spiritual Enlightenment (see chapter 4, second section).

4. In his book *Self Consciousness* (1994), Cohen argues that there is a common anthropological mistake in assuming that cultures determine the individual selves of their members, and he suggests that it is more like a dance: "I think of society and the self," says Cohen, "as dancing an improvised *pas de deux*: Each tries to cover the moves of the other; sometimes they merge, at others they separate" (1994, 71).

5. Martha Nussbaum defines emotions as "acknowledgements of neediness and lack of self-sufficiency" (2001, 22), which are constant in human interaction. This lack of self-sufficiency is most patent in the domestic

life, while it is a kind of nuisance for the liberal conception of an autonomous self.

6. Although modern life in the cities is artificial enough for us to be able to ignore the natural cycles of the earth (besides, maybe, concern about the weather), and this artificiality may also dull perception of the personal cycles of being embodied, perception of the need for work to survive is very much alive. Yet, the need for work is perceived to be created by the social system, which organizes work in the most differentiated environments. But when an intricate social system is absent, raw nature demands work and constantly improvised creativity for the human communities to survive. An important part of the Marxist cosmology is based on observation of this pragmatic feature of human experience.

7. Synchronically speaking, from a contemporary perspective, this is observable in modern societies as subcultures, with the prefix "sub" because they lack legitimacy to order interaction, they represent a vernacular view of reality, through the "not-really-true-life" realm in which contemporary mass practices of consumption, of spirituality, entertainment/advertisement, and fashion dominate.

8. And this entails a hermeneutical exercise.

9. Moore prefers to translate *durée* as "durance," eventhough its translation into "duration" had Bergson's authorization. "But it seems to me," says Moore, "that the most natural use of this word in English is to refer to a measurable period of time during which something happens. It is perfectly true that the French word '*durée*' also has this meaning. However, my sense is that the French word can more readily be applied to *the fact or property of going through time* than the English 'duration' " (Moore 1996, 58).

10. For humans, these behaviors also take place only within an environment that *does* have articulated discursive intentions and embodies and enacts the different disciplined practices that are learnt.

11. This imaginary "relational space" may expand to include transcendental concepts and experiences that might even overcome the initial local quality of the space in the notions of "universality," "eternal," or "infinite."

12. However, I do not follow Ruddick to her conclusions on a politics of peace based on maternal thinking. I do not believe that any prescriptive model for political theory can emerge from considering the primitive need of comfort and peace in the midst of domestic life. Yet, I do consider it essential in the portrayal of human beings as ethical entities.

13. But this business of classification is not without its deep and unsolvable paradoxes. See Gould (1977).

14. Much like in the contractual liberal tradition in political theory, the contracting individuals are seen as rational adult entities that surged like "mushrooms" (Hobbes [1651] 1948) from the soil and did not have an infancy or were not nurtured into adulthood, unencumbered and unrestrained by social and intimate bonds.

15. According to Maturana and Varela, behavior and cognition can be observed in all living organisms, "for the observer will see behavior when

he looks at any living being in its environment" (1987, 138). As we have said before, in their theory, the "notion of cognition is extended to cover all the effective interactions that an organism has" (Mingers 1991, 321). To Maturana and Varela, behavior and cognition are not limited to second-order (multicellular) autopoietic organisms with a nervous system, but as human beings are this kind of organism, behavior and cognition will be considered in this work only for multicellular autopoietic organisms with a nervous system.

16. The more general use of cognition regards it as the process of acquiring and using knowledge by a nervous system whose role is generally taken to be the collection of information that will allow the organism to survive. This view is heavily criticized by the theory of Maturana and Varela, as will become clear later on in the discussion.

17. Five kingdoms of living beings have been differentiated: monera, proctitis, animals, plants, and fungi (Margulis and Scwartz 1982). "Behavior" is generally associated with the animal kingdom, but Maturana and Varela find it hard to establish a clear basis for differentiating behavior from observation of any living organism in its environment (see Maturana and Varela 1987, chapter 7).

18. The transfer functions of the nerve cell involve the communication of impulses from its collector area (dendrites and, in some cases, also the cell body and part of the axon) through its distributive element (the axon and, in some cases, also the cell body and main dendrites) to its effector area (the terminal branching of the axon) (Maturana 1970, 18).

19. Otherwise, with no nervous system, as in the behavior of an amoeba, only the physicochemical effect of *autopoiesis* in an environment can be observed. While this example is not without its own vast perspectival complexity, the amount of observable behaviors of this living entity is comparatively reduced at the level of the observation of its motility.

20. In his theory of social systems, Niklas Luhmann (1995) argues that language can never go beyond itself as it is self-referential; it is determined by its own autopoiesis. I agree with him on this, but do not follow him in his theoretical need to dispose of human consciousness altogether in order to reject the modern idea of individuality. Nevertheless, the reason I have introduced Maturana and Varela's own notion of "autopoiesis" is because I want to argue (contrary to Luhmann) that language depends on human consciousness of self, be it individual in a modern idealized sense, or not.

21. The synchronic perspective allows for at least another type of morality, one that universalizes love as a unifying principle—more on this, in chapter 5.

4   THE HISTORICAL IDEAL TYPE OF REALITY

1. Eliade defines hierophany as: "[A] term designating the manifestation of the sacred. The term involves no further specification. Herein lies its

advantage: it refers to any manifestation of the sacred in whatever object throughout history. Whether the sacred appear in a stone, a tree, or an incarnate human being, a hierophany denotes the same act: A reality of an entirely different order than those of this world becomes manifest in an object that is part of the natural or profane sphere" (1993, 313).

2. In Modernity, this identity is enacted and lived either in shame, denial, or practice of organic habits and conversations and practices, such as recycling one's garbage or refusing to trade in a savage non-environmentally friendly manner. For a living example of this kind of conversation or culture, see Andruss et al. (1990).

3. What Hegel regarded as positive fetishist religion in his *Early Theological Writings* (1948), but he also applies this idea on the Enlightenment's deification of reason that made the latter into a kind of fetish.

4. As he developed in his *Critique of Pure Reason* ([1781] 1929), *Critique of Practical Reason* ([1798] 1996), and *Groundwork of the Metaphysics of Morals* ([1785] 1998).

5. Voegelin uses the term *ecumene* to signify humanity unified by awareness of each other through imperial expansion, which became a term to refer to unified humanity in the Christian cosmos. The imperial drive that is the root of European supremacy is linked to an eclectic creation of human history that is based not only on pragmatic knowledge and evidence, but also on values and beliefs: "No single society, but the whole geographical and civilizational horizon of the Mediterranean and Near Eastern peoples, from the Atlantic to the Indus, becomes the theatre of pragmatic history. This new phenomenon requires a new terminology, for one can no longer speak of societies and their order when the events converge toward their destruction. What takes their place is the ecumene. The term ecumene, which originally means no more than the inhabited world in the sense of cultural geography, has received through Polybius the technical meaning of the peoples who are drawn into the process of imperial expansion. On this Polybian stratum of meaning could later be superimposed the meaning of the mankind under Roman Jurisdiction (Luke 2:1; Acts 17:6; 24:5), and ultimately of the messianic world to come (Heb. 2:5)" (Voegelin 1974, 124).

6. Nishitani refers to the field of consciousness as the perspective where we relate to objects *without* from a position *within* the subject, where "self and things remain fundamentally separated from one another. This standpoint of separation of subject and object, or opposition between within and without is what we call the field of 'consciousness'. And it is from this field that we ordinarily relate to things by means of concepts and representations" (1982, 9).

7. The domain of facticity to which awareness of a transhistorical "near side" realm gives birth is essentially related to the particularity of a human lifetime.

8. The concept of church belongs to the Christian tradition and describes a form of religious communal life, inherited from Hellenic political organization. "The ideals of the political philosophy of the ancient Greek city-state

entered the discussion of the new Christian type of human community, now called the church, but in Greek *ekklesia* . . . originally meant the assembly of the citizens of a Greek polis" (Jaeger 1962, 15).

9. In chapter 6 of this book, I propose a theoretical solution to the moral predicament in which Modernity finds itself today. I argue for allowing the historical type to converge with the mystic type for a universal basis of morality. Even as the mystic type of reality aspires to overcome embodied individuality, this convergence requires individual consciousness as a theoretical standpoint. This is the reason why I conceive of mine as a liberal position.

10. However, it is not clear where one can draw a line between his concepts of "practice" and "tradition," except for the difference in size and expansion.

5   The Mystic Ideal Type of Reality

1. The notion of "conversion" is very much at home in the religions of the Book that emanate from the house of Abraham.

2. Here, I sometimes refer to this tradition as Western to point toward the self-identity of its source and for heuristic purposes, but it is important to bear in mind that it is now a global tradition of knowledge and practice.

3. See chapter 4, second section for an explanation of Nishitani's "near side" and "far side" transhistorical realms (1982).

4. I have defined the present moment of meaningful experience in chapter 3 as a phenomenological center of embodied awareness for human cognition.

5. Similar to ontogeny, phylogeny is a biological concept that means "The evolutionary history of a group or a lineage" or "The origin and evolution of higher taxa" (Lincoln et al. 1982, 192).

BIBLIOGRAPHY

Abe, M. 1985. *Zen and Western Thought*. Ed. W. R. La Fleur. Honolulu: University of Hawaii Press.

Adorno, T. W. and M. Horkheimer. 1972. *Dialectic of Enlightenment*. London: Verso.

Ahmad, A. 1987. "Jameson's Rhetoric of Otherness and the 'National Allegory.' " *Social Text* 17: 3–25.

———. 1992. *In Theory: Classes, Nations, Literatures*. London: Verso.

———. 1995. "The Politics of Literary Postcoloniality." *Race and Class* 36(3): 1–20.

Alcoff, L. and E. Potter, eds. 1993. *Feminist Epistemologies*. London and New York: Routledge.

Al-Daffa', A. A. 1977. *The Muslim Contribution to Mathematics*. London: Croom Helm/Humanities.

Alessandrini, A. 1997. "Fanon and the Post-Colonial Future." *Jouvert: A Journal of Postcolonial Studies* 1(2): 22–40.

Althusser, L. 1984. *Essays on Ideology*. London: Verso.

Andrea, B. 1996. "Early Modern Women, 'Race,' and the (Post)Colonial Writing." *Ariel* 27(3): 127–49.

Andruss, A., C. Plant, J. Plant, and E. Wright. 1990. *Home! A Bioregional Reader*. Gabriola Island BC, Canada: New Society.

An-Naim, A. 1992. "Toward a Cross-Cultural Approach to Defining International Standards of Human Rights: The Meaning of Cruel, Inhuman, or Degrading Treatment or Punishment." In *Human Rights in Cross-Cultural Perspectives: A Quest for Consensus*. Ed. A. An-Naim. Philadelphia: University of Pennsylvania Press, pp. 19–43.

Ansell, P., B. Parry, and J. Squires, eds. 1997. *Cultural Readings of Imperialism: Edward Said and the Gravity of History*. New York: St. Martin's Press.

Appiah, K. A. 1991. "Is the Post- in Postmodernism the Post- in Postcolonial?" *Critical Inquiry* 17(3): 336–57.

———. 1992. *In My Father's House: Africa in the Philosophy of Culture*. London: Methuen.

Ashcroft, W. D. 1989a. "Intersecting Marginalities: Post-Colonialism and Feminism." *Kunapipi* 11(1): 58–73.

———. 1989b. "Is that the Congo? Language as Metonymy in the Post-Colonial Text." *World Literature Written in English* 29(2): 3–10.

Ashcroft, W. D., G. Griffith, and H. Tiffin, eds. 1989. *The Empire Writes Back: Theory and Practice in Post-Colonial Literatures*. London: Routledge.

Ashcroft, W. D., G. Griffith, and H. Tiffin, eds. 1995. *The Post-Colonial Studies Reader*. London: Routledge.

Auerbach, E. 1953. *Mimesis: The Representation of Reality in Western Literature*. Trans. W. R. Trask. Princeton, NJ: Princeton University Press.

Avineri, S. 1993. *Communitarianism and Its Critics*. Oxford: Clarendon Press.

———. 1995a. "A Communitarian Critique of Authoritarianism." *Society* (July/August): 38–43.

———. 1995b. "Residential Community Associations: Community or Disunity." *The Responsive Community* (Fall): 25–36.

Avineri, S. and A. de-Shalit, eds. 1992. *Communitarianism and Individualism*. Oxford: Clarendon Press.

Baillie, J. 1945. *What is Christian Civilization?* London: Humphrey Milford and Oxford University Press.

———. 1950. *The Belief in Progress*. London: Oxford University Press.

Bakhtin, M. 1981. *The Dialogic Imagination: Four Essays*. Trans. M. Holquist and C. Emerson. Austin: University of Texas Press.

Barfoot, C. 1993. *Shades of Empire in Colonial and Post-Colonial Literatures*. Amsterdam: Rodopi.

Barker, F., P. Hulme, and M. Iversen, eds. 1985. *Europe and Its Others*. Essex: University of Essex Press.

Barthes, R. 1970. *Empire of Signs*. London: Jonathan Cape.

Beckles, H. 1997. "Capitalism, Slavery and Caribbean Modernity." *Callaloo* 20(4): 777–89.

Bell, C. 1992. *Ritual Theory, Ritual Practice*. Oxford: Oxford University Press.

Bellah, R. et al. 1985. *Habits of the Heart*. Berkeley: University of California Press.

Belnap, J. 1993. *The Post-Colonial State and the "Hybrid" Intellect: Carpentier, Ngugi, and Spivak*. Irvine CA: University of California Press.

Benhabib, S. 1992. *Situating the Self; Gender, Community and Postmodernism in Contemporary Ethics*. New York: Routledge.

Benjamin, W. 1979. *One Way Street and Other Writings*. Trans. E. Jephcott and K. Shorter. London: NLB.

Benn, S. 1988. *A Theory of Freedom*. Cambridge: Cambridge University Press.

Bennet, C. 1996. *In Search of the Sacred: Anthropology and the Study of Religions*. London: Cassell.

Berger P. and T. Luckmann. 1966. *The Social Construction of Reality; a Treatise in the Sociology of Knowledge*. London: Penguin.

Bergson, H. 1965. *Duration and Simultaneity. With Reference to Einstein's Theory*. Trans. L. Jacobson. Indianapolis: Bobbs-Merril.

Berlin, I. 1969. *Four Essays on Liberty*. Oxford: Oxford University Press.

Berlin, B., D. E. Breedlove, and P. H. Raven. 1974. *Principles of Tzeltal Plant Classification*. New York: Academic Press.

Berman, M. 1992. *Cuerpo y espíritu: la historia oculta de occidente*. Santiago, Chile: Cuatro Vientos.

Bernhard, L. 1986. *Wisdom and the Book of Proverbs: An Israelite Goddess Redefined*. New York: Pilgrim.

Berten, A., P. da Silveira, and H. Pourtois, eds. 1997. *Liberaux et Communautariens*. Paris: PUF.

Beveridge, W. 1944. *Full Employment in a Free Society*. London: Allen and Unwin.

Bhabha, H. 1990. *Nation and Narration*. New York: Routledge.

———. 1996. *Location of Culture: Discussing Post-Colonial Culture*. London: Routledge.

Biardeau, M. 1989. *Hinduism: The Anthropology of a Civilization*. Delhi: Oxford University Press.

Block, N., O. Flanagan, and G. Güzeldere, eds. 1997. *The Nature of Consciousness: Philosophical Debates*. Cambridge, MA: The Massachusetts Institute of Technology Press.

Blodgett, E. 1995. "Toward and Ethnic Style." *Canadian Review of Comparative Literature* 22(3): 623–38.

Bohm, D. 1980. *Wholeness and the Implicate Order*. London: Routledge.

Bosanquet, B. [1923] 2002. *Philosophical Theory of the State and Related Essays*. Ed. G. F. Gaus and W. Sweet. Indianapolis: St. Augustine Press.

Brennan, T. 1992. "Rushdie, Islam, and Postcolonial Criticism." *Social Text* 10(3): 271–75.

Bruun, H. H. 1972. *Science, Values and Politics in Max Weber's Methodology*. Copenhagen: Munksgaard.

Burger, T. 1976. *Max Weber's Theory of Concept Formation: History, Laws, and Ideal Types*. Durham, NC: Duke University Press.

Burke, E. [1790] 1999. *Reflection on the Revolution in France. Select Works of Edmund Burke*, vol. 2. Indianapolis: Liberty Fund.

Burrel, G. 1997. *Pandemonium; Towards a Retro-Organization Theory*. London: Sage.

Campbell, J. 1997. *Arguing with the Phallus: Feminist, Queer and Postcolonial Theory: A Psychoanalytic Contribution*. Atlantic Highlands, NJ: Humanities Press International.

Camus, A. [1942] 1989. *The Stranger*. Trans. M. Ward. New York: Vintage International.

Caney, S. 1992. "Liberalism and Communitarianism: A Misconceived Debate." *Political Studies* (June): 273–90.

Capra, F. 1982. *The Tao of Physics: An Exploration of the Parallels between Modern Physics and Eastern Mysticism*, 3rd edn. Glasgow: Flamingo.

———. 1983. *The Turning Point*. London: Flamingo.

Card, C. 1990. "Caring and Evil." *Hypatia: A Journal of Feminist Philosophy* 2(2): 101–08.

———, ed. 1991. *Feminist Ethics*. Lawrence: University of Kansas.

Carmagnani, M. 2004. *El Otro Occidente. América Latina desde la Invasión Europea hasta la Globalización*. Mexico City: El Colegio de México/ Fideicomiso Historia de las Américas/ Fondo de Cultura Económica.

Chakrabarty, D. 1992. "Postcoloniality and the Artifice of History: Who Speaks for 'Indian' Past?" *Representations* 37: 1–26.

Chatterjee, P. 1993a. *Nation and Its Fragments: Colonial and Postcolonial Histories*. Princeton: Princeton University Press.

———. 1993b. *Nationalist Thought and the Colonial World: A Derivative Discourse*. Minneapolis, MN: University of Minnesota Press.

Cherniavsky, E. 1996. "Subalterns Studies on a U.S. Frame." *Boundary* 2(23): 85–110.

Chow, R. 1993. *Writing Diaspora: Tactics of Intervention in Contemporary Cultural Studies*. Bloomington, IN: Indiana University Press.

Chrisman, L. 1995. "Inventing Post-Colonial Theory: Polemical Observation." *Pretexts: Studies in Writing and Culture* 51(1): 205–12.

Chrisman, L. and B. Parry, eds. 2000. *Postcolonial Theory and Criticism*. Cambridge: D.S. Brewer.

Clayton, D. and D. Gregory, eds. 1996. *Colonialism, Postcolonialism and the Production of Space*. Oxford: Blackwell.

Clendinnen, I. 1991. *Aztecs: An Interpretation*. Cambridge: Cambridge University Press.

Clifford, J. 1988. *The Predicament of Culture*. Cambridge, MA: Harvard University Press.

Cohen, A. P. 1994. *Self Consciousness: An Alternative Anthropology of Identity*. London: Routledge.

Costa de Beauregard, O. 1984. "Quanta and Relativity, Cosmos and Consciousness." In *The Science and Praxis of Complexity*. Ed. S. Aida et al. Montpellier, France: The United Nations University Press, pp. 153–69.

Coupe, L. 1997. *Myth*. New Critical Idiom. Ed. J. Drakakis. London: Routledge.

Cross, F. L. 1955. *The Jung Codex: A Newly Recovered Gnostic Papyrus*. London: A.R. Mowbray & Co.

Culler, J. 1981. *The Pursuit of Signs: Semiotics, Literature, Deconstruction*. London: Routledge.

Czarniawska, B. 1992. *Exploring Complex Organizations: A Cultural Perspective*. London: Sage.

———. 1997. *Narrating the Organization: Dramas of Institutional Identities*. Chicago: The University of Chicago Press.

———. 1998. *A Narrative Approach to Organization Studies*. Qualitative Research Methods Series 43. London: Sage.

Dagger, R. 1997. *Civic Virtue: Rights, Citizenship and Republican Liberalism*. Oxford: Oxford University Press.

Dallmayr, F. 1996. *Beyond Orientalism: Essays on Cross-Cultural Encounter*. Albany, NY: State University of New York Press.

Danzin, A. 1984. "The Pervasiveness of Complexity: Common Trends, New Paradigms, and Research Orientations." In *The Science and Praxis of Complexity*. Ed. S. Aida et al. Montpellier, France: The United Nations University Press, pp. 69–80.

Davies, T. 1997. *Humanism the New Critical Idiom*. Ed. J. Drakakis. London: Routledge.

Dawson, R. 1981. *Confucius*. Oxford: Oxford University Press.

de Zeeuw, G. 1992. "Autopoiesis and Social Science: A Counterresponse." *International Journal of General Systems* 21: 261–62.

Delanty, G. 1997. *Social Science; Beyond Constructivism and Realism.* Buckingham: Open University Press.

Dewey, J. 1929. *Characters and Events.* Ed. Joseph Ratner. New York: Henry Holt.

Dirlik, A. 1995. "Confucius in the Borderland: Global Capitalism and the Reinvention of Confucianism." *Boundary* 2(22): 229–73.

———. 1996. "The Postcolonial Aura: Third World Criticism in the Age of Global Capitalism." In *Contemporary Postcolonial Theory. A Reader.* Ed. P. Mongia. London: Arnold, pp. 294–320.

Donaldson, L. 1993. *Decolonizing Feminism.* London: Routledge.

Donnell, A. 1995. "She Ties Her Tongue: The Problems of Cultural Paralysis in Postcolonial Criticism." *Ariel* 2(1): 101–16.

Doppelt, G. 1989. "Is Rawls Kantian Liberalism Coherent and Defensible?" *Ethics* (July): 820–21.

Dorfman, A. 1983. *Empire's Old Clothes.* New York: Pantheon Books.

Douglas, M. 1986. *How Institutions Think.* London: Routledge & Kegan Paul.

Dunbar, R. 1996. *Grooming, Gossip and the Evolution of Language.* London: Faber and Faber.

Dupuy, J. 1984. "Autonomy and Complexity in Sociology." In *The Science and Praxis of Complexity.* Ed. S. Aida et al. Montpellier, France: The United Nations University Press, pp. 255–67.

Dworkin, G. 1988. *The Theory and Practice of Autonomy.* Cambridge: Cambridge University Press.

———. 1989. "Liberal Community." *California Law Review* 77(3): 479–504.

Eden, R. 1987. "Weber and Nietzsche: Questioning the Liberation of Social Science from Historicism." In *Max Weber and His Contemporaries.* Ed. W. J. Mommsen and J. Osterhammel. London: Allen & Unwin, pp. 350–70.

Eisenstadt, S. N. 1973. *Tradition, Change, and Modernity.* London: John Wiley & Sons.

———. 1982. "The Axial Age: The Emergence of Transcendental Visions and the Rise of Clerics." *European Journal of Sociology* 23: 294–314.

Eliade, M. 1955. *The Myth of the Eternal Return.* London: Routledge and Kegan Paul.

———. 1967. *Essential Sacred Writings from Around the World.* San Francisco: Harper Collins.

———, ed. 1993. *The Encyclopedia of Religion,* 16 vols. New York: Macmillan Publishing Company.

Elias, N. 1989. *El proceso de la civilización.* 2nd edn in Spanish of the 1st in German. Mexico City: Fondo de Cultura Económica.

Erikson, E. H. 1968. *Identity Youth and Crisis.* London: Faber & Faber.

Ermarth, E. D. 1995. "Ph(r)ase Time: Chaos Theory and Post Modern Reports on Knowledge." *Time and Society* 4(1): 91–110.

Etzioni, A. 1993. *The Spirit of Community.* New York: Crown Publishers.

Etzioni, A. 1995a. *New Communitarian Thinking.* Charlottesville: University of Virginia Press.

———. 1995b. *Rights and the Common Good: The Communitarian Perspective.* New York: St. Martin's Press.

———. 1996. *The New Golden Rule.* New York: Basic Books.

———. 1998. *The Essential Communitarian Reader.* Lanham: Rowman & Littlefield.

———. 2001. *The Monochrome Society.* Princeton: Princeton University Press.

Fanon, F. 1961. *The Wretched of the Earth.* New York: Grove Press.

———. 1965. *Studies in Dying Colonialism.* New York: Grove Press.

———. 1967. *Black Skin, White Masks.* New York: Grove Press.

Farrellkrell, D. 1986. *Intimations of Mortality: Time, Truth and Finitude in Heiddeger's Thinking of Being.* University Park, PA: The Pennsylvania State University Press.

Fleischaker, G. R. 1992. "It's not Mine and It's not a Dictum." *International Journal of General Systems* 21: 257–58.

Fludernik, M. 1998. *Hybridity and Postcolonialism: Twentieth-Century Indian Literature.* Tubinger, Germany: Stauffenburg.

Foucault, M. 1988. "The Art of Telling the Truth." In *Politics, Philosophy, Culture: Interviews and Other Writings, 1977–1984.* Trans. A. Sheridan. London: Routledge.

Frazer, E. 1999. *The Problems of Communitarian Politics.* Oxford: Oxford University Press.

Frazer, E. and N. Lacey. 1993. *The Politics of Community: A Feminist Critique of the Liberal-Communitarian Debate.* Hemel Hempstead: Harvester Wheatsheaf.

Freeden, M. 1978. *The New Liberalism: An Ideology of Social Reform.* Oxford: Clarendon Press.

Friedman, M. 1987. "Beyond Caring: The De-Moralization of Gender." *Canadian Journal of Philosophy* 13: 87–110.

Frug, G. 1999. *City Making: Building Communities Without Building Walls.* Princeton: Princeton University Press.

Frye, N. 1964. *The Educated Imagination.* Bloomington: Indiana University Press.

———. 1971. *Anatomy of Criticism.* Princeton: Princeton University Press.

———. 1982. *The Great Code: The Bible and Literature.* Toronto, Canada: Academic Press Canada.

Fukuyama, F. 1992. *The End of History and the Last Man.* New York: Free Press.

Fuss, D. 1994. "Interior Colonies: Frantz Fanon and the Politic of Identification." *Diacritics* 24(2): 20–42.

Gadamer, H. G. 1989. *Truth and Method.* Ed. J. C. Weinsheimer and D. G. Marshall. New York: Continuum International Publishing Group.

Galston, W. 1980. *Justice and the Human Good.* Chicago: University of Chicago Press.

Gandhi, L. 1998. *Postcolonial Theory: A Critical Introduction.* New York: Columbia University Press.

Gaus, G. 1981. "The Convergence of Rights and Utility: The Case of Rawls and Mill." *Ethics* 92: 57–72.

———. 1983a. "Public and Private Interests in Liberal Political Economy, Old and New." In *Public and Private in Social Life.* Ed. S. I. Benn and G. Gaus. New York: St. Martin's Press, pp. 183–221.

———. 1983b. *The Modern Liberal Theory of Man.* New York: St. Martin's Press.

———. 1990. *Value and Justification.* Cambridge: Cambridge University Press.

———. 1994a. "Green, Bosanquet and the Philosophy of Coherence." In *The Routledge History of Philosophy,* vol. 7. Ed. C. L. Ten. London: Routledge, pp. 708–33.

———. 1994b. "Property, Rights and Freedom." *Social Philosophy and Policy* 11: 209–40.

———. 1996. *Justificatory Liberalism: An Essay on Epistemology and Political Theory.* New York: Oxford University Press.

———. 2003. "Backwards into the Future: Neorepublicanism as a Postsocialist Critique of Market Society." *Social Philosophy and Policy* 20: 59–92.

Gauthier, D. 1986. *Morals by Agreement.* Oxford: Oxford University Press.

Geertz, C. 1973. *The Interpretation of Cultures.* London: Fontana.

Geyer, F. 1992. "Answer to Zeleny and Hufford." *International Journal of General Systems* 21: 259–60.

Giarini, O. 1984. "The Consequences of Complexity in Economics: Vulnerability, Risk, and Rigidity Factors in Supply." In *The Science and Praxis of Complexity.* Ed. S. Aida et al. Montpellier, France: The United Nations University Press, pp. 133–45.

Giddens, A. 1990. *The Consequence of Modernity.* Oxford: Polity.

Gilligan, C. 1982. *In a Different Voice: Psychological Theory and Women's Development.* Cambridge, MA: Harvard University Press.

———. 1995. "Hearing the Difference: Theorizing Connection." *Hypatia: A Journal of Feminist Philosophy* 10(2): 120–27.

Gilligan, C., J. V. Ward, and J. M. Taylor, eds. 1989. *Mapping the Moral Domain: A Contribution of Women's Thinking to Psychological Theory and Education.* Cambridge, MA: Harvard University Press.

Gilroy, P. 1993. *The Black Atlantic: Modernity and Double Consciousness.* Cambridge, MA: Harvard University Press.

Glage, L. 2000. *Being/s in Transit: Travelling, Migration, Dislocation.* Amsterdam: Rodopi.

Glendon, M. A. 1991. *Rights Talk: The Impoverishment of Political Discourse.* New York: The Free Press.

Goss, J. 1996. "Postcolonialism: Subverting Whose Empire?" *Third World Quarterly* 17(2): 239–50.

Gould, S. J. 1977. *Ever since Darwin: Reflections in Natural History.* London: Penguin.

Gramsci, A. 1991. *Prison Notebooks.* New York: Columbia University Press.

Green, T. H. 1986 [1895]. *Lectures on the Principles of Political Obligation and Other Essays.* Ed. Paul Harris and John Morrow. Cambridge: Cambridge University Press.

Green, V. 1996. *A New History of Christianity.* Gloucestershire, UK: Sutton.

Griffiths, G. 1987. "Imitation, Abrogation and Appropriation: The Production of the Post-Colonial Text." *Kunapipi* 9(1): 13–20.

———. 1993. "An Imaginary Life: The Post-Colonial Text as Transformative Representation." *Commonwealth Essays and Studies* 16(2): 61–69.

Gunew, S. 1994. "Postcolonialism and Multiculturalism: Between Race and Ethnicity." *Yearbook of English Studies* 27: 22–39.

Gutmann, A., ed. 1992. *Multiculturalism and "The Politics of Recognition."* Princeton: Princeton University Press.

Habermas, J. 1984. *Reason and the Rationalization of Society,* vol. 1 *The Theory of Communicative Action.* Boston, MA: Beacon.

———. 1990a. *Critica de la razón funcionalista,* vol. 2 *Teoría de la acción comunicativa.* Buenos Aires, Argentina: Taurus.

———. 1990b. *Moral Consciousness and Communicative Action.* Boston: MIT Press.

———. 1995. "Reconciliation Through the Public Use of Reason: Remarks on John Rawls's Political Liberalism." *The Journal of Philosophy* 92(3) (March): 109–31.

———. 1996. *Die Einbeziehung des Anderen.* Frankfurt: Suhrkamp Verlag.

———. 1998. *Between Facts and Norms. Contributions to a Discourse Theory of Law and Democracy.* Trans. William Rehg. Cambridge, MA: The MIT Press.

Habermas, J. and J. Rawls. 1998. *Debate sobre el liberalismo político.* Trans. Gerard Vilar Roca. Barcelona: Paidós/Instituto de Ciencias de la Educación de la Universidad Autónoma de Barcelona.

Habib, I. 1998. "Othello, Sir Peter Negro, and the Black of Early Modern England: Colonial Inscription and Postcolonial Excavation." *Literature-Interpretation-Theory* 9(1): 15–30.

Hall, P. A. and R. C. R. Taylor. 1996. "Political Science and the Three New Institutionalisms." *Political Studies* XLIV: 936–57.

Hammond, M., J. Howarth, and R. Keat. 1991. *Understanding Phenomenology.* Oxford: Blackwell.

Hampton, J. 1989. "Should Political Philosophy by Done without Metaphysics?" *Ethics* 99: 791–814.

Harding, S. 1993. "After Eurocentrism? Challenges for the Philosophy of Science." *Proceeding of the Philosophy of Science Association* 2: 311–19.

———. 1998. *Is Science Multicultural? Postcolonialism, Feminism and Epistemologies.* Bloomington, IN: Indiana University Press.

Harlow, B. 1993. *Barred: Women, Writing, and Political Detention.* Hanover: Wesleyan University Press.

Harnack, A. 1904. *What is Christianity?,* 3rd edn. London: Williams & Norgate.

———. 1910. *The Constitution and Law of the Church in the First Two Centuries.* London: Williams & Norgate.

Havelock, E. A. 1963. *Preface to Plato.* Oxford: Basil and Blackwell.

Hawley, J. 1996. *Writing the Nation: Self and Country in the Post-Colonial Imagination.* Amsterdam: Rodopi.

Hayek, F. A. 1976. *The Mirage of Social Justice.* Chicago: University of Chicago Press.

———. 1978. *New Studies in Philosophy, Politics, Economics and the History of Ideas.* London: Routledge and Kegan Paul.

Held, V. 1993. *Feminist Morality: Transforming Culture, Society, and Politics.* Chicago: The University of Chicago Press.

———, ed. 1995. *Justice and Care: Essential Reading in Feminist Ethics.* Boulder: Westview Press.

Hennis, W. 1988. *Max Weber: Essays in Reconstruction.* Trans. K. Tribe. London: Allen & Unwin.

Hobbes, T. [1651] 1948. *Leviathan.* Ed. Michael Oakeshott. Oxford: Blackwell.

Hobson, J. A. 1922. *The Economics of Unemployment.* London: Allen & Unwin.

Hodgson, G. M. 1993. *Economics and Evolution: Bringing Life Back into Economics.* Cambridge: Polity.

Hofstadter, D. R. 1979. *Göedel, Escher, Bach: An Eternal Golden Braid; A Metaphorical Fugue on Minds and Machines in the Spirit of Lewis Carrol.* London: Penguin.

Hofstadter, D. R. and D. Dennett, eds. 1981. *The Mind's Eye: Fantasies and Reflections on Self and Soul.* New York: Basic Books.

Hunn, E. S. 1977. *Tzeltal Folk Zoology; the Classification of Discontinuities in Nature.* New York: Academic Press.

Husserl, E. 1977. *Cartesian Meditations.* New York: Kluwer Academic Publishers.

Hutcheon, L. 1994. "The Post Always Rings Twice: The Postmodern and the Postcolonial." *Practice* 8(2): 205–38.

Ingold, T. 1983. "The Architect and the Bee: Reflections on the Work of Animals and Men." *Man* 18: 1–20.

———. 1986. *Evolution and Social Life.* Cambridge: Cambridge University Press.

———. 1989. "An Anthropologist Looks at Biology." *Man* 25: 208–29.

Inoue, T. 1993. "The Poverty of Rights-Blind Communality: Looking Through the Window of Japan." *Brigham Young University Law Review* (January): 534.

Jacob, F. 1977. "Evolution and Tinkering." *Science* 196: 1161–66.

Jacobs, J. 1965. *The Death and Life of American Cities.* New York: Random House.

Jaeger, W. 1962. *Early Christianity and Greek Paideia.* London: Oxford University Press.

Jakobson, R. 1956. "Two Aspects of Language and Two Types of Aphasic Disturbances." In *Fundamental of Language.* Ed. R. Jakobson and Halle. The Hague: Mouton, pp. 115–33.

Jaspers, K. 1953. *The Origin and Goal of History*. London: Routledge and Kegan Paul.

———. 1964. *Leonardo, Descartes, Max Weber*. London: Routledge and Kegan Paul.

Jay, M. 1993. *Downcast Eyes: The Denigration of Vision in Twentieth-Century French Thought*. Los Angeles: The University of California Press.

Jonas, H. 1966. "The Nobility of Sight: A Study in the Phenomenology of the Senses." In *The Phenomenon of Life: Toward a Philosophical Biology*. Ed. H. Jonas. Chicago: The University of Chicago Press, pp. 135–56.

Kant, I. [1781] 1929. *Immanuel Kant's Critique of Pure Reason*. Trans. N. K. Smith. London: Macmillan.

———. [1797] 1965. *The Metaphysical Elements of Justice*. Trans. J. Ladd. Indianapolis: Bobbs-Merrill.

———. [1784] 1991. "An Answer to the Question: 'What Is Enlightenment?' " In *Kant. Political Writings*, 2nd edn. Ed. H. Reiss, trans. H. B. Nisbet. Cambridge: Cambridge University Press.

———. [1798] 1996. *Critique of Practical Reason*. Trans. T. K. Abbott. New York: Prometheus Books.

———. [1785] 1998. *Groundwork of the Metaphysics of Morals*. Ed. M. Gregor. Cambridge: Cambridge University Press.

Kauffman, S. 1995. *At Home in the Universe; the Search for Laws of Complexity*. London: Penguin.

Kavka, G. S. 1986. *Hobbesian Moral and Political Theory*. Princeton: Princeton University Press.

Kavolis, V. 1993. *Moralizing Cultures*. Lanham, Maryland: University Press of America.

Kenny, V. 1992a. "On the Subject of Autopoiesis and Its Boundaries: Does the Subject Matter?" *International Journal of General Systems* 21: 187–96.

———. 1992b. "The Spockian Paradox." *International Journal of General Systems* 21: 263–64.

Keynes, J. M. [1936] 1973. *The General Theory of Employment, Interest and Money*. London: Macmillan/Cambridge University Press.

King, R. 1999. *Orientalism and Religion: Post-Colonial Theory, India and the Mystic East*. New York: Routledge.

Kirby, M. J. L. 1984. "Complexity, Democracy and Governance." In *The Science and Praxis of Complexity*. Ed. S. Aida et al. Montpellier, France: The United Nations University Press, pp. 329–37.

Kittay, E. F. and D. T. Meyers, eds. 1987. *Women and Moral Theory*. Yorkshire: Rowman & Littlefield.

Klir, G. J. 1984. "The Many Faces of Complexity." In *The Science and Praxis of Complexity*. Ed. S. Aida et al. Montpellier, France: The United Nations University Press, pp. 81–98.

Knox, R. A. 1950. *Enthusiasm: A Chapter in the History of Religion*. Oxford: Clarendon.

Kocis, R. A. 1980. "Reason, Development and the Conflict of Human Ends: Sir Isaiah Berlin's Vision of Politics." *American Political Science Review* 74: 38–52.

Kohlbergh, L. 1981. *Essays on Moral Development. The Philosophy of Moral Development*, vol. 1. New York: Harper and Row.

———. 1984. *Essays on Moral Development. The Psychology of Moral Development*, vol. 2. San Francisco: Harper and Row.

Kosko, B. 1994. *Fuzzy Thinking: The New Science of Fuzzy Logic*. London: Flamingo.

Kroner, R. 1948. Introduction to *Early Theological Writings*, by G. W. F. Hegel. Trans. T. M. Knox and R. Kroner. Chicago: The University of Chicago Press.

Kulananda. 1997. *Western Buddhism*. London: Harper Collins.

Kymlicka, W. 1989. *Liberalism, Community and Culture*. Oxford: Clarendon Press.

———. 1995. *Multicultural Citizenship*. Oxford: Clarendon Press.

———. 2002. *Contemporary Political Philosophy; An Introduction*, 2nd edn. Oxford: Oxford University Press.

Lacan, J. [1968] 1997. *The Languages of the Self: The Function of Language in Psychoanalysis*. Trans. A. Wilden. Baltimore, MD: Johns Hopkins University Press.

Lai, M. 1998. "The Intellectual's Deaf-Mute, or (How) Can We Speak Beyond Postcoloniality?" *Cultural Critique* 39: 31–58.

Lakoff, G. 1987. *Women, Fire, and Dangerous Things: What Categories Reveal about the Mind*. Chicago: The University of Chicago Press.

———. 1988. "Cognitive Semantics." In *Meaning and Mental Representations*. Ed. U. Eco, M. Santambrogio, and P. Violi. Indianapolis: Indiana University Press, pp. 119–54.

Lakoff, G. and M. Johnson. 1980. *Metaphors We Live By*. Chicago: The University of Chicago Press.

Latour, B. 1993. *We Have Never Been Modern*. London: Harvester and Wheatsheaf.

Le Moigne, J. 1984. "The Intelligence of Complexity." In *The Science and Praxis of Complexity*. Ed. S. Aida et al. Montpellier, France: The United Nations University Press, pp. 35–61.

Leeming, D. and J. Page. 1994. *Goddess, Myths of the Female Divine*. Oxford: Oxford University Press.

Leeuw, G. van der. 1940. *L'homme primitif et la Religion*. Paris: Alcan.

Levine, L. 1977. *Black Culture and Black Consciousness: Afro-American Folk Thought from Slavery to Freedom*. Oxford: Oxford University Press.

Levy, R. G. 1948. *The Gate of Horn*. London: Faber & Faber.

Lewis, I. M. 1989. *Ecstatic Religion: A Study of Shamanism and Spirit Possession*, 2nd edn. London: Routledge.

Lincoln, R. J., G. A. Boxshall, and P. F. Clark. 1982. *A Dictionary of Ecology, Evolution and Systematics*. Cambridge, UK: Cambridge University Press.

Locke, J. [1706] 1975. *An Essay Concerning Human Understanding.* Ed. P. H. Nidditch. Oxford: Clarendon Press.

Lovejoy, A. O. 1960. *The Great Chain of Being: A Study of the History of an Idea.* New York: Harper & Row.

Löwith, K. 1993. *Max Weber and Karl Marx.* London: Routledge.

Luhmann, N. 1979. *Trust and Power: Two Works by Niklas Luhmann.* New York: John Wiley & Sons.

———. 1984. "Complexity and Meaning." In *The Science and Praxis of Complexity.* Ed. S. Aida et al. Montpellier, France: The United Nations University Press, pp. 99–104.

———. 1995. *Social Systems.* Stanford, California: Stanford University Press.

Luijpen, W. A. 1964. *Phenomenology of Atheism.* Pittsburgh: Duquesne University Press.

Macedo, S. 1990. *Liberal Virtues: Citizenship, Virtue and Community in Liberal Constitutionalism.* Oxford: Clarendon Press.

———. 2000. *Diversity and Distrust.* Cambridge: Harvard University Press.

Machiavelli, N. [1513] 1950. *The Prince and the Discourses.* Trans. L. Ricci and C. E. Detmold. New York: Random House.

MacIntyre, A. 1978. *Against the Self-Images of the Age.* Notre Dame: University of Notre Dame Press.

———. 1981. *After Virtue.* London: Gerald Duckworth & Co. Ltd.

———. 1984. *After Virtue,* 2nd edn. Notre Dame: University of Notre Dame Press.

———. 1988. *Whose Justice? Which Rationality?* Notre Dame: University of Notre Dame Press.

Macpherson, C. B. 1973. *Democratic Theory: Essays in Retrieval.* Oxford: Clarendon Press.

Majid, A. 1995. "Can the Postcolonial Critic Speak? Orientalism and the Rushdie Affair." *Cultural Critique* 32: 5–42.

Manzo, K. 1997. "Critical Humanism: Postcolonialism and Postmodern Ethics." *Alternatives* 32(3): 381–408.

March, J. G. and J. P. Olsen. 1989. *Rediscovering Institutions; the Organizational Basis of Politics.* London: The Free Press.

Margulis, L. and K. Scwartz. 1982. *Five Kingdoms.* San Francisco: Freeman.

Mason, A. 2000. *Community, Solidarity and Belonging: Levels of Community and Their Normative Significance.* Cambridge: Cambridge University Press.

Maturana, H. 1970. Biology of Cognition. B. C. L. Report No. 9, University of Illinois.

———. 1992. "Todo lo dice un observador." In *Gaia: Implicaciones de la nueva biología,* 2nd edn. Ed. W. I. Thompson. Barcelona: Kairós.

———. 1997. The Biological Foundations of Self-Consciousness and the Physical Domain of Existence. Lecture delivered at The Open University, Milton Keynes, U.K.

Maturana, H. and F. Varela. 1987. *The Tree of Knowledge: The Biological Roots of Human Understanding.* London: Shambala.

Maturana, H. and G. Verden-Zöler. 1995. *Amor y juego: fundamentos olvidados de lo humano*, 4th edn. Santiago de Chile: Instituto de Terapia Cognitiva.

McClintock, A. 1995. *Imperial Leather: Race, Gender, and Sexuality in the Colonial Context*. New York: Routledge.

McGee, P. 1992. *Telling the Other: The Question of Value in Modern and Postcolonial Writing*. Ithaca, NY: Cornell University Press.

McKenzie, E. 1994. *Privatopia*. New Haven: Yale University Press.

Memmi, A. 1965. *The Colonizer and the Colonized*. New York: Orion Books.

Merquior, J. G. 1986. *From Prague to Paris; a Critique of Structuralist and Post-structuralist Thought*. London: Verso.

———. 1988. El otro occidente (Un poco de filosofía de la historia desde Latinoamérica). Lecture presented at Romance Languages and Literatures Department of Harvard University, Boston.

Meyer, J. W. 1986. "Myths of Socialization and Personality." In *Reconstructing Individualism; Autonomy, Individuality, and the Self in Western Thought*. Ed. T. C. Heller, M. Sosna, and D. E. Wellbery. Stanford, CA: Stanford University Press, pp. 208–21.

Meyer, J. W., J. Boli, and G. M. Thomas. 1987. "Ontology and Rationalization in the Western Cultural Account." In *Institutional Structure: Constituting State, Society, and the Individual*. Ed. G. M. Thomas et al. Newbury Park, CA: Sage, pp. 12–37.

Mignolo, W. 1993. "Colonial and Postcolonial Discourse: Cultural Critique or Academic Colonialism?" *Latin American Research Review* 28(3): 120–34.

Mill, J. S. [1871] 1976. *Principles of Political Economy*. Fairfield: Augustus M. Kelley.

———. [1859] 1991. *On Liberty and Other Essays*. Ed. J. Gray. New York: Oxford University Press.

Miller, D. 2000. *Citizenship and National Identity*. Cambridge: Polity Press.

Mills, S. 1992. *Discourses of Difference: An Analysis of Women's Travel Writing and Colonialism*. London: Routledge.

———. 1995. "Discontinuity and Postcolonial Discourse." *Ariel* 26(3): 73–88.

Mingers, J. 1991. "The Cognitive Theories of Maturana and Varela." *Systems Practice* 4(4): 319–38.

———. 1992a. "The Problems of Social Autopoiesis." *International Journal of General Systems* 21: 229–36.

———. 1992b. "Reply to Zeleny and Hufford." *International Journal of General Systems* 21: 271–80.

Misztal, B. A. 1996. *Trust in Modern Societies*. Cambridge: Polity.

Mohanty, C., A. Russo, and L. Torres, eds. 1991. *Third World Women and the Politics of Feminism*. Bloomington IN: Indiana University Press.

Mongia, P., ed. 2003. *Contemporary Postcolonial Theory: A Reader*. London: Arnold Publishers.

Moore, F. C. T. 1996. *Bergson. Thinking Backwards*. Cambridge: Cambridge University Press.

Morgan, G. 1986. *Images of Organization*. London: Sage.

Morgan, K. P. 1987. "Women and Moral Madness." *Canadian Journal of Philosophy* 13: 201–26.

Morin, E. 1984. "On the Definition of Complexity." In *The Science and Praxis of Complexity*. Ed. S. Aida et al. Montpellier, France: The United Nations University Press, pp. 62–68.

Mulhall, S. and A. Swift. 1996. *Liberals & Communitarians*, 2nd edn. Oxford: Blackwell.

Mumford, L. 1967. *The Myth of the Machine. Technics and Human Development*, vol. 1, New York: Harcourt, Brace.

Narayan, U. and S. Harding, eds. 2000. *Decentering the Center: Philosophy for a Multicultural, Postcolonial, and Feminist World*. Bloomington, IN: Indiana University Press.

Neumann, E. 1954. *The Origins and History of Human Consciousness*. Princeton, NJ: Princeton University Press.

Ngugi, T. 1986. *Writing Against Neocolonialism*. Wembley, UK: Vita Books.

———. 1993. *Moving the Centre: The Struggle for Cultural Freedoms*. London: James Currey.

Nisbet, R. A. 1969. *Social Change and History: Aspects of the Western Theory of Development*. London: Oxford University Press.

———. 1994. *History of the Idea of Progress*. London: Transaction.

Nishitani, K. 1982. *Religion and Nothingness*. Trans. J. Van Bragt. Los Angeles: University of California Press.

North, D. C. 1990. *Institutions, Institutional Change and Economic Performance*. Cambridge: Cambridge University Press.

Nussbaum, Martha. 1986. *The Fragility of Goodness: Luck and Ethics in Greek Tragedy and Philosophy*. Cambridge: Cambridge University Press.

———. 2001. *Upheavals of Thought; the Intelligence of Emotions*. Cambridge, UK: Cambridge University Press.

O'Brien, E. 1965. *Varieties of Mystic Experience*. London: Mentor-Omega Paperbacks.

O'Flaherty, W. D., ed. 1980. *Karma and Rebirth in Classical Indian Traditions*. London: University of California Press.

Oakes, G. 1987. "Weber and the Southwest German School: The Genesis of the Concept of the Historical Individual." In *Max Weber and His Contemporaries*. Ed. W. J. Mommsen and J. Osterhammel. London: Allen & Unwin, pp. 80–115.

Ochoa, P. 1996. "The Historical Moments of Postcolonial Writing: Beyond Colonialism's Bynary." *Tulsa Studies in Women's Literature* 15: 221–29.

Ogus, A. I. 1989. "Law and Spontaneous Order: Hayek's Contribution to Legal Theory." *Journal of Law and Society* 16(4) (Winter): 393–409.

Olson, G. and L. Worsham. 1999. *Race, Rhetoric, and the Postcolonial*. Albany, NY: State University of New York Press.

Ortega y Gasset, J. 1937. *La rebelión de las masas*. Mexico City: Espasa-Calpe.

Oyama, S. 1985. *The Ontogeny of Information.* Cambridge, UK: Cambridge University Press.

Pandey, S. N. 1999. *Writing in a Post-Colonial Space.* New Delhi: Atlantic Publishers.

Parmar, P. and V. Amos. 1984. "Challenging Imperial Feminism." *Feminist Review* 17: 3–19f.

Parry, B. 1987. "Problems in Current Theories of Colonial Discourse." *Oxford Literary Review* 9: 27–58.

———. 1997. "The Postcolonial: Conceptual Category or Chimera?" *Yearbook of English Studies* 27: 3–21.

Paz, O. 1993. *El laberinto de la soledad. Postdata. Vuelta a el laberinto de la soledad,* 2nd edn. Mexico City: Fondo de Cultura Económica.

Perrow, C. 1979. *Complex Organizations: A Critical Essay.* New York: Random House.

Petersen K. and A. Rutherford, eds. 1986. *A Double Colonization: Colonial and Post-Colonial Women's Writing.* Sidney: Dangeroo.

Pettit, P. 1996. "Freedom as Antipower." *Ethics* 106: 576–604.

———. 1997. *Republicanism: A Theory of Freedom and Government.* Oxford: Clarendon Press.

Pieterse, J. N., ed. 1992. *Emancipations, Modern and Postmodern.* London: Sage.

Popper, K. R. [1962] 1995. *The Open Society and Its Enemies.* London: Routledge.

Powell, W. W. and P. J. DiMaggio. 1991. *The New Institutionalism in Organizational Analysis.* Chicago: The University of Chicago Press.

Prakash, G., ed. 1994. *After Colonialism: Imperial Histories and Postcolonial Displacements.* Princeton, NJ: Princeton University Press.

Pratt, M. L. 1992. *Imperial Eyes: Travel Writing and Transculturation.* London: Routledge.

Pribram, K. H. 1984. "Complexity and Causality." In *The Science and Praxis of Complexity.* Ed. S. Aida et al. Montpellier, France: The United Nations University Press, pp. 119–32.

Prigogine, I. 1984. "New Perspectives on Complexity." In *The Science and Praxis of Complexity.* Ed. S. Aida et al. Montpellier, France: The United Nations University Press, pp. 107–18.

———. 1997. *The End of Certainty; Time, Chaos, and the New Laws of Nature.* London: The Free Press.

Radhakrishnam, R. 1993. "Postcoloniality and the Boundaries of Identity." *Callaloo* 16(4): 750–71.

Radin, P. 1953. *The World of the Primitive Man.* New York: Henry Schuman.

Rasmussen, D., ed. 1990. *Universalism vs. Communitarianism.* Cambridge: MIT Press.

Rawls, J. 1971. *A Theory of Justice.* Cambridge, MA: Harvard University Press.

———. 1985. "Justice as Fairness: Political not Metaphysical." *Philosophy and Public Affairs* 14: 223–39.

Rawls, J. 1993. *Political Liberalism*. New York: Columbia University Press.

———. 1996. *Political Liberalism; with a New Introduction and the "Reply to Habermas."* New York: Columbia University Press.

———. 1999. *The Law of Peoples; with the Idea of Public Reason Revisited*. Cambridge: Harvard University Press.

Ray, S. 1992. "Shifting Subjects Shifting Grounds: The Names and Spaces of the Post-Colonial." *Hypatia: A Journal of Feminist Philosophy* 7(2): 188–201.

Raz, J. 1986. *The Morality of Freedom*. Oxford: Clarendon Press.

———. 1990. "Facing Diversity: The Case of Epistemic Abstinence." *Philosophy and Public Affairs* 19: 3–46.

Reid, T. R. 1999. *Confucius Lives Next Door*. New York: Random House.

Reiman, J. 1990. *Justice and Modern Moral Philosophy*. New Haven, CT: Yale University Press.

Richards, T. 1993. *The Imperial Archive: Knowledge and the Fantasy of Empire*. London: Verso.

Rickert, H. 1962. *Science and History: A Critique of Positivist Epistemology*. London: D. Van Nostrand Company.

Ricoeur, P. 1967a. *The Symbolism of Evil*. Boston: Beacon.

———. 1967b. *Husserl: An Analysis of His Phenomenology*. Evanston, IL: North Western University Press.

———. 1981. *Hermeneutics & the Human Sciences*. Trans. and ed. J. B. Thompson. Cambridge, UK and Paris: Cambridge University Press/Editions de la Maison de Science de l'Homme.

Riley, J. 1988. *Liberal Utilitarianism*. Cambridge: Cambridge University Press.

Riney, T. J. 1998. "Pre-Colonial System of Writing and Post-Colonial Languages of Publication." *Journal of Multilingual and Multicultural Development* 19(1): 64–83.

Ritchie, D. G. 1896. *Principles of State Interference*, 2nd edn. London: Swan Sonnenschein.

Robb, F. F. 1992. "Guilty as Charged but Unrepentant!" *International Journal of General Systems* 21: 265–66.

Rorty, R. 1980. *Philosophy and the Mirror of Nature*. Oxford: Basil Blackwell.

Rosenblum, N. 1998. *Membership and Morals*. Princeton: Princeton University Press.

Roth, G. and W. Schluchter. 1979. *Max Weber's Vision of History: Ethics and Methods*. Berkeley: University of California Press.

Rotman, B. 1987. *Signifying Nothing: The Semiotics of Zero*. Stanford, CA: Stanford University Press.

Rousseau, J. J. [1762] 1973. *The Social Contract and Discourses*. Trans. G. D. H. Cole. New York: Dutton.

Ruddick, S. 1990. *Maternal Thinking: Towards a Politics of Peace*. New York: Ballantine.

Rushdie, S. 1992. *Imaginary Homelands: Essays and Criticism, 1981–1991*. London: Penguin Books.

Said, E. W. 1978. *Orientalism*. New York: Pantheon Books.

———. 1992. *Edward Said: A Critical Reader*. Ed. M. Sprinker. Oxford: Blackwell.

———. 1994. *Culture and Imperialism*. New York: Vintage Books.

San Juan Jr., E. 1984. *Toward a People's Literature: Essays in the Dialectics of Praxis and Contradiction in Philippine Writing*. Quezon City: University of Philippines Press.

———. 1999. *Beyond Postcolonial Theory*. New York: St. Martin's Press.

Sandel, M. 1981. *Liberalism and the Limits of Justice*. Cambridge: Cambridge University Press.

———. 1996. *Democracy's Discontent*. Cambridge: Harvard University Press.

———. 1998. *Liberalism and the Limits of Justice*, 2nd edn. Cambridge: Cambridge University Press.

Sartre, J. [1943] 1995. *Being and Nothingness*. Washington: Washington Square Press.

Scanlon, T. 1982 "Contractualism and Utilitarianism." In *Utilitarianism and Beyond*. Ed. Amartya Sen and Bernard Williams, Cambridge: Cambridge University Press, pp. 103–28.

Schulze-Engler, F. 1996. "Universalism with a Difference: The Politics of Postcolonial." *Studies in English and Comparative Literature* 10: 41–46.

Searle, J. R. 1979. "The Intentionality of Intention and Action." *Inquiry* 22: 253–80.

———. 1995. *The Construction of Social Reality*. London: Penguin.

Seligman, A. B. 1994. *Innerwordly Individualism: Charismatic Community and Its Institutionalization*. London: Transaction.

Shapin, S. 1994. *A Social History of Truth: Civility and Science in Seventeenth-Century England*. Chicago: University of Chicago Press.

Shils, E. 1975. *Center and Periphery: Essays in Macrosociology*. Chicago: The University of Chicago Press.

Sica, A. 1988. *Weber, Irrationality and Social Order*. Berkeley: University of California Press.

Siedentop, L. 1979. "Two Liberal Traditions." In *The Idea of Freedom*, Ed. Alan Ryan. Oxford: Oxford University Press, pp. 70–93.

Skinner, Quentin. 1998. *Liberty Before Liberalism*. Cambridge: Cambridge University Press.

Slemon, S. 1988. "Post-Colonial Allegory and the Transformation of History." *Journal of Commonwealth Literature* 23(1): 157–68.

Snell, B. 1953. *The Discovery of the Mind: The Greek Origins of European Thought*. Oxford: Blackwell.

Sober, E. 1993. *Philosophy of Biology*. Oxford: Oxford University Press.

Sogyal Rinpoche. 1992. *The Tibetan Book of Living and Dying*. London: Rider.

Sommers, C. H. 2001. *The War against Boys: How Misguided Feminism is Harming Our Young Men*. New York: Simon & Schuster.

Spector, H. 1992. *Autonomy and Rights: The Moral Foundations of Liberalism*. Oxford: Clarendon.

Spivak, G. C. 1986. "Imperialism and Sexual Difference." *Oxford Literary Review* 8(1): 225–40.

Spivak, G. C. 1988. "Can the Subalterns Speak?" In *Marxism and the Interpretation of Culture*. Ed. C. Nelson and L. Grossberg. Urbana: University of Illinois Press, pp. 271–313.

Starr Sered, S. 1994. *Priestess, Mother, Sacred Sister: Religions Dominated by Women*. Oxford: Oxford University Press.

Stearn, S. 1982. "On Fitness." In *Environmental Adaptation and Evolution*, Ed. D. Mossakowski and G. Roth. Stuttgart: Gustav Fisher.

Steiner, H. 1994. *An Essay on Rights*. Oxford: Basil Blackwell.

Swenson, R. 1992. "Galileo, Babel, and Autopoiesis (it's Turtles All the Way Down)." *International Journal of General Systems* 21: 267–69.

Tae, H. 1997. "Toward Postcolonial Feminist Ethics: Gayatri Spivak and French Feminism." *Journal of English Language and Literature* 43(1): 151–69.

Tamir, Y. 1993. *Liberal Nationalism*. Princeton: Princeton University Press.

Tams, H. 1998. *Communitarianism: A New Agenda for Politics and Citizenship*. Basingstoke: Macmillan.

Taylor, C. 1985. *Philosophy and the Human Sciences: Philosophical Papers* 2. Cambridge: Cambridge University Press.

———. 1989. *Sources of the Self: The Making of the Modern Identity*. Cambridge: Cambridge University Press.

———. 1999. "Conditions of an Unforced Consensus on Human Rights." In *The East Asian Challenge for Human Rights*. Ed. J. R. Bauer and D. Bell. New York: Cambridge University Press, pp. 124–44.

Tellenbach, G. 1940. *Church, State and Christian Society at the Time of the Investiture Contest*. Oxford: Basil Blackwell.

Tiffin, H. 1988. "Post-Colonialism, Post-Modernism and the Rehabilitation of Post-Colonial History." *Journal of Commonwealth Literature* 23(1): 169–81.

Trigger, B. G. 1998. *Sociocultural Evolution; New Perspectives on the Past*. Oxford: Blackwell.

Trinh, M. 1989. *Woman, Native, Other: Writing Postcoloniality and Feminism*. Bloomington, IN: University of Indiana Press.

Tutu, D. 1999. *No Future without Forgiveness*. London: Rider

Underhill, E. 1995. *Mysticism*, 14th edn. London: Bracken Books.

Varela, F., E. Thompson, and E. Rosch. 1991. *The Embodied Mind: Cognitive Science and Human Experience*. Cambridge, MA: The Massachusetts Institute of Technology Press.

Viroli, M. 2002. *Republicanism*. Trans. A. Shugaar. New York: Hill and Wang.

Voegelin, E. 1957. *Order and History: The World of the Polis*. Louisiana: Louisiana State University Press.

———. 1974. *Order and History: The Ecumenic Age*. Louisiana: Louisiana State University Press.

Voge, J. 1984. "Management of Complexity." In *The Science and Praxis of Complexity*. Ed. S. Aida et al. Montpellier, France: The United Nations University Press, pp. 298–311.

Wade, I. O. 1971. *The Intellectual Origins of the French Enlightenment*. Princeton: Princeton University Press.

Waldo, D. 1961. "Organization Theory: An Elephantine Problem." *Public Administration Review* 21: 210–25.

Walzer, M. 1983. *Spheres of Justice.* Oxford: Blackwell.

———. 1987. *Interpretation and Social Criticism.* Cambridge: Harvard University Press.

———. 1994. *Thick and Thin.* Notre Dame: University of Notre Dame Press.

Warner, M. 1980. *Alone of All Her Sex: The Myth and the Cult of the Virgin Mary.* London: Picador.

———. 1994. *Six Myths of Our Time; Managing Monsters.* London: Vintage.

Warnock, M. 1970. *Existentialism.* Oxford: Oxford University Press.

Waters, C. K. 1986. "Natural Selection without Survival of the Fittest." *Biology and Philosophy* 2(1) (April): 207–25.

Weber, M. [1904] 1949. " 'Objectivity' in Social Science and Social Policy." In *The Methodology of the Social Sciences.* Ed. E. A. Shils and H. A. Finch. New York: The Free Press, pp. 49–112.

———. [1905] 1958. *The Protestant Ethic and the Spirit of Capitalism: The Relationships between Religion and the Economic and Social Life in Modern Culture.* Trans. T. Parsons. New York: Charles Scribner's Sons.

———. [1922a] 1965. *The Sociology of Religion,* 4th edn. in English from the 4th in German. London: Methuen & Co. Ltd.

———. [1922b] 1987. *Economía y sociedad,* 2nd edn. in Spanish from the 4th in German. Mexico City: Fondo de Cultura Económica.

Wilden, A. 1972. *System and Structure; Essays in Communication and Exchange.* London: Tavistock.

Winograd, T. and F. Flores. 1987. *Understanding Computers and Cognition; a New Foundation for Design.* Wokingham, UK: Addison-Wesley.

Wolfe, A. 1989. *Whose Keepers? Social Science and Moral Obligation.* Berkeley, CA: The University of California Press.

Wright, R. 1994. *The Moral Animal: Why We Are the Way We Are.* London: Abacus.

Young, I. M. 1990. *Justice and the Politics of Difference.* Princeton: Princeton University Press.

Young, M. E., ed. 2002. *From Early Child Development to Human Development.* Washington, DC: The World Bank.

Young, R. J. C. 1990. *White Mythologies: Writing History and the West.* London: Routledge.

———. 1995. *Colonial Desire: Hybridity in Theory, Culture, and Race.* London: Routledge.

Zadeh, L. 1965. "Fuzzy Sets." *Information and Control* 8: 338–53.

Zeleny, M. 1984. "Spontaneous Social Orders." In *The Science and Praxis of Complexity.* Ed. S. Aida et al. Montpellier, France: The United Nations University Press, pp. 312–28.

Zeleny, M. and K. D. Hufford. 1992. "The Ordering of the Unknown by Causing it to Order Itself." *International Journal of General Systems* 21: 239–53.

INDEX